A PRIMER OF LINGUISTICS

A PRIMER OF LINGUISTICS

Anne Fremantle

St. Martin's Press — New York

First Printing

Library of Congress Catalogue #72-89425
Manufactured in the United States of America

St. Martin's Press, 175 Fifth Avenue, New York, N.Y. 10010

AFFILIATED PUBLISHER: Macmillan Limited, London
—also at Bombay, Calcutta, Madras and Melbourne

Dedication

For A.J. who will never read it, and for C.F. who might.

Acknowledgements

I wish to thank my editor, Thomas Dunne, for patience and perseverance above the call of duty. Also Dr. Samuel Anderson for contributing his invaluable introduction and his summary of one aspect of Ludwig Wittgenstein's analysis. And his wife for her devoted care of the MSS and its author.

Contents

Language In The Early Christian Era

The Medieval Period And After

New Worlds, New Theories

From Romantics to Naturalists

The Nineteenth Century

The Twentieth Century

The Contemporary Scene: The Naturalists

The Contemporary Scene II

Preface

A preface is not a place to present, and certainly is not one in which it is possible to justify, a historiographic analysis of linguistics. But a few classificatory remarks about the field may be of value to the reader for interpreting the chronologically organized material in the book. First, however, a comment about what this book is not.

Primer of Linguistics is manifestly not an introductory text, nor a compendium of curious facts about languages. Less obviously, it is not a history-of-a-science with the inevitable evolutionary story that begins with a primeval glimmer and ends with a bask in the triumphs of some contemporary culture. Although early chapters are given standard Western historical titles, and the earliest quotations are taken from the only known writers on their respective traditions, most of the selected writings in the book are here reprinted for the first time in any collected work, and all have been chosen to characterize views man has held of himself within the universe by virtue of what he has understood his language capacity to be. This characterization clearly ceases to be historically exhaustive by the time of the Renaissance, and by the nineteenth century only a sampling is possible of the direct philosophical backgrounds of modern linguistics — naturalism, dialectical formalism and logistic.

The introductory reader must be advised, then, to seek a standard linguistics history for an appreciation of the preeminence of de Saussure, Bloomfield, Jakobson, and L. H. Morgan, Boas and Whorf, to mention only some.

It is now accepted that phonology is both the oldest and most completely understood branch of linguistics. Many believe that

Panini provided an entirely adequate description of the Sanskrit sound system, although he employed a narrow, conventional orthography that permitted no comparison whatever between Sanskrit and even the neighboring Indic languages. Narrow though it was, Panini's Vedic articulatory phonetics identifies what are the general loci of articulation for most human speech sounds, and his treatment of the degrees of occlusion in the vocal tract, while incomplete, is remarkable for a work done more than two millennia prior to the invention of X-ray, spectrograph and oscilloscope. It has been suggested by Jozef Cohen that it was the behavioral phonetic code of Melville Bell (Alexander Graham's father) that supplied Henry Sweet with the necessary technical idea for universal comparative phonetics — a long time indeed to wait for a theoretical improvement on Panini.

Syntax is the branch of linguistics which is intermediate in development. Important major issues remain unsettled, particularly regarding the proper relationship between syntax and the other branches, phonology and semantics. A principal question is whether any phonologically naive work can offer anything rigorously useful to the enterprise of syntactic description, or whether, as Bloomfield held, a science of the relations among sounds presupposes that one has already worked out a theory of the sounds themselves. Chomsky, who argues that a science of phonology can no more stand alone than can one of syntax, and should never be pursued independently, has encouraged an increasing number of workers to appreciate Descartes and his immediate successors no less than the recent mathematicians Turing, Gödel and Post, as direct precursors of the syntactic concepts implicit within the modern notion of a generative grammar. It is generally agreed, though, that significant fragments of many natural languages have been supplied with adequate syntactic descriptions, and dispute is largely limited to formulating these descriptions to generalize appropriately to newly created sentences within a given language and to permit all natural languages to be treated within a single framework.

The newest and most controversial branch of linguistics is generative semantics, viewed by "transformationalists" such as Lakoff as capable of amending and replacing the syntactic hypotheses of the "lexicalist" Chomsky. While the issues are largely technical, a straightforward solution to the problem is made difficult by the evident fact that words frequently take on different meanings as a function of their syntactic arrangement among other words. For example, the word *need* in the sentence *Bees need flowers* connotes nutrition, while the same word in the sentence *Flowers need bees* connotes not nutrition, but sex. The necessarily abstract and hidden nature of this type of distinction lends itself to both syntactic and semantic interpretations, and no criterion for choosing between them seems remotely close to general acceptance.

Moulton has described linguistics as "the most scientific of the humanities and the most humanistic of the sciences." Anne Fremantle's book is a documentation, and I think a convincing one, that this has probably always been so. Contrary to the views of some contemporary psychological observers to the effect that man's mind either can never be the subject of science or, at best, may be rigorously investigated only at some indefinite time in the future, it is possible to discern coherent models for judgment and decision in the records of cultural epochs in the past. A chronological examination of what we choose to call linguistic prescience, linguistic science and what have become the linguistic sciences, shows an unbroken thread of theoretical explicitness and logical concern that inescapably suggests a very early and continually recurring human desire for self-understanding through the analysis of language. This desire is apparently contemporary with, and possibly antecedent to, the early formal accomplishments in geometry and astronomy that have too long been unchallenged conventional criteria by which a culture proclaims its capability for scientific thought.

SAMUEL W. ANDERSON

Excerpt from *Salvation by Words*, Blackfield Address, given by Iris Murdoch to American Academy of Arts and Letters, March 17, 1972.

. . . Words constitute the ultimate texture and stuff of our moral being, since they are the most refined and delicate and detailed, as well as the most universally used and understood, of the symbolisms whereby we express ourselves into existence. We became spiritual animals. The *fundamental* distinctions can only be made in words. Words are spirit. Of course eloquence is no guarantee of goodness, and an inarticulate man can be virtuous. But the quality of a civilization depends upon its ability to discern and reveal truth, and this depends upon the scope and purity of its language.

Author's Foreword

A primer is essentially a *first* reader, and the purpose of this primer is to provide an historical anthology of basic texts important in the history of the development of linguistics as a discipline, and relevant to the changes in human attitudes towards linguistics, from B.C. 2100 to our own day. As far as possible, easily obtained texts have been avoided, so that if this collection seems to lean heavily on early Sanskrit and on eighteenth-century French authors, it is because these are not readily available except in research libraries. As a corollary, if the nineteenth-century giants in the linguistic field seem short-changed here, it is because all of them, from Antoine Meillet and De Saussure through Otto Jespersen and Roman Jakonsen, are readily obtainable.

A primer is a beginning book, and this primer is for beginners in linguistics, by a beginner who claims no competence in the field other than a passion for language, an affection for grammar, and an abiding belief in causality: "this happened; therefore, that followed inevitably." The development of human speech, of languages and, finally, of the science of linguistics, is as historical as the development of dogma. Some of the milestones of that journey may, it is hoped, be found in this primer.

Linguistics is the science of language, "the study of the nature and structure of human speech." Language itself (according to the *American Heritage Dictionary*) is the aspect of human behaviour "that involves the use of vocal cords in meaningful patterns, and, when they exist, corresponding written symbols to form, express and communicate thoughts and feelings." No one has given any date for the beginning of language: probably human speech began about the same time as the use of tools, somewhere between five hundred thousand and one million years ago.

Human beings have from earliest times been conscious of the power the capacity for communication through speech gives them. They early assumed that they themselves, and the whole world, or worlds, were created by the word of the gods, or a god. The Hymn of Bel Marduk, written down some time between 2100 and 2080 B.C., declares:

Of his word, the splendor is like the sun above the earth
When it rises, who will make known that it contains?
The word of the God Goula is like the sun when it rises above the earth
What it contains who will make known?
The word which on high brings the skies to submit to its power
The word which below makes the earth motionless
The word which establishes the God Anunnalu prince of lamentations and which makes him die
For the divine man's growing, the brightness of his word bears plenteous fruit.

> Herodotus, the Greek historian (484-420 B.C.), describes "how the Egyptians, before the reign of Psammitichus, considered themselves to be the most ancient of mankind. But afterward Psammitichus, having come to the throne, endeavoured to ascertain who were the most ancient. From the time they considered the Phrygians to have been before them, and themselves before all others. Now, when Psammitichus was unable, by inquiry, to discover any solution of this question, who were the most ancient of men, he devised the following expedient: He gave two new-born children of poor parents to a shepherd, to be brought up among his flocks in the following manner: he gave strict orders that no one should utter a word in their presence, that they should lie in a solitary room by themselves, and that he should bring goats to them at certain times, and that when he had satisfied them with milk he should attend to his other employments. Psammitichus contrived and

ordered this, for the purpose of hearing what word the children would first articulate after they have given over their insignificant mewlings; and such accordingly was the result. For when the shepherd had pursued this plan for the space of two years, one day as he opened the door and went in, both the children falling upon him, and holding out their hands, cried "Becos." The shepherd when he first heard it said nothing; but when this same word was constantly repeated to him whenever he went and tended the children, he acquainted his master. By his command he brought the children into his presence. When Psammitichus heard the same, he enquired what people called anything by name "Becos" and discovered that the Phrygians called bread by that name. Thus the Egyptians, convinced, allowed that the Phrygians were more ancient than they. I had this from the priests of Vulcan at the temple of Memphis."

(Herodotus, *The Histories*, Bk. 11.)

Plato (B.C. 428-348), in his dialogue the *Phaedros*, in a conversation between Socrates (B.C. 470-399) and Phaedros, makes Socrates also credit the Egyptians with inventing writing, if not language.

Socrates: I have heard a tradition of antiquity, whether true or not only antiquity knows . . .

Phaedros: I wish you would tell it to me!

Socrates: In Egypt, in the city of Naukratis, there was a famous old god, Theuth. He was the inventor of many arts: arithmetic, calculations, geometry, astronomy, draughts and dice. But his great discovery was the use of letters. Now in those days Thammus was king of the whole of Upper Egypt, which is the district surrounding that great city called by the Hellenes, Egyptian Thebes, and they call the god himself Ammon. To Thammus comes Theuth and showed him his inventions, desiring that all other Egyptians might have the benefit of them. He went through them and Thammus inquired about their several uses, and praised some and censured others and approved or disapproved of them. When they came to letters, "This," said Theuth, "will make the Egyptians wiser and give them better memories, for this is the cure for forgetfulness and folly." Thammus replied: "O most ingenious Theuth, he who has the gift of invention is not always the best judge of the utility or intelligence of his own invention or the uses of them. And in this instance paternal love for your own child has led you to say what is not, in fact. For this invention of yours will create forgetfulness in the learners' souls, because they will not use their memories, they will trust to the written characters and will not remember of themselves. You have found a specific, not for memory, but for reminiscence, and you give your disciples only the pretence of wisdom. They will be hearers of many things and will have learned nothing; they will appear to be omniscient and will generally know nothing; they will be tiresome company having a show of wisdom without the reality."

Phaedros: Yes, Socrates, you can easily invent tales of Egypt, or of any other country.

(*The Dialogues of Plato*. Trans. B. Jowett; Macmillan, 1894.)

Out of Egypt came the Hebrew Moses (between 2000 and 1200 B.C.), who wrote the account of the Creation accepted by Jews and Christians. This account, in the first chapter of Genesis, refers to the creation as the result of God's words.

Genesis: Chapter 1.

1 In the beginning God created the heaven and the earth.

2 And the earth was without form, and void, and darkness was upon the face of the deep.
And the Spirit of God moved upon the face of the water.

3 And God said: Let there be light, and there was light. . . .

5 And God called the light Day, and the darkness he called Night.
And God said: Let there be a firmament in the midst of the water, and let it divide the waters from the waters. . . .

26 And God said: Let us make man in our image, after our likeness; and let them have dominion over the fish of the sea, and over the fowl of the air, and over the cattle, and over all the earth, and over every creeping thing that creepeth upon the earth.

28 And God blessed them, and said unto them, be fruitful and multiply and replenish the earth and subdue it.

Genesis: Chapter 2.

19 And out of the ground the Lord God formed every beast of the field and every fowl of the air, and brought them unto Adam to see what he would call them; and whatsoever Adam called every living creature, that was the name thereof.

20 And Adam gave names to all cattle, and to the fowl of the air, and to every beast of the field, but for Adam there was not found an helpmate for him.

(The Holy Bible, Authorized Version.)

ANCIENT INDIA

The Phrygians flourished in Asia Minor around 1300 B.C. Sometime between 1500 and 1000 B.C. in India, the Vedas were written down in Sanskrit — a language no longer spoken anywhere, but in which Hindu philosophy, religion and literature were written and are read, and from which are derived all the Indo-European languages, including English. "Vedanam Vedam," the Veda of Vedas, is what grammar is called in the Vedas, and the god Indra, one of the greatest in the Hindu pantheon, is said to have divided speech from thought; speech thereafter was to be called "analysed speech." The Vedas consist of four collections of writings, of which the most ancient are the Rig-Veda, hymns to the gods; the Sama-Veda, priests' chants; the Yajur-Veda, sacrificial formulae, and the Atharva-Veda, magical chants. Each Veda is further divided into Mantra, hymns, and Bramana, precepts which latter are further subdivided into a) Aranyakas, or theology; and b) Upanishads, or philosophy. There are over one hundred Upanishads, which are the basis of all Hindu philosophy, and there are thirteen major Upanishads, thought to be the oldest. These include the Chandogya, which discusses the whole question of the importance of speech. It probably dates from around 1000 B.C.

CHĀNDOGYA UPANISHAD

First Prapāṭhaka

A Glorification of the Chanting of the Sama-Veda

The Udgītha identified with the sacred syllable "Om"

FIRST KHAṆḌA

1. *Om*! One should reverence the Udgītha (Loud Chant) as this syllable, for one sings the loud chant [beginning] with "*Om*"

The further explanation thereof [is as follows].—

2. The essence of things here is the earth.

The essence of the earth is water.

The essence of water is plants.

The essence of plants is a person (*puruṣa*).

The essence of a person is speech.

The essence of speech is the Rig ("hymn").

The essence of the Rig is the Sāman ("chant").

The essence of the Sāman is the Udgītha ("loud singing").

3. This is the quintessence of the essences, the highest, the supreme, the eighth—namely the Udgītha.

4. "Which one is the Rig? Which one is the Sāman? Which one is the Udgītha?"—Thus has there been a discussion.

5. The Rig is speech. The Sāman is breath (*prāṇa*). The Udgītha is this syllable "*Om*."

Verily, this is a pair—namely speech and breath, and also the Rig and the Sāman.

Seventh Prapāṭhaka

The instruction of Nārada by Sanatkumāra

Progressive worship of Brahma up to the Universal Soul

FIRST KHAṆḌA

1. *Om*! "Teach me, sir!"—with these words Nārada came to Sanatkumāra.

To him he then said: "Come to me with what you know. Then I will tell you still further."

2. Then he said to him: "Sir, I know the Rig-Veda, the Yajur-Veda, the Sāma-Veda, the Atharva-Veda as the fourth, Legend and Ancient Lore (*itihāsa-purāṇa*) as the fifth, the Veda of the Vedas [i.e. Grammar], Propitiation of the Manes, Mathematics, Augury (*daiva*), Chronology, Logic, Polity, the Science of the Gods (*deva-vidyā*), the Science of Sacred Knowledge (*brahma-vidyā*), Demonology (*bhūta-vidyā*), the Science of Rulership (*kṣatra-vidyā*), Astrology (*nakṣatra-vidyā*), the Science of Snake-charming, and the Fine Arts (*sarpa-devajana-vidyā*). This, sir, I know.

3. Such a one am I, sir, knowing the sacred sayings (*mantravid*), but not knowing the Soul (Ātman). It has been heard by me from those who are like you, sir, that he who knows the Soul (Ātman) crosses over sorrow. Such a sorrowing one am I, sir. Do you, sir, cause me, who am such a one, to cross over to the other side of sorrow."

To him he then said: "Verily, whatever you have here learned, verily, that is mere name (*nāman*).

4. Verily, a Name are the Rig-Veda, the Yajur-Veda, the Sāma-Veda, the Atharva-Veda as the fourth, Legend and Ancient Lore (*itihāsa-purāṇa*) as the fifth, the Veda of the Vedas [i.e.Grammar], Propitiation of the Manes, Mathematics, Augury (*daiva*), Chronology, Logic, Polity, the Science of the Gods (*deva-vidyā*), the Science of Sacred Knowledge (*brahma-vidyā*), Demonology (*bhūta-vidyā*), the Science of Rulership (*kṣatra-vidyā*), Astrology (*nakṣatra-vidyā*), the Science of Snake-charming, and the Fine Arts (*sarpa-devajana-vidyā*). This is mere Name. Reverence Name.

5. He who reverences Name as Brahma—as far as Name goes, so far he has unlimited freedom, he who reverences Name as Brahma."

"Is there, sir, more than Name?"

"There is, assuredly, more than Name."

"Do you, sir, tell me it."

SECOND KHAṆḌA

1. "Speech (*vāc*), assuredly, is more than Name. Speech, verily,

makes known the Rig-Veda, the Yajur-Veda, the Sāma-Veda, the Atharva-Veda as the fourth, Legend and Ancient Lore as the fifth, the Veda of the Vedas [i.e. Grammar], Propitiation of the Manes, Mathematics, Augury, Chronology, Logic, Polity, the Science of the Gods, the Science of Sacred Knowledge, Demonology, the Science of Rulership, Astrology, the Science of Snake-charming, and the Fine Arts, as well as heaven and earth, wind and space, water and heat, gods and men, beasts and birds, grass and trees, animals together with worms, flies, and ants, right and wrong, true and false, good and bad, pleasant and unpleasant. Verily, if there were no speech, neither right nor wrong would be known, neither true nor false, neither good nor bad, neither pleasant nor unpleasant. Speech, indeed, makes all this known. Reverence Speech.

2. He who reverences Speech as Brahma—as far as Speech goes, so far he has unlimited freedom, he who reverences Speech as Brahma."

"Is there, sir, more than Speech?"

"There is, assuredly, more than Speech."

"Do you, sir, tell me it."

THIRD KHAṆḌA

1. "Mind (*manas*), assuredly, is more than Speech. Verily, as the closed hand compasses two acorns, or two kola-berries, or two dice-nuts, so Mind compasses both Speech and Name. When through Mind one has in mind 'I wish to learn the sacred sayings (*mantra*),' then he learns them; 'I wish to perform sacred works (*karma*),' then he performs them; 'I would desire sons and cattle,' then he desires them; 'I would desire this world and the yonder,' then he desires them. Truly the self (*ātman*) is Mind. Truly, the world (*loka*) is Mind. Truly, Brahma is Mind.

2. He who reverences Mind as Brahma—as far as Mind goes, so far he has unlimited freedom, he who reverences Mind as Brahma."

"Is there, sir, more than Mind?"

"There is, assuredly, more than Mind."

"Do you, sir, tell me it."

* * *

FOURTH KHAṆḌA

1. "Conception (*samkalpa*), assuredly, is more than Mind. Verily, when one forms a Conception, then he has in Mind, then he utters Speech, and he utters it in Name. The sacred sayings (*mantra*) are included in Name, and sacred works in the sacred sayings.

2. Verily, these have Conception as their union-point, have Conception as their soul, are established on Conception. Heaven and earth were formed through Conception. Wind and space were formed through Conception. Water and heat were formed through Conception. Through their having been formed, rain becomes formed. Through rain having been formed, food becomes formed. Through food having been formed, living creatures (*prāṇa*) become formed. Through living creatures having been formed, sacred sayings (*mantra*) become formed. Through sacred sayings having been formed, sacred works (*karma*) become [per]formed. Through sacred works having been [per]formed, the world becomes formed. Through the world having been formed, everything becomes formed. Such is Conception. Reverence Conception.

3. He who reverences Conception as Brahma—he, verily, attains the Conception-worlds; himself being enduring, the enduring worlds; himself established, the established worlds; himself unwavering, the unwavering worlds. As far as Conception goes, so far he has unlimited freedom, he who reverences Conception as Brahma."

"Is there, sir, more than Conception?"

"There is, assuredly, more than Conception."

"Do you, sir, tell me it."

FIFTH KHAṆḌA

1. "Thought (*citta*), assuredly, is more than Conception. Verily, when one thinks, then he forms a conception, then he has in Mind, then he utters Speech, and he utters it in Name. The sacred sayings (*mantra*) are included in Name, and sacred works in the sacred sayings.

2. Verily, these things have Thought as their union-point, have

Thought as their soul, are established on Thought. Therefore, even if one who knows much is without Thought, people say of him: 'He is not anybody, whatever he knows! Verily, if he did know, he would not be so without Thought!' On the other hand, if one who knows little possesses Thought, people are desirous of listening to him. Truly, indeed, Thought is the union-point, Thought is the soul (*ātman*), Thought is the support of these things. Reverence Thought.

Since "the Veda of the Vedas is grammar," there are many words used to designate speech and thought (expressed in word). The Vedic speculations, as Louis Renou, among others, has brought out, are based on the primacy of speech. A Vedic word like *vac* is the equivalent of the later Greek *logos*, the "Word" that for Christians from the beginning was "with God and was God." It is the prototype of the notion of the Atman-brahman, of God as the creative principle all-powerful, "marvellous, eternal, which in each generation sounds again." Thought is conceived of in the Vedas as Light, and *arka*, which means both "light" and "song," is used of Agni, the fire god. The *tapas* is the interior flame that illumines and burns the poet, and another term, *susa*, is used for "word" in the sense of the word that is breathed out as inspiration.

Already in the Rig-Veda is the idea of a proto-speech preceeding human speech: "The word is measured in four stages known to intelligent brahmans; three are hidden and immobile; humans use the fourth as speech." (1. 164.45) "Those who by intuition arrive at the source of speech or who by reflexion have expressed exact reality by the third formulation arrive at the fourth." (10.125) Thus the very origin of grammar is organically and intimately connected with the deep study of the Vedas. Around 700 B.C. Yaska wrote the *Nirukta* to explain the meaning of the Vedic texts. Herein already he divides words into four classes, and speech into four parts.

THE NIRUKTA

Translated by Lashman Sarup

CHAPTER ONE

A traditional list (of words) has been handed down (to us). It is to be (here) explained. This same list is called *Ni-ghaṇṭavas*. From what (root) is (the word) *Ni-ghaṇṭavas* derived? They are words quoted from the Vedas (*ni-gamāḥ*). Having been repeatedly gathered together from Vedic hymns, they have been handed down by tradition. Aupamanyava holds that, as these are the quoted words of the Vedas, they are called *Ni-ghaṇṭavas* on account of their being quoted (*ni-gamanāt*). Or else (the word *Ni-ghaṇṭavas*) may be (so called) from being fixed only (√*han*), i.e. (a list, in which) they (the words) are fixed together, or collected together (√*hṛ*).

Now, what (are) the four classes of words? They are the following: noun and verb; prepositions and particles. With reference to this, they thus prescribe the definition of noun and verb: the verb has *becoming* as its fundamental notion, nouns have *being* as their fundamental notion. But where both are dominated by *becoming*, a *becoming* arising from a former to a later state is denoted by a verb, as "he goes", "he cooks", &c. The embodiment of the whole process from the beginning to the end, which has assumed the character of *being*, is denoted by a noun, as "going", "cooking", &c. The demonstrative pronoun is a reference to *beings*, as "cow", "horse", "man", "elephant", &c.; "to be", to *becoming*, as "he sits", "he sleeps", "he goes", "he stands", &c.

According to Audumbarāyaṇa speech is permanent in the organs only.

(Here ends the first section.)

In that case the fourfold division (of words) will not hold good, nor the grammatical connexion, nor the mutual reference of sounds which are not produced simultaneously. Words are used to designate objects, with regard to everyday affairs in the world, on account of their comprehensiveness and minuteness. They, too, are the names of gods as well as of human beings. On account of the impermanence of human knowledge, the stanza, (directing) the accomplishment of action, is (to be found) in the Veda.

According to Vārṣyāyaṇi, there are six modifications of *becoming*: genesis, existence, alteration, growth, decay, and destruction. Genesis denotes only the commencement of the first state, but neither affirms nor denies the later. Existence affirms a being that has been produced. Alteration connotes the modification of elements of a non-decaying being. Growth denotes the increase of one's own limbs or of objects which are associated (with one's self), as he grows by means of victory, or he grows with his body. The term decay denotes its antithesis. Destruction denotes the commencement of the later state, but neither affirms nor denies the former.

(Here ends the second section.)

Hence, other modifications of *becoming* are only further developments of those (enumerated above), and should be inferred according to the occasion.

"Unconnected prepositions", says Śākaṭayana, "have no meaning, but only express a subordinate sense of nouns and verbs." "They have various meanings," says Gārgya; "hence, whatever their meaning may be, they express that meaning (which brings about) modification in the sense of the noun and the verb." The word *ā* is used in the sense of "hitherward"; *pra* and *parā* are its antitheses: *abhi*, "towards"; *prati* is its antithesis: *ati* and *su*, "approval"; *nir* and *dur* are their antitheses: *ni* and *ava*, "downwards"; *ud* is their antithesis: *sam*, "combination"; *vi* and *apa* are its antitheses: *anu*, "similarity" and "succession": *api*, "contact": *upa*, "accession": *pari*, "being all around": *adhi*, "being above", or "supremacy". Thus they express various meanings to which attention should be paid.

(Here ends the third section.)

Now the particles occur in various senses, both in a comparative sense, in a conjunctive sense, and as expletives. Of them, the following four are used in the sense of comparison. *Iva* (has this sense) both in the classical and the Vedic Sanskrit thus "like Agni", "like Indra", &c. The word *na* has the sense of negation in classical, and both (i.e. the sense of negation and comparison) in Vedic Sanskrit: thus in the passage, "They did not recognize Indra as a god", it has the sense of negation. The established use is (to place it immediately) before that which it makes negative. In the passage "Like hard drinkers of wine", it has the sense of comparison. The established use is (to place it immediately) after that with which it compares. The word *cid* has many meanings. In the sentence "Will the teacher kindly explain it?" it is used in the (sense of) respect. [From what root is (the word) *ā*cārya derived?] *Ā-cā*rya (teacher) is so called because he imparts traditional precepts (*ā*-cāra); or because he systematically arranges (*ā*+√ci+artha) the various objects (of knowledge), or because he systematically develops the intellectual faculty. In the expression "like curd", it is used in the sense of comparison; in "bring even the sour gruel", it is used in the sense of contempt. *Kul-mā*ṣāḥ (sour gruels) are so called because they are wasted away (*sidanti*) in families (*kuleṣu*). The word *nu* has many meanings. In the sentence "therefore he will do it", it is used in assigning a reason; in "how pray will he do it?" in asking a question, as well as in "has he really done it?" It is also used in the sense of comparison (as follows):

Of thee like the branches of a tree, O widely invoked one!

*Vayā*ḥ means branches, (and) is derived from (the root) *vi* (to move): they move in the wind. *Śā*-khāḥ (branches) are so called because they rest in the sky (*kha-śayā*ḥ), or (the word) may be derived from (the root) *śak* (to be able).

Now a conjunctive particle is that by whose addition separateness of notions is indeed recognized, but not like an enumerative one, i.e. because of a separation by isolation. The word *ca* is used in the sense of "aggregation", and is joined together with both, as "I and you, O slayer of Vṛtra!" *ā* is used in the same sense, as "for gods and for manes". The word *vā* is used in the sense of deliberation, as "Ah, shall I put this earth here or there?" Moreover, it is used in the sense of "aggregation" (as follows).

(Here ends the fourth section.)

"Vāyu and thee, Manu and thee." The words *aha* and *ha* have the sense of "mutual opposition", and are combined with the former (member), as "let this man do this, the other that", and "this man will do this, not that", &c. The letter *u* is also used in the same sense, (being joined) with the later (member), as "these people tell a lie, those the truth"; it is further used as an expletive, as "this", "that". The word *hi* has many meanings: in (the sentence) "therefore he will do it", it (is used) to point out the reason; in (the sentence) "how pray will he do it?" to ask a question; in (the sentence) "how *can* he analyse it?" to (indicate) displeasure. The word *kila* (is used to express) superiority of knowledge, as "thus truly it happened".

Moreover, it is combined with the two (particles) *na* and *nanu* in asking a question, as "was it not so?" and "was it so, pray?" The word *mā* denotes prohibition, as "do not do it", and "do not take". The word *khalu* also (denotes prohibition), as "enough of doing this", and "have done with it"; further, it is used as an expletive, as "thus it happened". The word *śaśvat* has the sense of uncertainty in classical Sanskrit: (in the sentence) "was it ever so?" it (is used) in an interrogation; (in the sentence) "was it ever so pray?" in an interrogation but not to oneself. The word *nū*nam has the sense of uncertainty in the classical language, both, i.e. the sense of uncertainty and that of an expletive, in Vedic Sanskrit.

Agastya, having assigned an oblation to Indra, desired to offer it to the Maruts. Indra, having presented himself, lamented (as follows).

(Here ends the fifth section.)

There, it seems, it does not exist; there is no to-morrow; who knows that which is not past? The mind of another is apt to waver; lo! the expected is lost.

There, it seems, it does not exist, i.e. there is no to-day nor indeed to-morrow. To-day, on this day. *Dyuḥ* is a synonym of day (so called) because it is bright (√*dyut*). To-morrow, the time that is still expected. Yesterday, the time that has expired. "Who knows that which is not past?" i.e. who knows that which is yet to come (i.e. the future)? . . . With these words, the four word classes are explained: i.e. the noun and the verb, the preposition and the particles in order. Sakata holds nouns are derived from verbs. This too is the doctrine of the etymologists. Not all say this, only some of the grammarians, "but only those, the accent and grammatical form of which are regular and which are accompanied by an explanatory radical modification. Those (nouns), such as cow, horse, man, elephant, &c., are conventional (terms, and hence are underivable)."

Now, if all nouns are derived from verbs, every person who performs a particular action should be called by the same name, i.e. whosoever runs on the road should be called "runner" (*aśva*, "horse"); whatever pricks (like needle, &c.), "pricker" (*tṛṇam*, "grass"). Further, if all nouns are derived from verbs, a substantive should obtain as many names as the actions with which it is connected; thus a column should also be called "beam-supporter", and "that which rests in a hole".

(Here ends the twelfth section.)

Moreover, substantives should be named according to the regular and correct grammatical form of a verb, so that their meanings may be indubitable, e.g. *puruṣa* (man) should take the form of *puri-śaya* (city-dweller); *aśva* (horse), of *aṣṭā* (runner); *tṛṇam* (grass), of *tardanam* (pricker). Further, people indulge in sophistry with regard to current expressions, e.g. they declare that earth (*pṛthivī*) is (so called) on account of being spread (√*prath*); but who spread it, and what was the base? Again, Śākaṭāyana derived parts of one word from different verbs, in spite of the meaning being irrelevant, and of the explanatory radical modification being non-existent, e.g. (explaining *sat-ya*) he derived the later syllable *ya* from the causal form of (the root) *i* (to go), and the former syllable *sat* from the regular form of (the root) *as* (to be). Further, it is said that a *becoming* is preceded by a *being*, (hence) the designation of a prior (*being*) from a posterior (*becoming*) is not tenable; consequently this (theory of the derivation of nouns from verbs) is not tenable.

(Here ends the thirteenth section.)

As to (the statement) that all those (nouns), the accent and grammatical form of which are regular, and which are accompanied by an explanatory radical modification, are derived, (we reply that) in that case it is quite evident. As to (the point) that every person whoever performs a particular action should be called by the same name, we see that in some cases the performers of the action do obtain a common name, while in others they do not, e.g. a carpenter or ascetic, enlivener, earth-born, &c. With this, the following objection is answered as well. As to (the point) that substantives should be named in such a way that their meanings may be indubitable, (we reply that) there are words (of that character), words of rare occurrence, i.e. single words formed by primary suffixes, as creeper, guest, one having matted locks, a wanderer, wakeful, one who sacrifices with a ladle, &c. As to (the objection) that people indulge in sophistry with regard to current expressions, (we reply that) it is with regard to current expressions alone that (etymological) examination is most desirable. With regard to "they declare that earth (*pṛthivi*) is (so called) on account of being spread (*prath*); but who spread it, and what was the base?" (we reply that) it is indeed broad to look at, even if it is not spread by others. Moreover, in this way all known words, without any exception, can be found fault with. As to (the point) that a certain individual derived parts of one word from different verbs, (we reply that) the person who made such a derivation in spite of the meaning being irrelevant should be blamed; it is the fault of an individual, not of the science (of etymology).

As to (the argument) that the designation of a prior (*being*) from a posterior *becoming* is not tenable, we see that in some cases prior *beings* do obtain their names from posterior *becomings*, but not in others, as "a woodpecker", "one having long locks", &c. *Bilva* is (so called) from being supported or from sprouting.

(Here ends the fourteenth section.)

Moreover, without it (etymology) the precise meaning of Vedic stanzas cannot be understood. For one who does not understand the meaning, a thorough investigation of accent and grammatical form is not possible.

* * *

Panini, who wrote the first extant Sanskrit grammar, the *Astadhyayi*—the word means eight books—was born, probably in the fifth or fourth century B.C., in Gandhara, India, a town then part of the Achaemenid empire. The *Astadhyayi* represents "the first attempt in the history of the world to describe and analyse the components of a language on scientific lines." Panini is regarded with immense reverence by all Hindus; he is said to have received fourteen *Sutras* (aphoristic doctrinal summaries) from the Lord Shiva, a member of the Hindu supreme triad.

Panini is regarded no less highly by contemporary philologists and can be considered the founder of both the Sanskrit philosophy of language and the science of linguistics. "It is not always easy," the late Professor Louis Renou wrote, "to gauge exactly what Panini wanted to teach." Also, to a certain degree, "Panini has built a special language. . . . in short he has created a meta-language flexible enough to describe the facts of language."[1] However, it is possible to conclude, as J. F. Staal said in 1963, that "From a historical point of view, Panini's grammatical method has been as central to Indian thought as Euclid's geometrical method to Western thought."

Extracts from the *Astadhyayi* follow (edited and translated by the late Srisa C. Vasu; published by Mohtal Banarsidass, 1962, under a scheme for reprinting important out-of-print Sanskrit books, sponsored by the Government of India).

From the ASTADHYAYI

That which is pronounced by the nose along with the mouth is called *Anunâsika* or nasal. . . .

A letter partially uttered by the nose and partially by the mouth would be called *anunâsika*. Therefore the nasals are those letters which are pronounced from two organs or places, *i.e.*, the mouth and the nose. The pure nasal is *anusvâra*, while *anunasikas* are different from this, in as much as, that in pronouncing these, the breath passes through the nose and the mouth.

The vowels are generally so nasalised. If, instead of emitting the vowel sound freely through the mouth, we allow the *velum pendulum* to drop and the air to vibrate through the cavities which connect the nose with the pharynx, we hear the nasal vowels (*anunâsika*). . . . The consonants are also *anunâsika*. . . . Semi-vowels are also nasalised and are then called *anunâsika*. . . . Why have we used the word "by the mouth"? This definition will not include *anusvâra* or the pure nasal, which is pronounced wholly through the nose. Why have we used the word "by the nose"? In order to exclude those consonants . . . which are pronounced wholly and solely through the mouth. . . .

Those whose place of utterance and effort are equal are called *savarna* or homogeneous letters.

This defines the word *savarṇa* or a homogeneous letter. The *sûtra* consists of four words: "equal or similar," "mouth or place of pronunciation," "effort" and "words of the same class."

The places or portions of the mouth by contact with which various sounds are formed are chiefly the following:—1. "throat" 2. "palate," 3. "head," 4. "teeth," 5. "lips," 6. "nose."

The quality or effort is of two sorts primarily, "internal" and "external." The first is again sub-divided into five parts:—

1. Complete contact of the organs. Twenty-five letters belong to this class. In pronouncing these there is a complete contact of the root or the tongue with the various places, such as throat, palate, dome of the palate, teeth and lip.

2. Slight contact. "In pronouncing these semi-vowels the two organs, the active and passive, which are necessary for the production of all consonantal noises, are not allowed to touch each other, but only to approach."

3. Complete opening. The vowels belong to this class.

4. Slight opening. Some place the vowels and these into one group and call them all *vivṛita*.

5. Contracted. In actual use, the organ in the enunciation is contracted but it is considered to be open only, as in the case of the other vowels, when the vowel is in the state of taking part in some operation of grammar.

The *âbhyantara prayatna* is the mode of articulation preparatory to the utterance of the sound, the *bâhya-prayatna* is the mode of articulation at the close of the utterance of the sound.

The division of letters according to *âbhyantra prayatna* has been already given. By that we get, 1. the sparsa or mute letters, 2. the *antastha* or intermediate between *sparsas* and *ushmans*, or semi-vowel or liquid letters, 3. the *svaras* or vowels or *vivrita* letters, 4. the *ushmans* or *sibilants* or *flatus* letters.

The division of letters according to *bâhya prayatna* gives us first surds or *aghosha* letters, 2. sonants or *ghosha* letters. The *aghosha* are also called *svâsa* letters, the *ghoshas* are called *nâda* letters.

The second division of letters according to *bâhya prayatna* is into:

1. Aspirated (*mahâprâṇa*). 2. Unaspirated (*alpaprâṇa*).

One vowel has eighteen forms. The *acute (udâtta), grave (anudâtta)* and *circumflexed (svarita)*. Each one of these three may be nasalised (*anunâsika*), or not (*niranunâsika*).

Similarly 3 letters have also eighteen forms. One letter has no long form; it has therefore 12 modifications. The diphthongs have no short forms, they have therefore, only 12 forms. The *antastha* or semi-vowels with one exception have two forms each *viz.*, nasalised and un-nasalised. The semi-vowels have no homogeneous letters corresponding to them. All letters of a *varga* or "class" are homogeneous to each other.

Thus then the homogeneous or *savarna* letters must satisfy two conditions before they could be called *savarṇa*. First, their place of pronunciation must be the same. Secondly their quality must be equal. If one condition be present and the other be absent, there can be no *savarṇa-* hood. . . .

There is an exception to this rule in one case, and which though having different quality is still called *savarṇa* by virtue of the *vârttika* of Kâtyâyana . . . The word *savarṇa* occurs in *sûtras* (VI. 1. 101).

Why do we say "the place of pronunciation"? So that there may not be homogeneous relationship between those whose *prayatna* is the same but whose *âsya* is different. . . .

Why do we say "effort"? That there may be no homogeneity between the palatals, and these whose organ of pronunciation is the same, but whose *prayatna* is different. . . . Then elison would occur.

There is however no homogeneity between vowels and consonants, through their place and effort be equal.

This *sûtra* lays down an exception to the former *sûtra*. There can be no homogeneity or *savarṇa* relationship between vowels and consonants. . . .

A dual case affix is called *Pragrihya*, or excepted vowels which do not admit of *sandhi* or conjunction.

As a general rule, Sanskrit allows of no hiatus in a sentence. If a word ends in a vowel, and the next word begins with a vowel, the two vowels coalesce, according to certain rules. This is called *sandhi*. But *pragṛihyas* are exceptions to this *sandhi*, "they are certain terminations, the final vowels of which are not liable to any *sandhi* rules." . . .

A finite verb is unaccented, when a word precedes it, which is not a finite verb. . . .

Why do we say "when the preceding word is not a finite verb"? Observe "the act of cooking exists". Here the word is a finite verb, therefore the verb *pachati* does not lose its accent. So also "successful he conquers, rules, thrives". "For us conquer and fight". In one simple sentence, two finite verbs cannot be employed; one sentence consists of one finite verb only. But the very fact of this *sûtra* indicates that this condition does not apply to this *sûtra*; so that the two words need not be portions of the *same* sentence, for the application of this *nighâta*. . . .

But the Periphrastic Future is not unaccented, when it is preceded by a word which is not a finite verb. . . .

This restricts the scope of the last *sûtra* which was rather too wide.

The finite verb retains its accent in connection with the particles "that", "because", "if", "also"!, "O!", "well", "not", "if", "if", (interrogative particle, implying "I hope" or "I hope not)", and "where". . . .

The finite verb retains its accent . . . when employed in the sense of forbidding.

When something urged by one, is rejected insultingly by another, then the reply made by the first tauntingly, with a negation, is *pratyârambha*. Thus A says to B: "Eat this please". B rejects the offer repeatedly, in anger or jest. Then A in anger or jest says "No, you will eat"—here its accent, which is acute on the middle, is retained.

Another example is "No, you will study". Why do we say, "when asseverative"? Observe "Verily in that world they do not wish for fee". Here it is pure negation.

The finite verb retains its accent when used in asking a question.

Thus "Truly will you eat"?

The finite verb retains its accent when used in a friendly assertion.

Anything done to injure another is *prati-loma*, opposite of this is *apratiloma*, or friendliness. In fact, it is equal to *anuloma*. Thus "yes, you may cook". Here *anga* has the force of friendly permission. But when it has the force of *pratiloma*, we have:— "Well, chuckle O sinner! soon wilt thou learn, O coward". Here the verb is used in the sense of censure, for chuckling is a thing not liked by the person: and is *pratiloma* action. . . .

A finite verb loses its accent when it denotes "praise".

The last *sûtra* taught that the verb loses its accent when *immediately* preceded. This qualifies the word "immediately" and teaches that the intervention of a Preposition does not debar immediateness. . . .

A finite verb retains its accent when meaning "praise".

In the Veda, the finite verb retains its accent, though not always, when it stands in correlation to another verb, even more than one.

That is, sometimes one verb, sometimes more than one verb, retain their accent. Thus of more than one verb, we have the following example:— "Because the drunkard tells falsehood, therefore sin will make him impure: i.e. he does incur sin". Here both verbs retain their accent. According to Kaiyyata the meaning of this sentence is i.e. a drunkard does not incur the sin of telling a falsehood, because he is not in his senses. . . .

A finite verb retains its accent optionally when it means "haste". Why do we say when "asking for permission"? Observe: "Devadatta hast thou made the mat? Well, I am making it".

A finite verb retains its accent when a question is asked relating to an action, and when the verb is not preceded by a Preposition or by a Negation.

When however "action" is not added in asking such a question, the finite verb may optionally retain its accent.

The Paniniya Śikṣā has also been ascribed to Panini, and the following extracts from it are from the edition published by the University of Calcutta in 1938, with translation and notes by Manomohan Gosh.

PANINIYA ŚIKṢA

Now I shall give out the Sikṣā according to the views of Panini. In pursuance of the traditional lore, one should learn it with reference to the popular and the Vedic languages. Though words and their meanings are well known, yet these are not within the knowledge of persons intellectually deficient, (hence) I shall dwell once more on the rules regarding the pronunciation of words. That speech-sounds in Prakrit and Sanskrit are sixty-three or sixty-four, according to their origin, has been said by Brahman (Svayambhu) himself.

Ātmā with *buddhi* perceives things and sets the mind to an intention of speaking; the mind (then) gives impetus to the fire within the body, and the latter drives the breath out.

The breath circulating within the lungs creates the soft (*mandra*) tone; this is connected with the morning offering (*prātaḥ-savana*) and rests in the Gāyatrī (metre).

(The same breath circulating) in the throat (produces) the middle (*madhyama*) tone and relates to the midday offering (*mādhyandina-savana*) and follows the *Triṣṭubh* (metre); and the shrill (*tāra*) tone (which is produced by the breath circulating) in the roof of the mouth relates to the third (i.e., evening) offering (of the day) and follows the *Jagatī* (metre).

(The breath which is thus) sent upwards and is checked by the roof of the mouth attains to the mouth and produces speech-sounds (*varṇas*), which have a fivefold classification—according to their pitch, quantity, place of articulation, the primary effort and the secondary effort. So said those who were versed in (pronouncing) speech-sounds. Learn this carefully.

There are three kinds of (pitch) accent: *udātta, anudātta*, and *svarita*. Among vowels short, long and pluta varieties are distinguished by their time (of articulation).

Of the seven musical notes *niṣā* and *gāndhāra* can arise in the high pitch (*udātta*), *ṛṣabha* and *dhaivata* in the low pitch (*anudātta*), while *ṣaḍja, madhyama* and *pañcama* have their source in the medium pitch (*svarita*).

The speech-sounds have eight places (of articulation): chest, throat, roof of the mouth (*lit.* head), root of the tongue, teeth, nostril, lips and palate.

Uṣmans (spirants) have eight ways (of development): change to *o*, hiatus, *ś, ṣ, s, r, jihvāmūlīya* and *upadhmānīya*.

When a word ending in *o* (out of an *ūṣman*) is followed by another word beginning with *u*, the former should be considered as ending in a vowel coming from an *ūṣman*.

When combined with nasal stops (*lit.* fifth ones) and semi-vowels, *ḥ* should be known (as arising) from the chest; while *h* not so combined is said to be from the throat.

A and h are throat sounds; i, *cu* (i.e., c, ch, j, jh and ñ) and ś are palatals; u and *pu* (i.e., p, ph, b, bh and m) labials; ṛ, *ṭu* (i.e., ṭ, ṭh, ḍ, ḍh and ṇ) and ṣ cerebrals; and l, *tu* (i.e., t, th, d, dh and n) and s are dentals.

Ku (i.e., k, kh, g, gh and ṅ) is uttered from the root of the tongue, and v is a denti-labial sound; e and ai are throat-palatal, and o and au are throat-labial sounds.

The throat element of e and o is half a *mātrā* and of ai and au is (one) *mātrā*; these two latter (i.e., ai and au) are open-close sounds (i.e., their first half or the *a*-element is open and the second half or *i*- and *u*- element is closed).

Svarāṇām ūṣmaṇāṃ câiva vivṛtaṃ karaṇaṃ smṛtam
tebhyo'pi vivṛtāv eṅau tābhyām aicau tathâiva ca

Vowels and sibilants are open in enunciation; e and o are more open than they, and ai and au are still more so.

Anusvāra and *yamas* have the nose for their place (of articulation); *upadhmāniya, ūṣman* (i.e., *visarjanīya*), *jihvāmūlīya* as well as *nāsikyas* (i.e., the *anusvāra* and *yamas*) are *ayogavāhas* and as such they share the place of articulation of sounds on which they are dependent.

The *anusvāra* after the vowels not pronounced at the root of the teeth, should be made sonorous like the sound of an *alābu-vīnā*, but when it stands before h, ś, ṣ and s this pronunciation is compulsory.

NOTE. All the recensions except the Astadhyayi contain the above couplet. The *anusvāra* being a frequent sound in Vedas and the classical Skt., it appears very much likely that Panini gave attention to it. Besides this for interpreting *śaṣaseṣu ca* we must invoke the help of Panini's Paribhāṣā *tasminn iti nirdiṣṭe pūrvasya*. (I. 1. 66) This also may be taken to show that this couplet belongs to the original Paniniya Siksā.

NOTE. From this passage we derive a hint about an alternative pronunciation which the *anusvāra* had before stops. This alternative pronunciation has been provided for by Panini in his grammar (*anusvārasya yayi parasavarnah, vā padāntasya*. VIII. 4. 58, 59),* and it is equivalent to the pronunciation of what according to Prof. S. K. Chatterji is a "reduced" nasal occurring also in the late Middle Indo-Aryan.

Anusvāre vivṛtyāṃ tu virāme cákṣara-dvaye
dvir oṣṭhau tu vigṛhṇiyād yatrâukāra-vakārayoḥ

* The anusvāra followed by consonants other than *ś, ṣ, s* and *h* is changed to the *savarṇa* (homogeneous nasal sound) of the following sound; the possible homogeneous sounds in the above case are *ṅ, ñ, ṇ, n* and *m*. This rule is optional when the anusvāra stands at the end of a word.

In the *anusvāra*, hiatus, *virāma* and double consonant, the two lips should be separated as also in case of au and v.

As the tigress carries her cubs between two (rows of) teeth taking care lest they should either be dropped or bitten, so should one pronounce the (Vedic) speech-sounds lest they should be dropped (i.e., elided) or differentiated (i.e., mis-pronounced).

NOTE. There is pun in the words *patana* and *bheda*. The fact that the couplet mentions the dropping of *varṇaṣ* in the Vedic recitation shows that the upper limit to the date of the composition of the couplet is c. 200 B.C. . . .

In memorizing the Vedas one should make his reading quick but in applying the same in rituals the recitation should be of medium speed, while at the time of instructing pupils, the Vedic passages should be recited slowly.

Gitī śighrī śiraḥ-kampī tathā likhita-pāṭhakaḥ
Anarthajño 'lpa-kaṇṭhaś ca ṣaḍ ete pāṭhakâdhamāḥ
Mādhurnyam akṣara-vyaktiḥ padacchedas to susvaraḥ
dhairyaṃ laya-samarthaṃ ca ṣaḍ ete pāṭhake guṇāḥ

Those who recite the Veda in a singsong manner, (too) quickly, with a nodding of the head, use a written text at the time of recitation, do not know the meaning of the passages read, and have a low voice, are six kinds of bad reciters. Sweetness, clearness, separation of words, right accent, patience and ability to observe time are six merits in a reciter.

Śaṅkitaṃ bhītam udghuṣṭam avyaktam anunāsikam
kāka-svaraṃ śirasigam tathā sthāna-vivarjitam

Shyness, fear, extreme loudness, indistinctness, undue nasalisation, repressed tone, undue cerebralization, non-observance of the places of articulation (in general) and (proper) accent, and harshness, creating undue separation between words, uneven tone, hastiness, want of due palatalisation: these are the fourteen faults in the Vedic chant.

One should not recite a Vedic passage in under-tone, between one's teeth, quickly, haltingly, slowly, with a hoarse voice, in a sing-song manner, with repressed voice, omitting (occasionally) words and syllables and in a plaintive voice.

In the morning (the Vedic student) should read (*mantras*) with a voice from the chest, which should be (as deep-toned) as the growl of a tiger. In the midday he should read it with voice from his throat, which should be like that of a *cakravāka*. In the third *savana* (i.e., the evening offering) he should recite it in the highest pitch from the roof of his mouth and his voice should be like that of a peacock, goose or cuckoo.

The vowels are without touch, semi-vowels slightly touched, ś, ṣ and s are half-touched sounds, and the remaining consonants are touched (i.e., stops).

NOTE. The degree of touch in this connexion is with regard to the cavity of the mouth or rather the space between the two parts of the mouth which touch or approach each other before speech-sounds are produced.

Ñam (i.e., ñ, ṅ, m, ṇ, and n) are produced through nose, and h except when it is combined with r; and *jhas* (i.e., gh, jh, ḍh, dh, bh) are voiced, semivowels (y, r, l, v) and *jas* (i.e., j, b, g, ḍ, d) slightly voiced, the group beginning with kh and ph (i.e., kh, ch, ṭh, th and ph) breathed, *car* (i.e., k, c, ṭ, t, p) slightly breathed. This has been called the basis of speech.

By Pāṇini, the son of Dākṣi, who has promulgated in this world this science which is as it were a jewel, has also revealed it to the world (for the first time).

(First) Metrics which is the two legs (of the Veda) is read and then the Kalpa which is its two hands. The Science of the Movement of Luminaries (Astronomy) is its eyes, and the Nirukta is called its ears; the Śikṣā is the nose of the Veda, and Grammar is its mouth. It is for this reason that one studying the Veda with all its limbs (i.e., accessory studies) attains a high position in the realm of Brahman.

One ought not to repeat *mantras* with teeth shown, lips unduly protruded and with indistinct, unduly nasalised and half choked-up voice and immobile tongue.

A *mantra* uttered either with a defective accent or pronunciation is badly done and it does not carry the proper sense. And it is like a thunderbolt of speech and kills the *yajamāna* just as

"*Indrasatruh*" did on account of its wrong accent.

(When a *mantra* is) deficient in a syllable it tends to diminish life, and (when it is) lacking in proper accent it makes the reciter troubled with illness, and the syllable (wrongly treated) will strike one at the head as a thunderbolt.

Hasta-hīnaṃ yo'dhīte svara-varṇa-vivarjitam
Rg-Yajuḥ-Sāmabhir dagdho viyonim adhigacchati

If anybody reads (the Veda) without a show of hands and does not observe proper accents and places of articulation Ṛk, Yajus and Sāman burn him and (on death) he attains rebirth as an inferior animal.

And a person who reads the Veda with a show of hands, observes proper accent and places of articulation and knows the meaning of what he reads is purified by the Ṛk, Yajus and the Sāman and is placed high in the realm of Brahman.

Drawing the divine words from the entire domain of speech (*vāṅmaya*) Śaṅkara gave this, his science (*Śāṅkarim*) to the wise son of Dākṣi. This is its basis.

Homage to that Pāṇini who having received the traditional lore of speech-sounds (*Varṇa-samāmnāya*) from Śiva has told us the entire grammar.

The most famous commentator on Panini was Patanjali, who probably lived between the second and first century B.C. Patanjali, a seer, sage and saint, said the preservation of the Veda was served by the study of grammar, and he refers to the ancient custom by which Brahmin students took up grammar first—and shows, too, the extent to which grammar was related to popular usage.

He was an adherent of the *Mimamsa* philosophy, originally founded by Jaimini, by which sound was considered to be eternal, as manifested by utterance and represented by letters. In this philosophy, the authority of the Vedas is upheld by *Vac*, the Word. Sound is neither produced by the vocal organ nor liable to disappear: the vocal apparatus serves to manifest the sound ever existing in all beings. The relations between sound and meaning are natural and eternal, and not brought about by any convention of human origin. His *Mahabhasya* is "an important work not only for grammar but also for logic, methodology and philosophy."[2] And Staat adds, "as a scholar and thinker on the one hand, and as a forerunner of innumerable themes of Indian scientific thought on the other, Patanjali could be compared in the West with no less a thinker than Aristotle."

In the *Mahabhasya*, Patanjali states that words and meanings have a permanently fixed and eternal relation. Creation itself is a manifestation of the unmanifest in the shape of the finite passage from the indeterminate to the determinate. The Creator gives names: there is no object without a name, and no name that does not call up an object. The relation of sound and sense is ultimately the same relation as *naman*, body and *rupa*, soul. Speech (*Vac*) is pure consciousness at work, evolved from *sabda*. As the word evolves from *sabda*, so perception and inference flow from it. The first manifestation of eternal consciousness, *nada*, is materialised into sound by the operation of the flowing of internal air: the four forms of speech correspond to the four shapes *nada* takes as it becomes the word: the relation of word to meaning can suffer no disruption. How is it known that words and meanings and their relations are eternal? From the experience of everyday life, Patanjali goes on to declare. In everyday life men first think of objects and then make use of words to denote them, but they never attempt to create words. With things, an attempt is made to produce whatever is needed, as, for example, "one needing a pot goes to the house of the potter and asks him 'make a pot and I shall do something with it.' One wishing to use words does not go to the house of the grammarian and ask him, 'make words and then I shall use them.' "

Against this *Mimamsa* theory of the eternity of words (followers of this theory were called *Mimasakas*), the *Nyaya* philosophical system declared the origin of sound to be the *sphota*, the undifferentiated shout. The Naiyayikas (followers of this theory) said *sabda* was a quality of the sky, was indeed a quality of space itself, and was not eternal, though invisible, but was liable to production and destruction.

Patanjali laid great stress on the *Samartha*, by which he denoted "semantic connection": i.e., the relationship between two or more meaningful units. This word he restricted solely to the province of syntax, as the following excerpts from Patanjali's *Mahabhasya* may make clear.

From the MAHABHASYA

(*Now starts the section on the purpose of the* samartha-paribhāṣā)

14. (*Bhāṣya:* Question)
Now, what is the purpose of mentioning (the word) *samartha*?

Kaiyaṭa:

Through the question regarding the purpose of the main word *samartha* the question about the purpose of the rule itself is raised. Although by this word we cannot generate semantic connection (between the elements to be compounded), because to generate semantic connection, when the elements themselves do not show it, falls outside the scope of this rule, still, the word *samartha* serves the purpose of providing the proviso "semantic connection" for the rules dealing with a finished word. Therefore, the word *samartha* is regarded as the main one.

Note (13):

For the meaning of *padavidhi*: "rule prescribing a grammatical operation for a finished word", i.e. rule dealing with a finished word.

15. (*Bhāṣya:* Answer)
(a) He (Pāṇini) will state (that a word in the) accusative case is compounded with (the words *śrita* etc., as in *kaṣṭaśritaḥ*: "who has resorted to effort", *narakaśritaḥ*: "who has taken his refuge in hell".
(a') What is the purpose of mentioning *samartha* here? (So that this rule will not become operative in the following example:) *paśya devadatta kaṣṭam śrito viṣnumitro gurukulam*: "see, o Devadatta, the (painful) effort, resorted to the house of his teacher has Viṣṇumitra".

Note (14):

The examples are given in the sub-sections indicated by accentless letters (a-f). The counterexamples follow in the sub-sections indicated by accented letters (a'-f'). The words underlined in the translation of the counterexamples correspond with the compound-constituents in the examples. The rules mentioned in this *Bhāṣya* prescribe compounding. The words given as examples are compounds. The counterexamples show how the words used as compound-constituents in the examples may occur in immediate sequence without semantic connection. Throughout these sections it is shown that the word *samartha* supplied in each rule quoted becomes purposeful by prohibiting compounding in the counterexamples. F.i. the word *samartha* becomes purposeful by prohibiting the formation of the compound of the semantically unconnected words *kaṣṭam* and *śritaḥ* which here form part of two different sentences.

(*Bhāṣya* continued)
(b) (Pāṇini will state:) *śaṅkulākhaṇḍaḥ*: "piece cut off by nippers", *kirikāṇaḥ*: "made blind in one eye by a hog".
(b') What is the purpose of mentioning *samartha*? (So that this rule will not become operative in the following example:) *tiṣṭha tvaṁ śāṅkulayā khaṇḍo dhāvati musalena*: "stop (cutting) by nippers, the piece (already cut off) by a pestle slips away".
Note (15):
This rule states that a word in the instrumental may be compounded with a semantically connected word denoting a quality; when it (the quality, f.i. *kāṇatva*: "blindness") is caused by the thing denoted by the word in the instrumental, and with the word *artha*. For further explanation see note (14).

(*Bhāṣya* continued)
(c) (Pāṇini will state:) *gohitam*: "good for cows", *aśvahitam*: "good for horses".
(c') What is the purpose of mentioning *samartha* here? (So that this rule will not become operative in the following example:) *sukhaṁ gobhyo hitaṁ devadattāya*: "pleasant for cows, good for Devadatta".
Note (16):
This rule states that a word in the dative may be compounded

with semantically connected words denoting things intended for the objects denoted by the words in the dative, and with the word *artha*: "for the sake of", *bali*: "a sacrifice", *hita*: "good", *sukha*: "pleasant", *rakṣita*: "reserved for". For further explanation see note (14).

(*Bhāṣya* continued)
(d) (Pāṇini will state:) *vṛkabhayam*: "fear of wolves" *dasyubhayam*: "fear of robbers", *caurabhayam*: "fear of thieves".
(d') What is the purpose of mentioning *samartha* here? (So that the rule will not become operative in the following example:) *gaccha tvaṁ mā vṛkebhyo bhayaṁ devadattāt yajñadattasya*: "do not go away because of the wolves, fear of Devadatta has Yajñadatta".
Note (17):
This rule states that a word in the ablative may be compounded with the semantically connected word *bhaya*: "fear". For further explanation see note (14).

(*Bhāṣya* continued)
(e) (Pāṇini will state that (a word in) the genitive is compounded with a case-inflected word. (By this rule we derive the compounds:) *rājapuruṣaḥ*: "king-man", *brāhmaṇakambalaḥ*: "brahmin-blanket".
(e') What is the purpose of mentioning *samartha* here? (So that the rule will not become operative in the following example:) *bhāryā rājñaḥ puruṣo devadattasya*: "wife of the king, man of Devadatta".

(*Bhāṣya* continued)
(f) (Pāṇini will state:) *akṣaśauṇḍaḥ*: "addicted to dice", *strīśauṇḍaḥ*: "addicted to women".
(f') What is the purpose of mentioning *samartha* here? (So that the rule will not become operative in the following example:) *kuśalo devadatto 'kṣeṣu śauṇḍaḥ, pibati pānāgāre*: "skilled is Devadatta in dice, the addict drinks in the winehouse".

* * *

Another of the great Sanskrit grammarians was Bhartrhari. On the word of a Chinese pilgrim, Yi-tsing, Bhartrahi was long thought to have died in 651 A.D. and to have been a Buddhist: supposedly he had been seven times a monk and finally a layman. Now it has been fairly firmly established that he was a fifth-century (A.D.) very orthodox Brahmin! While the Mimamsa philosophers declared only phonemes real, and Panini isolated prefixes, Bhartrhari proclaimed, in the Vakydiya Bramakanda, the reality of the complete phrase only, and its sense, which he declared to be different from the words composing the sentence. "The words have no separate existence apart from the sentence." For example, "when the word 'cow' has been said eight times, that does not mean that there are eight words for cow, nor that there are eight cows; thus we recognise the same word, and language is a natural duplication of reality, as real as are things, but it is only perceptible by transmission in practice." And again, Bhartrhari declared: "Words are the only basis of the true nature of the objects designated and of their use. Without grammar, one has no knowledge of the true reality of words." He elevates grammar to "near Brahma [the highest God]; it is the first annex of the vedic verse, as those say who know." Indeed, this Brahma-Word, from which comes the formation of words and their correct form, the object of whose formation is knowledge of correct forms,

> is near Him and is His direct auxiliary. It is the highest asceticism. Chastity, sleeping on the bare ground, remaining in water, fasting the phases of the moon, of all these things, Grammar has the most right to the name of asceticism, because it produces particular fruits, visible and invisible. This revaluation of language through the knowledge which one obtains as the fruit of the merits of all the Vedas, is truly the supreme essence of speech; this very holy light of grammar is the direct way to Him. Starting from the first undifferentiated Word, all succession is re-absorbed, which exists within all creatures. The Word, at the moment when phenomena disappear, re-absorbs them. From this word, the imperishable phoneme, proceeds the world. Language divides by acquiring differences coming from

articulation, and takes on the character of letters, words and phrases. Thanks to its eternal relation with objects, it acquires divisions like 'cow' insofar as objects have signification. Though a thing can exist without being perceived, still a hare's horn cannot be admitted, for there is no means of perceiving it. That is why the relation between words and their object cannot be the work of a man."

VAKYADIYA BRAMAKANDA[3]

"The relation between words and their meaning is eternal; this is what the great seers, the authors of the *sutra*, the *varttika*, and the *bhasya* have taught us."

"Eternal is the word, eternal the object it signifies, eternal their relation: this is the proposition at the basis of this treatise on grammar. What indeed one means by word, is in fact, the generic form of the word, according to what has been said." It is because of the eternity of the generic form that the word is eternal. It has been said indeed, "This treatise was established in reference to the generic form." This generic form is something different from the particular form of verbality. Indeed, verbality, in general, is what is inherent without contradiction in the same object as all the generic forms whose inherence to one and the same object would be contradictory; the different kinds of words, such as those of the word *vrksa* in general, are called "words" (only and simply) when (the audible object, being confused), they are represented by sounds which have become similar (to each other, lacking distinction). Just as in a jug are inherent without contradistinction materiality, the clayey nature in general, the type of jug etc., so also in the word *vrksa* the different generic forms of the quality of the word *vrksa*, of its verbality and so forth, are inherent without contradicting each other.

But, it will be said, in the case of things like a jug which has fixed parts, it is the totality (sum) of these parts which causes the manifestation of their special generic form. Whereas different individual words do not have fixed parts. Their parts are not produced at the same time and do not exist simultaneously; thus they cannot be described and, in consequence, since many of their inherent causes can be non-existent, they cannot form a different word in which different generic forms could be inherent. Whereas verbality (pure and simple) is complete in each part. Were one to admit that, in the same way the given generic form is completely present in each part, then, once a single part is stated, that is to say even if the *v* is stated separately, one could obtain an idea which would include the particular form of the word, *vrska*, for example.*

No, our position does not make this mistake. It is with the word as though there were different moves: throwing up into the air, turning around in circles, pouring out, etc. All the parts of a movement cannot constitute a new movement which would represent their entirety, and yet it is not true not to admit therein the inherence of special kinds of movements, such, for example, as that which consists in throwing up into the air, kinds differing from the movement in general. It is no less true that, if one sees only one part of a movement, the idea which would apprehend the form of a special kind of movement, such as turning around in a circle, does not arise.

Indeed, partial movements are doubtless produced by specific movements, but, although they each become the support of a particular kind of movement, such as throwing something up into

*Here the adversary (opposition) is Mimamsaka. For the Mimamsaka, generic form must be revealed by a perceptible physical structure—*akrti*—to the point that there can only be a generic form of the substance. Letters being conceived as substances perceptible by hearing, each possess completely the genus *sub-datva*. The first reply of the Vaiyakarana to the adversary accepts the hypothesis that the generic form should be present in each letter in order to be expressed by the word. Thus the generic form is revealed more and more clearly by the letters as they are pronounced. The structure is in time and not in space, as in the case of movement. The grammarian then gives a second reply. Ñ the generic form of a word, is not present in every letter under the pretext that the letters would manifest (express) it; it is completely revealed only in the final knowledge when it has the whole word for support and not the single letters. The *vrtti* here introduces a discussion on the type of generic form of words in relation to their permanent character, in a context where it is redundant. The permanence of words is for Bhartrhari that of the *sphota*, that is to say the sound entity essentially inaudible and which only becomes audible through impermanent sounds or *dhvani*. For Patanjali, the *akrti* is the permanent structure but the notion of *sphota* is structurally at the same level as that of *akrti*.

the air, each does not suggest the idea of this particular movement, for exactly what is particular about a movement is difficult to determine. In the same way, in the case of words like *vrksa* the letters v, etc., produced by specific efforts, are particularised, but in just what their particularity consists is difficult to determine, although each of their parts effects the manifestation of the particular kind of word involved, yet it is not possible to use those kinds of words whose particularities include several factors of non-apprehended manifestation. While, when the continuing series consists of parts perceived successively, then one can use it, because it includes limitation by a special kind of word.

Moreover, the procedure of revelation of a generic form admitted into another system is not necessarily accepted by grammarians. Indeed, it is not an absolute rule that that which is manifest is only manifest if it has the support of factors of manifestation. In the present case, even if the type of word is not inherent in the individual verbal elements, such a kind is first of all not apprehended or it is apprehended in an indistinct manner by ideas which are successively produced and acquire new disposition as the letters are perceived; then it is determined by the final idea in the internal organ thus prepared. As for the existence of this kind of word, one infers it from the identity of the idea which one has each time that an individual word *vrska*, for example, is used whether by a parrot, a myna bird or a man.

Even those who do not accept the use of a generic form still recognise that the individual word is itself eternal and that it can be manifested by multiple sounds. Some accept the division into letters within the individual word.

Others on the contrary maintain that in each letter, in each word, in each phrase, it is a unique verbal entity which is brought to light under the appearance of parts produced successively.

Others say that words are eternal because their usage is eternal; indeed, granted the absence of interruption of the transmission, and the eternity of their function, there was no moment when they were used for the first time by being created.

As to the signified objects too, some admit these are eternal because of the eternity of their generic form. Thus Patanjali said, "Relatively to what signified object is the following analysis correct: the word, its sense and their relation being established? It is said that this applies to their generic form." In all these theories relative to this affirmation of the Mahabhasya, the eternity of the signified object is explained in many ways; in any case, it must be admitted according to the Bhasya.

The relation is eternal because of the mutual appurtenance; the relation of identity between the word and its meaning is original and self-established, for it is impossible to forbid a meaning; there never was anyone to fabricate this relationship a first time, when it was unknown before, for the benefit of an interlocutor. That is why the relationship between a word and its meaning is without beginning and has never been interrupted. Or yet once again, the relationship between a word and its meaning has a certain natural appropriateness, limited by a convention which joins them like what is lighted and what lights in the way of a sensorial organ and its domain (sight and the eye). Or again, supposing it is admitted that ideas, taking on the appearance of things signified and converted into external objects, make one only domain with their signified objects, just as one imagines that a syllable (thought) is the cause of a syllable (heard) and the relation between the word and its meaning is in a ratio of cause to effect whose transmission was never interrupted. (Patanjali) said in effect "The speakers themselves, setting out the sequence of things from beginning to end, make the object of the ideas appear as real."

"This is what the great seers have transmitted to us" that is to say the authors of the *sutras*, etc. It is only the *sutras* and the other grammatical texts which are here described. Moreover, since the beginning of the *sutras*, the eternity of words has been recognised. Indeed, if the words and their meaning and the relationship between them were not eternal, there would be no reason for undertaking a Grammatical Treatise.

> And language is not learned by human beings. Children are born with an inborn intuition or instinct: "What makes the cuckoo sing in spring? What teaches the spider to weave its web, or the birds to build their nests? Who teaches beasts and birds to eat, make love, fight, swim? These activities are practised on account of heredity."

Guatama Siddhartha (563-483?), known as the Buddha, established a religion that prevailed for five hundred years in India, and is still the religion of one-third of the human race, flourishing in China, Japan, Ceylon and the Indonesian archipelago, with vigorous branches in the West. There was no Buddhist writing before the second century B.C., though the *Sangha*, the Buddhist monastery, is today the oldest surviving form of human association.

The Upanishads were based on causality: "Everything a man is, is the result of what he does." The Dhammapada, one of the earliest Buddhist writings, on the contrary, declared that "Everything a man is, is the result of what he thinks." The early Buddhist philosophy, written in Pali, considered that words were material. Later, the Buddhist schools taught that words indicate concepts or mental images and do not directly refer to things. Language which "has dialects and is subject to change is merely used for communication."

After the conquest of the Persian Empire by Alexander the Great (356-323), some of his generals and successors, Bactrian Greeks, conquered a large part of India. One of these Bactrians was King Menander, called Milinda in Asia. He was converted to Buddhism. The story of his conversion is a dialogue between the King and the Buddhist monk, Nagasena, and one chapter refers to problems of language. It follows here.

THE DISTINGUISHING CHARACTERISTICS OF ETHICAL QUALITIES.

CHAPTER ONE

1. Now Milinda the king went up to where the venerable Nâgasena was, and addressed him with the greetings and compliments of friendship and courtesy, and took his seat respectfully apart. And Nâgasena reciprocated his courtesy, so that the heart of the king was propitiated.

And Milinda began by asking, "How is your Reverence known, and what, Sir, is your name?"

"I am known as Nâgasena, O king, and it is by that name that my brethren in the faith address me. But although parents, O king, give such a name as Nâgasena, or Sûrasena, or Virasena, or Sihasena, yet this, Sire,—Nâgasena and so on—is only a generally understood term, a designation in common use. For there is no permanent individuality (no soul) involved in the matter."

Then Milinda called upon the Yonakas and the brethren to witness: "This Nâgasena says there is no permanent individuality (no soul) implied in his name. Is it now even possible to approve him in that?" And turning to Nâgasena, he said: "If, most reverend Nâgasena, there be no permanent individuality (no soul) involved in the matter, who is it, pray, who gives to you members of the Order your robes and food and lodging and necessaries for the sick? Who is it who enjoys such things when given? Who is it who lives a life of righteousness? Who is it who devotes himself to meditation? Who is it who attains to the goal of the Excellent Way, to the Nirvâ*n*a of Arahatship? And who is it who destroys living creatures? who is it who takes what is not his own? who is it who lives an evil life of worldly lusts, who speaks lies, who drinks strong drink, who (in a word) commits any one of the five sins which work out their bitter fruit even in this life? If that be so there is neither merit nor demerit; there is neither doer nor causer of good or evil deeds; there is neither fruit nor result of good or evil Karma.—If, most reverend Nâgasena, we are to think that were a man to kill you there would be no murder, then it follows that there are no real masters or teachers in your Order, and that your ordinations are void.—You tell me that your brethren in the Order are in the habit of addressing you as Nâgasena. Now what is that Nâgasena? Do you mean to say that the hair is Nâgasena?"

"I don't say that, great king."

"Or the hairs on the body, perhaps?"

"Certainly not."

"Or is it the nails, the teeth, the skin, the flesh, the nerves, the bones, the marrow, the kidneys, the heart, the liver, the abdomen, the spleen, the lungs, the larger intestines, the lower intestines, the stomach, the faeces, the bile, the phlegm, the pus, the blood, the sweat, the fat, the tears, the serum, the saliva, the mucus, the oil that lubricates the joints, the urine, or the brain, or any or all of these, that is Nâgasena?"

And to each of these he answered no.

"Is it the outward form then (*Rûpa*) that is Nâgasena, or the sensations (*Vedanâ*), or the ideas (*Saññâ*), or the confections (the constituent elements of character, *Samkhârâ*), or the consciousness (*Viññana*), that is Nâgasena?"

And to each of these also he answered no.

"Then is it all these *Skandhas* combined that are Nâgasena?"

"No! great king."

"But is there anything outside the five *Skandhas* that is Nâgasena?"

And still he answered no.

"Then thus, ask as I may, I can discover no Nâgasena. Nâgasena is a mere empty sound. Who then is the Nâgasena that we see before us? It is a falsehood that your reverence has spoken, an untruth!"

And the venerable Nâgasena said to Milinda the king: "You, Sire, have been brought up in great luxury, as beseems your noble birth. If you were to walk this dry weather on the hot and sandy ground, trampling under foot the gritty, gravelly grains of the hard sand, your feet would hurt you. And as your body would be in pain, your mind would be disturbed, and you would experience a sense of bodily suffering. How then did you come, on foot, or in a chariot?"

"I did not come, Sir, on foot. I came in a carriage."

"Then if you came, Sire, in a carriage, explain to me what that is. Is it the pole that is the chariot?"

"I did not say that."

"Is it the axle that is the chariot?"

"Certainly not."

"Is it the wheels, or the framework, or the ropes, or the yoke, or the spokes of the wheels, or the goad, that are the chariot?"

And to all these he still answered no.

"Then is it all these parts of it that are the chariot?"

"No, Sir."

"But is there anything outside them that is the chariot?"

And still he answered no.

"Then thus, ask as I may, I can discover no chariot. Chariot is a mere empty sound. What then is the chariot you say you came in? It is a falsehood that your Majesty has spoken, an untruth! There is no such thing as a chariot! You are king over all India, a mighty monarch. Of whom then are you afraid that you speak untruth? And he called upon the Yonakas and the brethren to witness, saying: "Milinda the king here has said that he came by carriage. But when asked in that case to explain what the carriage was, he is unable to establish what he averred. Is it, forsooth, possible to approve him in that?"

When he had thus spoken the five hundred Yonakas shouted their applause, and said to the king: "Now let your Majesty get out of that if you can?"

And Milinda the king replied to Nâgasena, and said: "I have spoken no untruth, reverend Sir. It is on account of its having all these things—the pole, and the axle, the wheels, and the framework, the ropes, the yoke, the spokes, and the goad—that it comes under the generally understood term, the designation in common use, of 'chariot.' "

"Very good! Your Majesty has rightly grasped the meaning of 'chariot.' And just even so it is on account of all those things you questioned me about—the thirty-two kinds of organic matter in a human body, and the five constituent elements of being—that I come under the generally understood term, the designation in common use, of 'Nâgasena.' For it was said, Sire, by our Sister Vagirâ in the presence of the Blessed One:

" 'Just as it is by the condition precedent of the co-existence of its various parts that the word "chariot" is used, just so is it that when the Skandhas are there we talk of a "being." ' "

"Most wonderful, Nâgasena, and most strange. Well has the puzzle put to you, most difficult though it was, been solved. Were the Buddha himself here he would approve your answer. Well done, well done, Nâgasena!"

2. "How many years seniority have you, Nâgasena?"

"Seven, your Majesty."

"But how can you say it is your 'seven?' Is it you who are 'seven,' or the number that is 'seven?' "

Now that moment the figure of the king, decked in all the finery of his royal ornaments, cast its shadow on the ground, and was reflected in a vessel of water. And Nâgasena asked him: "Your figure, O king, is now shadowed upon the ground, and reflected in the water, how now, are you the king, or is the reflection the king?"

"I am the king, Nâgasena, but the shadow comes into existence because of me."

"Just even so, O king, the number of the years is seven, I am not seven. But it is because of me, O king, that the number seven has come into existence; and it is mine in the same sense as the shadow is yours."

THE GREEKS

The Greeks

Knowing nothing of the Sanskrit language, philosophers or grammarians, the Greeks early became fascinated on their own account by the fact of human speech. From the sophists to the stoics, from Plato to Aristotle, they thrashed out the problems of language. Aristophanes (445-386 B.C.) in his comedy *The Clouds* makes Socrates (470-399 B.C.) ask a foolish youth: "Come, tell me, what would you like to learn first? Something you never were disciplined in before? Shall it be measures and rhythms, or the proper use of words?" The oafish student answers, "Measures for me! Some days ago I was chased by a corn-seller with his great measure." Socrates replies: "But there are other things you must first learn. For example, the names of the four-footed animals that are of the masculine gender." The student replies, "I know well enough which are of the masculine gender—or call me daft! Such are ram, billy-goat, bull, dog, rooster."

In his dialogue *Cratylus*, Plato (428-348 B.C.) has Socrates argue with student, Hermogenes, Cratylus and others, over linguistic problems.

From CRATYLUS[4]

Hermogenes. I have often talked over this matter, both with Cratylus and others, and cannot convince myself that there is any principle of correctness in names other than convention and agreement; any name which you give, in my opinion, is the right one, and if you change that and give another, the new name is as correct as the old—we frequently change the names of our slaves, and the newly-imposed name is as good as the old: for there is no name given to anything by nature; all is convention and habit of the users;—such is my view. But if I am mistaken I shall be happy to hear and learn of Cratylus, or of any one else.

Socrates. I dare say that you be right, Hermogenes: let us see;—Your meaning is, that the name of each thing is only that which anybody agrees to call it?

Her. That is my notion.

Soc. Whether the giver of the name be an individual or a city?

Her. Yes.

Soc. Well, now, let me take an instance;—suppose that I call a man a horse or a horse a man, you mean to say that a man will be rightly called a horse by me individually, and rightly called a man by the rest of the world; and a horse again would be rightly called a man by me and a horse by the world:—that is your meaning?

Her. He would, according to my view.

Soc. But how about truth, then? you would acknowledge that there is in words a true and a false?

Her. Certainly.

Soc. And there are true and false propositions?

Her. To be sure.

Soc. And a true proposition says that which is, and a false proposition says that which is not?

Her. Yes; what other answer is possible?

Soc. Then in a proposition there is a true and false?

Her. Certainly.

Soc. But is a proposition true as a whole only, and are the parts untrue?

Her. No; the parts are true as well as the whole.

Soc. Would you say the large parts and not the smaller ones, or every part?

Her. I should say that every part is true.

Soc. Is a proposition resolvable into any part smaller than a name?

Her. No; that is the smallest.

Soc. Then the name is a part of the true proposition?

Her. Yes.

Soc. Yes, and a true part, as you say.

Her. Yes.

Soc. And is not the part of a falsehood also a falsehood?

Her. Yes.

Soc. Then, if propositions may be true and false, names may be true and false?

Her. So we must infer.

Soc. And the name of anything is that which any one affirms to be the name?

Her. Yes.

Soc. And will there be so many names of each thing as everybody says that there are? and will they be true names at the time of uttering them?

Her. Yes, Socrates, I can conceive no correctness of names other than this; you give one name, and I another; and in different cities and countries there are different names for the same things; Hellenes differ from barbarians in their use of names, and the several Hellenic tribes from one another.

Soc. But would you say, Hermogenes, that the things differ as the names differ? and are they relative to individuals, as Protagoras tells us? For he says that man is the measure of all things, and that things are to me as they appear to me, and that they are to you as they appear to you. Do you agree with him, or would you say that things have a permanent essence of their own?

Her. There have been times, Socrates, when I have been driven in my perplexity to take refuge with Protagoras; not that I agree with him at all.

Soc. What! have you ever been driven to admit that there was no such thing as a bad man?

Her. No, indeed; but I have often had reason to think that there are very bad men, and a good many of them.

Soc. Well, and have you ever found any very good ones?

Her. Not many.

Soc. Still you have found them?

Her. Yes.

Soc. And would you hold that the very good were the very wise, and the very evil very foolish? Would that be your view?

Her. It would.

Soc. But if Protagoras is right, and the truth is that things are as they appear to any one, how can some of us be wise and some of us foolish?

Her. Impossible.

Soc. And if, on the other hand, wisdom and folly are really distinguishable, you will allow, I think, that the assertion of Protagoras can hardly be correct. For if what appears to each man is true to him, one man cannot in reality be wiser than another.

Her. He cannot.

Soc. Nor will you be disposed to say with Euthydemus, that all things equally belong to all men at the same moment and always; for neither on his view can there be some good and other bad, if virtue and vice are always equally to be attributed to all.

Her. There cannot.

Soc. But if neither is right, and things are not relative to individuals, and all things do not equally belong to all at the same moment and always, they must be supposed to have their own proper and permanent essence: they are not in relation to us, or influenced by us, fluctuating according to our fancy, but they are independent, and maintain to their own essence the relation prescribed by nature.

Her. I think, Socrates, that you have said the truth.

Soc. Does what I am saying apply only to the things themselves, or equally to the actions which proceed from them? Are not actions also a class of being?

Her. Yes, the actions are real as well as the things.

Soc. Then the actions also are done according to their proper nature, and not according to our opinion of them? In cutting, for example, we do not cut as we please, and with any chance instrument; but we cut with the proper instrument only, and according to the natural process of cutting; and the natural process is right and will succeed, but any other will fail and be of no use at all.

Her. I should say that the natural way is the right way.

Soc. Again, in burning, not every way is the right way; but the right way is the natural way, and the right instrument the natural instrument.

Her. True.

Soc. And this holds good of all actions?

Her. Yes.

Soc. And speech is a kind of action?

Her. True.

Soc. And will a man speak correctly who speaks as he pleases? Will not the successful speaker rather be he who speaks in the natural way of speaking, and as things ought to be spoken, and with the natural instrument? Any other mode of speaking will result in error and failure.

Her. I quite agree with you.

Soc. And is not naming a part of speaking? for in giving names men speak.

Her. That is true.

Soc. And if speaking is a sort of action and has a relation to acts, is not naming also a sort of action?

Her. True.

Soc. And we saw that actions were not relative to ourselves, but had a special nature of their own?

Her. Precisely.

Soc. Then the argument would lead us to infer that names ought to be given according to a natural process, and with a proper instrument, and not at our pleasure: in this and no other way shall we name with success.

Her. I agree.

Soc. But again, that which has to be cut has to be cut with something?

Her. Yes.

Soc. And that which has to be woven or pierced has to be woven or pierced with something?

Her. Certainly.

Soc. And that which has to be named has to be named with something?

Her. True.

Soc. What is that with which we pierce?

Her. An awl.

Soc. And with which we weave?

Her. A shuttle.

Soc. And with which we name?

Her. A name.

Soc. Very good: then a name is an instrument?

Her. Certainly.

Soc. Suppose that I ask, "What sort of instrument is a shuttle?" And you answer, "A weaving instrument."

Her. Well.

Soc. And I ask again, "What do we do when we weave?"—The answer is, that we separate or disengage the warp from the woof.

Her. Very true.

Soc. And may not a similar description be given of an awl, and of instruments in general?

Her. To be sure.

Soc. And now suppose that I ask a similar question about names: will you answer me? Regarding the name as an instrument, what do we do when we name?

Her. I cannot say.

Soc. Do we not give information to one another, and distinguish things according to their natures?

Her. Certainly we do.

Soc. Then a name is an instrument of teaching and of distinguishing natures, as the shuttle is of distinguishing the threads of the web.

Her. Yes.

Soc. And the shuttle is the instrument of the weaver?

Her. Assuredly.

Soc. Then the weaver will use the shuttle well—and well means like a weaver? and the teacher will use the name well—and well means like a teacher?

Her. Yes.

Soc. And when the weaver uses the shuttle, whose work will he be using well?

Her. That of the carpenter.

Soc. And is every man a carpenter, or the skilled only?

Her. Only the skilled.

Soc. And when the piercer uses the awl, whose work will he be using well?

Her. That of the smith.

Soc. And is every man a smith, or only the skilled?

Her. The skilled only.

Soc. And when the teacher uses the name, whose work will he be using?

Her. There again I am puzzled.

Soc. Cannot you at least say who gives us the names which we use?

Her. Indeed I cannot.

Soc. Does not the law seem to you to give us them?

Her. Yes, I suppose so.

Soc. Then the teacher, when he gives us a name, uses the work of the legislator?

Her. I agree.

Soc. And is every man a legislator, or the skilled only?

Her. The skilled only.

Soc. Then, Hermogenes, not every man is able to give a name, but only a maker of names; and this is the legislator, who of all skilled artisans in the world is the rarest.

Her. True.

Soc. And how does the legislator make names? and to what does he look? Consider this in the light of the previous instances: to what does the carpenter look in making the shuttle? Does he not look to that which is naturally fitted to act as a shuttle?

Her. Certainly.

Soc. And suppose the shuttle to be broken in making, will he make another, looking to the broken one? or will he look to the form according to which he made the other?

Her. To the latter, I should imagine.

Soc. Might not that be justly called the true or ideal shuttle?

Her. I think so.

Soc. And whatever shuttles are wanted, for the manufacture of garments, thin or thick, of flaxen, woollen, or other material, ought all of them to have the true form of the shuttle; and whatever is the shuttle best adapted to each kind of work, that ought to be the form which the maker produces in each case.

Her. Yes.

Soc. And the same holds of other instruments: when a man has discovered the instrument which is naturally adapted to each work, he must express this natural form, and not others which he fancies, in the material, whatever it may be, which he employs; for example, he ought to know how to put into iron the forms of awls adapted by nature to their several uses?

Her. Certainly.

Soc. And how to put into wood forms of shuttles adapted by nature to their uses?

Her. True.

Soc. For the several forms of shuttles naturally answer to the several kinds of webs; and this is true of instruments in general.

Her. Yes.

Soc. Then, as to names: ought not our legislator also to know how to put the true natural name of each thing into sounds and syllables, and to make and give all names with a view to the ideal name, if he is to be a namer in any true sense? And we must remember that different legislators will not use the same syllables. For neither does every smith, although he may be making the same instrument for the same purpose, make them all of the same iron. The form must be the same, but the material may vary, and still the instrument may be equally good of whatever iron made, whether in Hellas or in a foreign country;—there is no difference.

Her. Very true.

Soc. And the legislator, whether he be Hellene or barbarian, is not therefore to be deemed by you a worse legislator, provided he gives the true and proper form of the name in whatever syllables; this or that country makes no matter.

Her. Quite true.

Soc. But who then is to determine whether the proper form is given to the shuttle, whatever sort of wood may be used? the carpenter who makes, or the weaver who is to use them?

Her. I should say, he who is to use them, Socrates.

Soc. And who uses the work of the lyre-maker? Will not he be the man who knows how to direct what is being done, and who will know also whether the work is being well done or not?

Her. Certainly.

Soc. And who is he?

Her. The player of the lyre.

Soc. And who will direct the shipwright?

Her. The pilot.

Soc. And who will be best able to direct the legislator in his work, and will know whether the work is well done, in this or any other country? Will not the user be the man?

Her. Yes.

Soc. And this is he who knows how to ask questions?

Her. Yes.

Soc. And how to answer them?

Her. Yes.

Soc. And him who knows how to ask and answer you would call a dialectician?

Her. Yes; that would be his name.

Soc. Then the work of the carpenter is to make a rudder, and the pilot has to direct him, if the rudder is to be well made.

Her. True.

Soc. And the work of the legislator is to give names, and the dialectician must be his director if the names are to be rightly given?

Her. That is true.

Soc. Then, Hermogenes, I should say that this giving of names can be no such light matter as you fancy, or the work of light or chance persons; and Cratylus is right in saying that things have names by nature, and that not every man is an artificer of names, but he only who looks to the name which each thing by nature has and is able to express the true forms of things in letters and syllables.

Her. I cannot answer you, Socrates; but I find a difficulty in changing my opinion all in a moment, and I think that I should be more readily persuaded, if you would show me what this is which you term the natural fitness of names.

Soc. My good Hermogenes, I have none to show. Was I not telling you just now (but you have forgotten), that I knew nothing, and proposing to share the enquiry with you? But now that you and I have talked over the matter, a step has been gained; for we have discovered that names have by nature a truth, and that not every man knows how to give a thing a name.

Her. Very good.

Soc. And what is the nature of this truth or correctness of names? That, if you care to know, is the next question.

Her. Certainly, I care to know.

Soc. Then reflect.

Her. How shall I reflect?

Soc. The true way is to have the assistance of those who know, and you must pay them well both in money and in thanks; these are the Sophists, of whom your brother, Callias, has—rather dearly—bought the reputation of wisdom. But you have not yet come into your inheritance, and therefore you had better go to him, and beg and entreat him to tell you what he has learnt from Protagoras about the fitness of names.

Her. But how inconsistent should I be, if, whilst repudiating Protagoras and his truth, I were to attach any value to what he and his book affirm!

Soc. Then if you despise him, you must learn of Homer and the poets.

Her. And where does Homer say anything about names, and what does he say?

Soc. He often speaks of them; notably and nobly in the places where he distinguishes the different names which Gods and men give to the same things. Does he not in these passages make a remarkable statement about the correctness of names? For the Gods must clearly be supposed to call things by their right and natural names; do you not think so?

Her. Why, of course they call them rightly, if they call them at all. But to what are you referring?

Soc. Do you not know what he says about the river in Troy who had a single combat with Hephaestus?

"Whom," as he says, "the Gods call Xanthus, and men call Scamander."

Her. I remember.

Soc. Well, and about this river—to know that it ought to be called Xanthus and not Scamander—is not that a solemn lesson? Or about the bird which, as he says,

"The Gods call Chalcis, and men Cymindis:"

to be taught how much more correct the name Chalcis is than the name Cymindis,—do you deem that a light matter? Or about Batieia and Myrina? And there are many other observations of the same kind in Homer and other poets. Now, I think that this is beyond the understanding of you and me; but the names of Scamandrius and Astyanax, which he affirms to have been the names of Hector's son, are more within the range of human faculties, as I am disposed to think; and what the poet means by correctness may be more readily apprehended in that instance: you will remember I dare say the lines to which I refer.

Her. I do.

Soc. Let me ask you, then, which did Homer think the more correct of the names given to Hector's son—Astyanax or Scamandrius?

Her. I do not know.

Soc. How would you answer, if you were asked whether the wise or the unwise are more likely to give correct names?

Her. I should say the wise, of course.

Soc. And are the men or the women of a city, taken as a class, the wiser?

Her. I should say, the men.

Soc. And Homer, as you know, says that the Trojan men called him Astyanax (king of the city); but if the men called him Astyanax, the other name of Scamandrius could only have been given to him by the women.

Her. That may be inferred.

Soc. And must not Homer have imagined the Trojans to be wiser than their wives?

Her. To be sure.

Soc. Then he must have thought Astyanax to be a more correct name for the boy than Scamandrius?

Her. Clearly.

Soc. And what is the reason of this? Let us consider:—does he not himself suggest a very good reason, when he says,

"For he alone defended their city and long walls"?

This appears to be a good reason for calling the son of the saviour king of the city which his father was saving, as Homer observes.

Her. I see.

Soc. Why, Hermogenes, I do not as yet see myself; and do you?

Her. No, indeed; not I.

Soc. But tell me, friend, did not Homer himself also give Hector his name?

Her. What of that?

Soc. The name appears to me to be very nearly the same as the name of Astyanax—both are Hellenic; and a king and a holder have nearly the same meaning, and are both descriptive of a king; for a man is clearly the holder of that of which he is king; he rules, and owns, and holds it. But, perhaps, you may think that I am talking nonsense; and indeed I believe that I myself did not know what I meant when I imagined that I had found some indication of the opinion of Homer about the correctness of names.

Her. I assure you that I think otherwise, and I believe you to be on the right track.

Soc. There is reason, I think, in calling the lion's whelp a lion, and the foal of a horse a horse; I am speaking only of the ordinary course of nature, when an animal produces after his kind, and not of extraordinary births;—if contrary to nature a horse have a calf, then I should not call that a foal but a calf; nor do I call any inhuman birth a man, but only a natural birth. And the same may be said of trees and other things. Do you agree with me?

Her. Yes, I agree.

Soc. Very good. But you had better watch me and see that I do not play tricks with you. For on the same principle the son of a king is to be called a king. And whether the syllables of the name are the same or not the same, makes no difference, provided the meaning is retained; nor does the addition or subtraction of a letter make any difference so long as the essence of the thing remains in possession of the name and appears in it.

Her. What do you mean?

Soc. A very simple matter. I may illustrate my meaning by the names of letters, which you know are not the same as the letters themselves with the exception of the four; the names of ambiguous this word is, seeming rather to signify stopping the soul at things than going round with them; and therefore we should leave the beginning as at present, and not reject the one but make an insertion of another instead. . . . Thus the names which in these instances we find to have the worst sense, will turn out to be framed on the same principle as those which have the best.

And any one I believe who would take the trouble might find many other examples in which the giver of names indicates, not that things are in motion or progress, but that they are at rest; which is the opposite of motion.

Crat. Yes, Socrates, but observe; the greater number express motion.

Soc. What of that, Cratylus? Are we to count them like votes? and is correctness of names the voice of the majority? Are we to say of whichever sort there are most, those are the true ones?

Crat. No; that is not reasonable.

Soc. Certainly not. But let us have done with this question and proceed to another, about which I should like to know whether you think with me. Were we not lately acknowledging that the first givers of names in states, both Hellenic and barbarous, were the legislators, and that the art which gave names was the art of the legislator?

Crat. Quite true.

Soc. Tell me, then, did the first legislators, who were the givers of the first names, know or not know the things which they named?

Crat. They must have known, Socrates.

Soc. Why, yes, friend Cratylus, they could hardly have been ignorant.

Crat. I should say not.

Soc. Let us return to the point from which we digressed. You were saying, if you remember, that he who gave names must have known the things which he named; are you still of that opinion?

Crat. I am.

Soc. And would you say that the giver of the first names had also a knowledge of the things which he named?

Crat. I should.

Soc. But how could he have learned or discovered things from names if the primitive names were not yet given? For, if we are correct in our view, the only way of learning and discovering things, is either to discover names for ourselves or to learn them from others.

Crat. I think that there is a good deal in what you say, Socrates.

Soc. But if things are only to be known through names, how can we suppose that the givers of names had knowledge, or were legislators before there were names at all, and therefore before they could have known them?

Crat. I believe, Socrates, the true account of the matter to be, that a power more than human gave things their first names, and that the names which are thus given are necessarily their true names.

Soc. Then how came the giver of the names, if he was an inspired being or God, to contradict himself? For were we not saying just now that he made some names expressive of rest and others of motion? Were we mistaken?

Crat. But I suppose one of the two not to be names at all.

Soc. And which, then, did he make, my good friend; those which are expressive of rest, or those which are expressive of motion? This is a point which, as I said before, cannot be determined by counting them.

Crat. No; not in that way, Socrates.

Soc. But if this is a battle of names, some of them asserting that they are like the truth, others contending that *they* are, how or by what criterion are we to decide between them? For there are no other names to which appeal can be made, but obviously recourse must be had to another standard which, without employing names, will make clear which of the two are right; and this must be a standard which shows the truth of things.

Crat. I agree.

Soc. But if that is true, Cratylus, then I suppose that things may be known without names?

Crat. Clearly.

Soc. But how would you expect to know them? What other way can there be of knowing them, except the true and natural way, through their affinities, when they are akin to each other, and through themselves? For that which is other and different from them must signify something other and different from them.

Crat. What you are saying is, I think, true.

Soc. Well, but reflect; have we not several times acknowledged that names rightly given are the likenesses and images of the things which they name?

Crat. Yes.

Soc. Let us suppose that to any extent you please you can learn things through the medium of names, and suppose also that you can learn them from the things themselves—which is likely to be the nobler and clearer way; to learn of the image, whether the image and the truth of which the image is the expression have been rightly conceived, or to learn of the truth whether the truth and the image of it have been duly executed?

Crat. I should say that we must learn of the truth.

Soc. How real existence is to be studied or discovered is, I suspect, beyond you and me. But we may admit so much, that the knowledge of things is not to be derived from names. No; they must be studied and investigated in themselves.

Crat. Clearly, Socrates.

Soc. There is another point. I should not like us to be imposed upon by the appearance of such a multitude of names, all tending in the same direction. I myself do not deny that the givers of names did really give them under the idea that all things were in motion and flux; which was their sincere but, I think, mistaken opinion. And having fallen into a kind of whirlpool themselves, they are carried round, and want to drag us in after them. There is a matter, master Cratylus, about which I often dream, and should like to ask your opinion: Tell me, whether there is or is not any absolute beauty or good, or any other absolute existence?

Crat. Certainly, Socrates, I think so.

Soc. Then let us seek the true beauty: not asking whether a face is fair, or anything of that sort, for all such things appear to be in a flux; but let us ask whether the true beauty is not always beautiful.

Crat. Certainly.

Soc. And can we rightly speak of a beauty which is always passing away, and is first this and then that; must not the same thing be born and retire and vanish while the word is in our mouths?

Crat. Undoubtedly.

Soc. Then how can that be a real thing which is never in the same state? for obviously things which are the same cannot change while they remain the same; and if they are always the same and in the same state, and never depart from their original form, they can never change or be moved.

Crat. Certainly they cannot.

Soc. Nor yet can they be known by any one; for at the moment that the observer approaches, then they become other and of another nature, so that you cannot get any further in knowing their nature or state, for you cannot know that which has no state.

Crat. True.

Soc. Nor can we reasonably say, Cratylus, that there is knowledge at all, if everything is in a state of transition and there is nothing abiding; for knowledge too cannot continue to be knowledge unless continuing always to abide and exist. But if the very nature of knowledge changes, at the time when the change occurs there will be no knowledge; and if the transition is always going on, there will always be no knowledge, and, according to this view, there will be no one to know and nothing to be known: but if that which knows and that which is known exist ever, and the beautiful and the good and every other thing also exist, then I do not think that they can resemble a process or flux, as we were just now supposing. Whether there is this eternal nature in things, or whether the truth is what Heracleitus and his followers and many others say, is a question hard to determine; and no man of sense will like to put himself or the education of his mind in the power of names: neither will he so far trust names or the givers of names as to be confident in any knowledge which condemns himself and other existences to an unhealthy state of unreality; he will not believe that all things leak like a pot, or imagine that the world is a man who has a running at the nose. This may be true, Cratylus, but is also very likely to be untrue; and therefore I would not have you be too easily persuaded of it. Reflect well and like a man, and do not easily accept such a doctrine; for you are young and of an age to learn. And when you have found the truth, come and tell me.

Crat. I will do as you say, though I can assure you, Socrates, that I have been considering the matter already, and the result of a great deal of trouble and consideration is that I incline to Heracleitus.

Soc. Then, another day, my friend, when you come back, you shall give me a lesson; but at present, go into the country, as you are intending, and Hermogenes shall set you on your way.

Crat. Very good, Socrates; I hope, however, that you will continue to think about these things yourself.

Aristotle (445-386 B.C.), who for the West is *the* Philosopher par excellence, the "Father of those who know," was the tutor of Alexander the Great. He regarded language not as a work, *ergon*, but as an action, *energeia*. His *De Interpretatione* is a treatise on language.

DE INTERPRETATIONE[5]

First we must define the terms "noun" and "verb", then the terms "denial" and "affirmation", then "proposition" and "sentence".

Spoken words are the symbols of mental experience and written words are the symbols of spoken words. Just as all men have not the same writing, so all men have not the same speech sounds, but the mental experiences, which these directly symbolize, are the same for all, as also are those things of which our experiences are the images. This matter has, however, been discussed in my treatise about the soul, for it belongs to an investigation distinct from that which lies before us.

As there are in the mind thoughts which do not involve truth or falsity, and also those which must be either true or false, so it is in speech. For truth and falsity imply combination and separation. Nouns and verbs, provided nothing is added, are like thoughts without combination or separation; "man" and "white", as isolated terms, are not yet either true or false. In proof of this, consider the word "goat-stag". It has significance, but there is no truth or falsity about it, unless "is" or "is not" is added, either in the present or in some other tense.

By a noun we mean a sound significant by convention, which has no reference to time, and of which no part is significant apart from the rest. In the noun "Fairsteed", the part "steed" has no significance in and by itself, as in the phrase "fair steed". Yet there is a difference between simple and composite nouns; for in the former the part is in no way significant, in the latter it contributes to the meaning of the whole, although it has not an independent meaning. Thus in the word "pirate-boat" the word "boat" has no meaning except as part of the whole word.

The limitation "by convention" was introduced because nothing is by nature a noun or name—it is only so when it becomes a symbol; inarticulate sounds, such as those which brutes produce, are significant, yet none of these constitutes a noun.

The expression "not-man" is not a noun. There is indeed no recognized term by which we may denote such an expression, for it is not a sentence or a denial. Let it then be called an indefinite noun.

The expressions "of Philo", "to Philo", and so on, constitute not nouns, but cases of a noun. The definition of these cases of a noun is in other respects the same as that of the noun proper, but, when coupled with "is", "was", or "will be", they do not, as they are, form a proposition either true or false, and this the noun proper always does, under these conditions. Take the words "of Philo is" or "of Philo is not"; these words do not, as they stand, form either a true or a false proposition.

A verb is that which, in addition to its proper meaning, carries with it the notion of time. No part of it has any independent meaning, and it is a sign of something said of something else.

I will explain what I mean by saying that it carries with it the notion of time. "Health" is a noun, but "is healthy" is a verb; for besides its proper meaning it indicates the present existence of the state in question.

Moreover, a verb is always a sign of something said of something else, i.e. of something either predicable of or present in some other thing.

Such expressions as "is not-healthy", "is not-ill", I do not describe as verbs; for though they carry the additional note of time, and always form a predicate, there is no specified name for this variety; but let them be called indefinite verbs, since they apply equally well to that which exists and to that which does not.

Similarly "he was healthy", "he will be healthy", are not verbs, but tenses of a verb; the difference lies in the fact that the verb indicates present time, while the tenses of the verb indicate those times which lie outside the present.

Verbs in and by themselves are substantival and have significance, for he who uses such expressions arrests the hearer's mind, and fixes his attention; but they do not, as they stand, express any judgement, either positive or negative. For neither are "to be" and "not to be" and the participle "being" significant of any fact, unless something is added; for they do not themselves indicate anything, but imply a copulation, of which we cannot form a conception apart from the things coupled.

A sentence is a significant portion of speech, some parts of which have an independent meaning, that is to say, as an utterance, though not as the expression of any positive judgement. Let me explain. The word "human" has meaning, but does not constitute a proposition, either positive or negative. It is only when other words are added that the whole will form an affirmation or denial. But if we separate one syllable of the word "human" from the other, it has no meaning; similarly in the word "mouse", the part "-ouse" has no meaning in itself, but is merely a sound. In composite words, indeed, the parts contribute to the meaning of the whole; yet, as has been pointed out, they have not an independent meaning.

Every sentence has meaning, not as being the natural means by which a physical faculty is realized, but, as we have said, by convention. Yet every sentence is not a proposition; only such are propositions as have in them either truth or falsity. Thus a prayer is a sentence, but is neither true nor false.

Let us therefore dismiss all other types of sentence but the proposition, for this last concerns our present inquiry, whereas the investigation of the others belongs rather to the study of rhetoric or of poetry.

The first class of simple propositions is the simple affirmation, the next, the simple denial; all others are only one by conjunction.

Every proposition must contain a verb or the tense of a verb. The phrase which defines the species "man", if no verb in present, past, or future time be added, is not a proposition. It may be asked how the expression "a footed animal with two feet" can be called single; for it is not the circumstance that the words follow in unbroken succession that effects the unity. This inquiry, however, finds its place in an investigation foreign to that before us.

We call those propositions single which indicate a single fact, or the conjunction of the parts of which results in unity: those propositions, on the other hand, are separate and many in number, which indicate many facts, or whose parts have no conjunction.

Let us, moreover, consent to call a noun or a verb an expression only, and not a proposition, since it is not possible for a man to speak in this way when he is expressing something, in such a way as to make a statement, whether his utterance is an answer to a question or an act of his own initiation.

To return: of propositions one kind is simple, i.e. that which asserts or denies something of something, the other composite, i.e. that which is compounded of simple propositions. A simple proposition is a statement, with meaning, as to the presence of something in a subject or its absence, in the present, past, or future, according to the divisions of time.

An affirmation is a positive assertion of something about something, a denial a negative assertion.

Now it is possible both to affirm and to deny the presence of something which is present or of something which is not, and since these same affirmations and denials are possible with reference to those times which lie outside the present, it would be possible to contradict any affirmation or denial. Thus it is plain that every affirmation has an opposite denial, and similarly every denial an opposite affirmation.

We will call such a pair of propositions a pair of contradictories. Those positive and negative propositions are said to be contradictory which have the same subject and predicate. The identity of subject and of predicate must not be "equivocal". Indeed there are definitive qualifications besides this, which we make to meet the casuistries of sophists.

Some things are universal, others individual. By the term "universal" I mean that which is of such a nature as to be predicated by many subjects, by "individual" that which is not thus predicated. Thus "man" is a universal, "Callias" an individual.

Our propositions necessarily sometimes concern a universal subject, sometimes an individual.

If, then, a man states a positive and a negative proposition of universal character with regard to a universal, these two propositions are "contrary". By the expression "a proposition of universal character with regard to a universal", such propositions as "every man is white", "no man is white" are meant. When, on the other hand, the positive and negative propositions, though they have regard to a universal, are yet not of universal character, they will not be contrary, albeit the meaning intended is sometimes contrary. As instances of propositions made with regard to a universal, but not of universal character, we may take the propositions "man is white", "man is not white". "Man" is a universal, but the proposition is not made as of universal character; for the word "every" does not make the subject a universal, but rather gives the proposition a universal character. If, however, both predicate and subject are distributed, the proposition thus constituted is contrary to truth; no affirmation will, under such circumstances, be true. The proposition "every man is every animal" is an example of this type.

An affirmation is opposed to a denial in the sense which I denote by the term "contradictory", when, while the subject remains the same, the affirmation is of universal character and the denial is not. The affirmation "every man is white" is the *contradictory* of the denial "not every man is white", or again, the proposition "no man is white" is the *contradictory* of the proposition "some men are white". But propositions are opposed as *contraries* when both the affirmation and the denial are universal, as in the sentences "every man is white", "no man is white", "every man is just", "no man is just".

We see that in a pair of this sort both propositions cannot be true, but the contradictories of a pair of contraries can sometimes both be true with reference to the same subject; for instance "not every man is white" and "some men are white" are both true. Of such corresponding positive and negative propositions as refer to universals and have a universal character, one must be true and the other false. This is the case also when the reference is to individuals, as in the propositions "Socrates is white", "Socrates is not white".

When, on the other hand, the reference is to universals, but the propositions are not universal, it is not always the case that one is true and the other false, for it is possible to state truly that man is white and that man is not white and that man is beautiful and that man is not beautiful; for if a man is deformed he is the reverse of beautiful, also if he is progressing towards beauty he is not yet beautiful.

This statement might seem at first sight to carry with it a contradiction, owing to the fact that the proposition "man is not white" appears to be equivalent to the proposition "no man is white". This, however, is not the case, nor are they necessarily at the same time true or false.

It is evident also that the denial corresponding to a single affirmation is itself single; for the denial must deny just that which the affirmation affirms concerning the same subject, and must correspond with the affirmation both in the universal or particular character of the subject and in the distributed or undistributed sense in which it is understood.

For instance, the affirmation "Socrates is white" has its proper denial in the proposition "Socrates is not white". If anything else be negatively predicated of the subject or if anything else be the subject though the predicate remain the same, the denial will not be the denial proper to that affirmation, but one that is distinct.

The denial proper to the affirmation "every man is white" is "not every man is white"; that proper to the affirmation "some men are white" is "no man is white", while that proper to the affirmation "man is white" is "man is not white".

We have shown further that a single denial is contradictorily opposite to a single affirmation and we have explained which these are; we have also stated that contrary are distinct from contradictory propositions and which the contrary are; also that with regard to a pair of opposite propositions it is not always the case that one is true and the other false. We have pointed out, moreover, what the reason of this is and under what circumstances the truth of the one involves the falsity of the other.

An affirmation or denial is single, if it indicates some one fact about some one subject; it matters not whether the subject is universal and whether the statement has a universal character, or whether this is not so. Such single propositions are: "every man is white", "not every man is white"; "man is white", "man is not white"; "no man is white", "some men are white"; provided the word "white" has one meaning. If, on the other hand, one word has two meanings which do not combine to form one, the affirmation is not single. For instance, if a man should establish the symbol "garment" as significant both of a horse and of a man, the proposition "garment is white" would not be a single affirmation, nor its opposite a single denial. For it is equivalent to the proposition "horse and man are white", which, again, is equivalent to the two propositions "horse is white", "man is white". If, then, these two propositions have more than a single significance, and do not form a single proposition, it is plain that the first proposition either has more than one significance or else has none; for a particular man is not a horse.

This, then, is another instance of those propositions of which both the positive and the negative forms may be true or false simultaneously.

In the case of that which is or which has taken place, propositions, whether positive or negative, must be true or false. Again, in the case of a pair of contradictories, either when the subject is universal and the propositions are of a universal character, or when it is individual, as has been said, one of the two must be true and the other false; whereas when the subject is universal, but the propositions are not of a universal character, there is no such necessity. We have discussed this type also in a previous chapter.

When the subject, however, is individual, and that which is predicated of it relates to the future, the case is altered. For if all propositions whether positive or negative are either true or false, then any given predicate must either belong to the subject or not, so that if one man affirms that an event of a given character will take place and another denies it, it is plain that the statement of the one will correspond with reality and that of the other will not. For the predicate cannot both belong and not belong to the subject at one and the same time with regard to the future.

Thus, if it is true to say that a thing is white, it must necessarily be white; if the reverse proposition is true, it will of necessity not be white. Again, if it is white, the proposition stating that it is white was true; if it is not white, the proposition to the opposite effect was true. And if it is not white, the man who states that it is is making a false statement; and if the man who states that it is white is making a false statement, it follows that it is not white. It may therefore be argued that it is necessary that affirmations or denials must be either true or false.

Now if this be so, nothing is or takes place fortuitously, either in the present or in the future, and there are no real alternatives;

everything takes place of necessity and is fixed. For either he that affirms that it will take place or he that denies this is in correspondence with fact, whereas if things did not take place of necessity, an event might just as easily not happen as happen; for the meaning of the word "fortuitous" with regard to present or future events is that reality is so constituted that it may issue in either of two opposite directions.

Again, if a thing is white now, it was true before to say that it would be white, so that of anything that has taken place it was always true to say "it is" or "it will be". But if it was always true to say that a thing is or will be, it is not possible that it should not be or not be about to be, and when a thing cannot not come to be, it is impossible that it should not come to be, and when it is impossible that it should not come to be, it must come to be. All, then, that is about to be must of necessity take place. It results from this that nothing is uncertain or fortuitous, for if it were fortuitous it would not be necessary.

Again, to say that neither the affirmation nor the denial is true, maintaining, let us say, that an event neither will take place nor will not take place, is to take up a position impossible to defend. In the first place, though facts should prove the one proposition false, the opposite would still be untrue. Secondly, if it was true to say that a thing was both white and large, both these qualities must necessarily belong to it; and if they will belong to it the next day, they must necessarily belong to it the next day. But if an event is neither to take place nor not to take place the next day, the element of chance will be eliminated. For example, it would be necessary that a sea-fight should neither take place nor fail to take place on the next day.

These awkward results and others of the same kind follow, if it is an irrefragable law that of every pair of contradictory propositions, whether they have regard to universals and are stated as universally applicable, or whether they have regard to individuals, one must be true and the other false, and that there are no real alternatives, but that all that is or takes place is the outcome of necessity. There would be no need to deliberate or to take trouble, on the supposition that if we should adopt a certain course, a certain result would follow, while, if we did not, the result would not follow. For a man may predict an event ten thousand years beforehand, and another may predict the reverse; that which was truly predicted at the moment in the past will of necessity take place in the fullness of time.

Further, it makes no difference whether people have or have not actually made the contradictory statements. For it is manifest that the circumstances are not influenced by the fact of an affirmation or denial on the part of anyone. For events will not take place or fail to take place because it was stated that they would or would not take place, nor is this any more the case if the prediction dates back ten thousand years or any other space of time. Wherefore, if through all time the nature of things was so constituted that a prediction about an event was true, then through all time it was necessary that that prediction should find fulfilment; and with regard to all events, circumstances have always been such that their occurrence is a matter of necessity. For that of which someone has said truly that it will be, cannot fail to take place; and of that which takes place, it was always true to say that it would be.

Yet this view leads to an impossible conclusion; for we see that both deliberation and action are causative with regard to the future, and that, to speak more generally, in those things which are not continuously actual there is a potentiality in either direction. Such things may either be or not be; events also therefore may either take place or not take place. There are many obvious instances of this. It is possible that this coat may be cut in half, and yet it may not be cut in half, but wear out first. In the same way, it is possible that it should not be cut in half; unless this were so, it would not be possible that it should wear out first. So it is therefore with all other events which possess this kind of potentiality. It is therefore plain that it is not of necessity that everything is or takes place; but in some instances there are real alternatives, in which case the affirmation is no more true and no more false than the denial; while some exhibit a predisposition and general tendency in one direction or the other, and yet can issue in the opposite direction by exception.

Now that which is must needs be when it is, and that which is not must needs not be when it is not. Yet it cannot be said without qualification that all existence and non-existence is the outcome of necessity. For there is a difference between saying that

that which is, when it is, must needs be, and simply saying that all that is must needs be, and similarly in the case of that which is not. In the case, also, of two contradictory propositions this holds good. Everything must either be or not be, whether in the present or in the future, but it is not always possible to distinguish and state determinately which of these alternatives must necessarily come about.

Let me illustrate. A sea-fight must either take place to-morrow or not, but it is not necessary that it should take place to-morrow, neither is it necessary that it should not take place, yet it is necessary that it either should or should not take place to-morrow. Since propositions correspond with facts, it is evident that when in future events there is a real alternative, and a potentiality in contrary directions, the corresponding affirmation and denial have the same character.

This is the case with regard to that which is not always existent or not always non-existent. One of the two propositions in such instances must be true and the other false, but we cannot say determinately that this or that is false, but must leave the alternative undecided. One may indeed be more likely to be true than the other, but it cannot be either actually true or actually false. It is therefore plain that it is not necessary that of an affirmation and a denial one should be true and the other false. For in the case of that which exists potentially, but not actually, the rule which applies to that which exists actually does not hold good. The case is rather as we have indicated.

An affirmation is the statement of a fact with regard to a subject, and this subject is either a noun or that which has no name; the subject and predicate in an affirmation must each denote a single thing. I have already explained what is meant by a noun and by that which has no name; for I stated that the expression "not-man" was not a noun, in the proper sense of the word, but an indefinite noun, denoting as it does in a certain sense a single thing. Similarly the expression "does not enjoy health" is not a verb proper, but an indefinite verb. Every affirmation, then, and every denial, will consist of a noun and a verb, either definite or indefinite.

There can be no affirmation or denial without a verb; for the expressions "is", "will be", "was", "is coming to be", and the like are verbs according to our definition, since besides their specific meaning they convey the notion of time.

Thus the primary affirmation and denial are as follows: "man is", "man is not". Next to these, there are the propositions: "not-man is", "not-man is not". Again we have the propositions: "every man is", "every man is not", "all that is not-man is", "all that is not-man is not". The same classification holds good with regard to such periods of time as lie outside the present.

When the verb "is" is used as a third element in the sentence, there can be positive and negative propositions of two sorts. Thus in the sentence "man is just" the verb "is" is used as a third element, call it verb or noun, which you will. Four propositions, therefore, instead of two can be formed with these materials. Two of the four, as regards their affirmation and denial, correspond in their logical sequence with the propositions which deal with a condition of privation; the other two do not correspond with these.

I mean that the verb "is" is added either to the term "just" or to the term "not-just", and two negative propositions are formed in the same way. Thus we have the four propositions. Reference to the subjoined table will make matters clear:

A. Affirmation. Man is just.	B. Denial. Man is not just.
D. Denial. Man is not not-just.	C. Affirmation. Man is not-just.

Here "is" and "is not" are added either to "just" or to "not-just". This then is the proper scheme for these propositions, as has been said in the *Analytics*. The same rule holds good, if the subject is distributed. Thus we have the table:

A′. Affirmation. Every man is just.	B′. Denial. Not every man is just.
D′. Denial. Not every man is not-just.	C′. Affirmation. Every man is not-just.

Yet here it is not possible, in the same way as in the former case, that the propositions joined in the table by a diagonal line should both be true; though under certain circumstances this is the case.

We have thus set out two pairs of opposite propositions; there are moreover two other pairs, if a term be conjoined with "not-man", the latter forming a kind of subject. Thus:

A″. Not-man is just.	B″. Not-man is not just.
D″. Not-man is not not-just.	C″. Not-man is not-just.

This is an exhaustive enumeration of all the pairs of opposite propositions that can possibly be framed. This last group should remain distinct from those which preceded it, since it employs as its subject the expression "not-man".

When the verb "is" does not fit the structure of the sentence (for instance, when the verbs "walks", "enjoys health" are used), that scheme applies, which applied when the word "is" was added.

Thus we have the propositions: "every man enjoys health", "every man does-not-enjoy-health", "all that is not-man enjoys health", "all that is not-man does-not-enjoy-health".

We must not in these propositions use the expression "not every man". The negative must be attached to the word "man", for the word "every" does not give to the subject a universal significance, but implies that, as a subject, it is distributed. This is plain from the following pairs: "man enjoys health", "man does not enjoy health"; "not-man enjoys health", "not-man does not enjoy health". These propositions differ from the former in being indefinite and not universal in character. Thus the adjectives "every" and "no" have no additional significance except that the subject, whether in a positive or in a negative sentence, is distributed. The rest of the sentence, therefore, will in each case be the same.

Since the contrary of the proposition "every animal is just" is "no animal is just", it is plain that these two propositions will never both be true at the same time or with reference to the same subject. Sometimes, however, the contradictories of these contraries will both be true, as in the instance before us: the propositions "not every animal is just" and "some animals are just" are both true.

Further, the proposition "no man is just" follows from the proposition "every man is not-just" and the proposition "not every man is not-just", which is the opposite of "every man is not-just", follows from the proposition "some men are just"; for if this be true, there must be some just men.

It is evident, also, that when the subject is individual, if a question is asked and the negative answer is the true one, a certain positive proposition is also true. Thus, if the question is asked "Is Socrates wise?" and the negative answer were the true one, the positive inference "Then Socrates is unwise" is correct. But no such inference is correct in the case of universals, but rather a negative proposition. For instance, if to the question "Is every man wise?" the answer is "no", the inference "Then every man is unwise" is false. But under these circumstances the inference "Not every man is wise" is correct. This last is the contradictory, the former the contrary. Negative expressions, which consist of an indefinite noun or predicate, such as "not-man" or "not-just", may seem to be denials containing neither noun nor verb in the proper sense of the words. But they are not. For a denial must always be either true or false, and he that uses the expression "not-man", if nothing more be added, is not nearer but rather further from making a true or a false statement than he who uses the expression "man".

The propositions "everything that is not man is just", and the contradictory of this, are not equivalent to any of the other propositions; on the other hand, the proposition "everything that is not man is not just" is equivalent to the proposition "nothing that is not man is just".

The conversion of the position of subject and predicate in a sentence involves no difference in its meaning. Thus we say "man is white" and "white is man". If these were not equivalent, there would be more than one contradictory to the same proposition, whereas it has been demonstrated that each proposition has one proper contradictory and one only. For of the proposition "man is white" the appropriate contradictory is "man is not white", and of the proposition "white is man", if its meaning be different, the contradictory will either be "white is not not-man" or "white is not man". Now the former of these is the contradictory of the proposition "white is not-man", and the latter of these is the contradictory of the proposition "man is white"; thus there will be two contradictories to one proposition.

It is evident, therefore, that the inversion of the relative position of subject and predicate does not affect the sense of affirmations and denials.

There is no unity about an affirmation or denial which, either positively or negatively, predicates one thing of many subjects, or many things of the same subject, unless that which is indicated by the many is really some one thing.

I do not apply this word "one" to those things which, though they have a single recognized name, yet do not combine to form a unity. Thus, man may be an animal, and biped, and domesticated, but these three predicates combine to form a unity. On the other hand, the predicates "white", "man", and "walking" do not thus combine. Neither, therefore, if these three form the subject of an affirmation, nor if they form its predicate, is there any unity about that affirmation. In both cases the unity is linguistic, but not real.

Both Plato and Aristotle wrote against a pre-Socratic school of philosophy whose adherents called themselves Sophists, from the Greek word *sophos*, skilled, clever, wise. Plato and Aristotle disparaged the Sophists for being both "too clever by half" and also conceited: Plato and Aristotle called themselves *philosophers*—that is, lovers of wisdom (from *philo*, to love, and *sophia*, wisdom)—not Sophists, or "wise men." Plato's dialogue, *The Sophists*, does not deal specifically with language questions, but Aristotle's *Sophistes* does, as the following extract shows:

> "Thought and speech are the same, except that the interior dialogue of the soul with itself without the voice is called thought, while what comes from thought into

the mouth with articulated sounds is called speech. Moreover, there is something we know to be contained in discourse, affirmation and negation. When this is done in silence in the soul by thought, it is called opinion, and when this state of the soul is not the work of thought, but of sensation, it is called imagination."

And elsewhere he writes:

"I mean by thought a speech the soul addresses to itself about subjects it is considering. It seems to me that the soul when it thinks, is doing nothing more than conversing with itself, asking and answering, affirming and denying, and that when it decides, that is what we call passing judgment. Thus passing judgment I declare to be speaking, and judgment is a speech made not alone to another but also in silence to oneself; judging that something is other and telling oneself it is other."

Though Aristotle considered language "a diffuse and uncertain expedient for human reason," yet in the *Politics* he declared:

It is now clear why the term "animal designed for living in states" applies to man more than to bees or to any other animal living in herds. Nature, we are always saying, does nothing without a purpose. Now, man is the only animal with the power of speech. The mere voicing of sounds is an indication of pleasure and pain, which is why it is found among animals other than man; the point being that their nature has reached the point where they perceive what is pleasant or painful and can indicate this to one another. But speech is for pointing out what is useful or hurtful; it points out also what is just or unjust. This is peculiar to man, as compared with the other animals—the fact that he is the only animal to have a sense of good and evil, just and unjust, and so on. It is a common partnership in such ideas that brings about a household, and eventually a state.

* * *

Epicurus (341-276 B.C.), in a letter quoted by Diogenes Laertius (Book X), wrote: "The first notion which each word awakens in us is the correct one; in fact, we would not seek for anything if we had not previously some notion of it. To enable us to affirm that what we see at a distance is a horse or an ox, we must have some preconception in our minds which makes us acquainted with the form of a horse and an ox. We could not give names to things if we had not a preliminary notion of what the things were. These preconceptions then furnish us with certainty." And to Herodotus (484-420 B.C.) Epicurus wrote rhetorically:

> First of all then, Herodotus, one must determine with exactness the notion comprehended under each separate word, in order to be able to refer to it, as to a certain criterion, conceptions which emanate from ourselves—otherwise the judgment has no foundation. One goes on from demonstration to demonstration *ad infinitum*; or else one gains nothing beyond mere words. In fact, it is absolutely necessary that in every word we should perceive directly and without the assistance of any demonstration, the fundamental notion which it expresses, if we wish to have any foundation to which we may refer our researches, our difficulties and our personal judgments.

The quasi-sacred character of language is illustrated by the following story about Tiberius Caesar (42 B.C.-A.D. 37), the adopted son and successor of the Emperor Augustus (63 B.C.-A.D. 14). Tiberius made a mistake in a speech and was reproved for it by the grammarian Marcellus. Capito, a courtier, said "what the Emperor said was good Latin, or soon would be." Marcellus said to Capito: "Liar! Tiberius can give Roman citizenship to men; he cannot give it to words."

LANGUAGE IN THE EARLY CHRISTIAN ERA

Language in the Early Christian Era

Christianity dates from the birth of Jesus Christ, when the Western system of recording dates changed from A.U.C. (*ab urbe condita*—from the foundation of Rome) to A.D.—*anno Domini*. All Western dates before the birth of Christ are, since that birth, given as B.C.

Christian thought derives from three sources: the teaching of Jesus; the Hebrew Scriptures; and Greek philosophy. The Jews have such a tremendous feeling for the power of words that they will never speak or write the name of their God, Jehovah, who triumphed over, and succeeded to, the various gods of Asia Minor and Egypt. To this day they will not spell out, even in English, the Name, but write G-d. The Christians inherited this tremendous respect for the Name from the Jews, transferring it to Jesus: "At the name of Jesus, every knee shall bow," wrote St. Paul. Pious Christians today still bow their heads at the name of Jesus. They also inherited the Greek idea of the *Logos*, the creative Word, by which God created everything. The Greeks also believed, and many Christians followed them, in *logoi spermatikoi*—seed words, words as the hidden seeds of ideas. Philo (flourished A.D. 40, in Alexandria, Egypt), a Jew, wrote many books explaining the inner meaning of the stories told by Moses in the Jewish Scriptures. Philo wrote very interestingly about the Tower of Babel. According to the Bible, in the beginning mankind all spoke one language. Men started to build a huge tower to reach heaven, and God got alarmed.

6 And the Lord said, Behold, the people is one, and

> they have all one language, and this they begin to do, and now nothing will be restrained from them, which they have imagined to do.
> 7 Go to, let us go down, and there confound their language, that they may not understand one another's speech.
> 8 So the Lord scattered them abroad from thence upon the face of all the earth, and they left off to build the city.
> 9 Therefore is the name of it called Babel, because the Lord did there confound the language of all the earth.
> (Genesis, Chapter XI, Authorized Version.)

Many Christian writers also commented on Babel. The earliest Christian statement about the Word (Logos) is the first chapter of St. John's Gospel. St. John, who died around A.D. 100 in Patmos, wrote his Gospel in Greek. He may have known Philo.

> "In the beginning was the Word, and the Word was with God, and the Word was God. The same was in the beginning with God.
> All things were made by him, and without him was not anything made that was made.
> In Him was life; and the life was the light of men.
> And the light shineth in darkness, and the darkness comprehended it not.
> There was a man sent from God, whose name was John.
> The same came for a witness, to bear witness, of the Light, that through him all men might believe.
> He was not that Light, but was sent to bear witness of that Light.
> That was the true Light, that lighteth every man that cometh into the world.
> He was in the world and the world was made by him and the world knew him not.
> He came unto his own, and his own received him not.
> But as many as received him, to them gave he power

to become the sons of God, even to them that believe on his name.

Which were born, not of blood, nor of the will of the flesh, nor of the will of man, but of God.

And the Word was made flesh, and dwelt among us."

Ibid., John 1, 1-14

From the beginning of Christianity, there were heretics. Heretics are individuals who refuse to give up their ideas when the Church—that is, the dominant majority—orders them to do so. St. Hippolytus (A.D. 170-236), writing against a heretic called Simon Magus, a Gnostic, said that one of Simon Magus' erroneous ideas was that Moses allegorically gave the name of Paradise to the womb. God, said Simon Magus, forms every man in Paradise (the womb); the exodus from the womb is the fall, the afterbirth is Eden, and the four rivers that flow out of Eden (from the navel) are the two arteries (conduits from birth) and the two major veins that channel the blood. (St. Hippolytus, "Report of all Heresies." P. D. Migne, *Patres Graeci*.)

By the third century A.D. the Christians had triumphed. With the Emperor Constantine's victory at the Milvian Bridge in A.D. 312 Christianity became the dominant religion of the Roman Empire. The Fathers of the Church (as the Christian writers of that date are called) early became involved in linguistic theories. Nemesius (fl. third century), in his *"De natura hominis"*: Migne, *Patres Graeci*), wrote:

"Instruments of the voice include the muscles between the ribs and thorax and the lungs and the *aspera arteria* and the larynx and the cartilages between these and the nerves and ligaments and bones and all the muscles which move these parts." St. John Crysostom (A.D. 340-407) declared that "What distinguishes men from animals is not that we live or eat, but *speech*." Nemesius also raised a problem: "Those who are born deaf and who by misfortune or illness have lost their voice, still are able to use reason."

This was to become a perennial argument. One argument was between those who declared God invented speech and gave it to man, and those who said God invented man and man invented speech. St. Basil (A.D. 329-379) was accused by Eunomius of denying Divine Providence because he would not admit that God had created the names of things, but ascribed the invention of language to the facilities God had implanted in man. St. Gregory of Nyssa (A.D. 335-395) rushed to his brother St. Basil's defense, declaring: "Though God gave human nature its faculties it does not follow that he produces the actions we perform. . . . our facility of speaking is the work of him who has so framed our nature, but the invention of words and the naming of each object is the work of our mind."

Here follows an account of some of the Patristic squabbles about the origin of human speech.

From LA FILOSOFIA DEL LINGAGGIO NELLA PATRISTICA[7]

Already in the serious discussion in the fourth century between Gregory of Nyssa and Eunomius, the opposition to any kind of traditionalist tendency is clearly seen. Eunomius' great importance in the history of Christian religious thought stems from the fact that he was a great proponent of the doctrine of *homoiousia*, or the mere resemblance of the Son to the Father, as against the doctrine of *homousia*, or the identity of nature and equality, a doctrine sustained with much heat by the orthodox Fathers. As to the subject which concerns us, Eunomius was a most faithful follower of Philo the Jew, from whose mysticism he very probably directly took his own opinions on language, for Philo is known to have much influenced neo-Platonic thought in the fourth century, precisely Eunomius' period. Eunomius may be considered as a distant ancestor of the traditional theory, affirmed by certain post-Renaissance theologians and later by De Bonald, who wrote: "It is necessary for man to think his speech before he can speak his thought"[8] because "it was necessary for the Creator to give man both the instrument of speech and the manner of using it."[9] An almost identical opinion was expressed by Eunomius as early as the fourth century. Eunomius, moreover, was favorable to a supernatural solution of the problem of the origin of language; names, he said, or nouns, are the very essence of things and therefore are directly dependent on God. The exact opposite was held by St. Gregory of Nyssa, who declared:

> "We declare that nouns [names] of things and all words signifying things were invented by human ingenuity."

And with this statement, this other is in entire accord:

> "We ourselves have invented particular words as signs signifying things."

If, therefore, Moses spoke of the "language" of God, he did this not in connection with any real discourse of His, for He would have manifested in quite another manner His divine will, but rather "because of the childishness and stupidity of those who credit God with our human understanding." Moreover, where did Moses ever say that God gave the complete Decalogue in human language? (Gregory of Nyssa, Contra Eunomium, Chap XII, Migne, *PG* XLV, p 1002.) One should therefore hold, as the Sacred Scriptures conclude, that God did not infuse in us the gift of language completely developed, but rather made man capable of speech just as He made him capable of every sort of knowledge.

It would seem at first sight that this solution given to the problem of the origin of language by Gregory of Nyssa would be inconsistent with what was asserted shortly before as to the more generally Platonic rather than Aristotelian interpretation given by Patristic doctrine to the theory of the nature of words. However, this inconsistency is only apparent, since even if it is true that Gregory admitted language to be the work and discovery of man's logical faculties, a view in which he seems to be a follower of the explanation given by Aristotle of language as being placed in man for his subsequent use, yet although Gregory admits that language is a work and invention "of the human faculty of logic," he adds: "Things however are conceived by the intelligence according to the nature and expression of each intelligence."

Nor, as Boethius points out, is this all, since just as one may find sounds which have no sense, so also one may find sounds to which no reality corresponds, that is, *thoughts without reference to any real object* (Boethius, *De Interpretatione. Opera*. Basle, 1570, P. 296). Boethius, anticipating what was later more elaborately and more subtly said in this connection by Duns Scotus, explains this by the fact that "man's intelligence is the creator (artifex) not only of incorporeal things, but even of pure invention and even lies."

The relation between things and words having been thus established, Boethius takes up the other question already so much discussed by the Greek philosophers, on the position of the noun. Here also, in commenting on Aristotle's famous definition "A noun is a sound signifying whatever you will from which no significant part has been removed without any reference to time," he shows himself a vigorous upholder of the perfect independence of nature from names and/or objects. Here in fact are Boethius' own words, which may be read in his introduction to *Ad Categoricus Syllogismos* (*op. cit.*, p. 559): "one can add to the definition what one will, because no noun [name] signifies anything by its nature, except by the will of the person using it and making it up. So anyone uses words as they please him. Quite different are sounds naturally significant, such as a dog barking to show anger, and also different is a human being moaning in pain."

Another point is made by Aristotle himself and precisely in that most famous passage in *De Interpretatione* which, combined with another no less famous in *De Anima*, caused so much discussion and comment in antiquity and during the Middle Ages. We quote it here in the Latin translation of Boethius himself because it was best known in this version:

> Quae sunt in voce sunt notae passionum quae sunt in anima, et quae scribuntur sunt notae eorum quae sunt in voce, atque ut litterae non sunt apud omnes eaedem, ita neu voces sunt apud omnes, eaedem sunt etionam res hae passiones sunt simulacra.
>
> (What the voice sounds is notes of the passions in the soul, and what is written is notes of what is in the voice; and just as letters are not the same for all, nor are sounds the same for all those things of which these passions are the copies.)

Boethius also saw fit to comment at length concerning another point made by Aristotle, although by his time nobody any longer held the old-fashioned opinion of Plato concerning the natural fitness of names; this opinion had really lost its importance. We are talking about that passage in which the Stagirite declared that truth or falsehood did not lie so much in the names (words) as in their disposition, that is to say, their judgment, about which Boethius expresses himself as follows: "Every noun joined to a verb makes a statement, and thereby acquires the nature of truth or a lie"; and elsewhere: "Man in truth is not a noun [name]; nor can one find a word by which to call him, for he is neither a petition nor a denial, but is an infinite noun. Because it is the same whether the object named exists or does not exist, as, for example, a unicorn means something never true but once believed to be true, whether it is true or not true its meaning is a function of time." Boethius writes that this illustrates the old definition of a noun given by Aristotle, "a noun is a voluntarily chosen significant sound without temporal reference, without any part which qualifies it as true or false."

Boethius goes on to comment upon the parts of this definition which concern the absence of meaning or sense which is characteristic of the various parts of nouns, whether they are syllables or true words, such as occur in compound words. All this, however, was already clearly expressed in Aristotle. More interesting is the explanation of the trenchant phrase *sine tempore* (without, or outside of, time). Aristotle had made a distinction between *onoma* and *rema*: that is, between *noun* and *verb*; and Boethius, following in his footsteps, maintains in various statements that there are only two parts of a discourse, the noun and the verb, since "all other words are not parts but supplementary."

The specific difference between the two is that the *noun* is expressive *sine tempore* (without reference to time), whereas the verb expresses *cum tempore* (with, or within, time). In fact the verb, according to Boethius, follows the definition given by the Stagirite: "A verb is a significant sound with a time-value arbitrarily chosen, from which no significant part can be removed, designating something finite and present."

In other words, let us explain that the noun is unaffected by the category of time since what it means is true in all cases, since it is equally true in the possible, as in the real and necessary situation. The noun, because it represents a static condition, is always in relation to the more or less perfect logical term; the verb represents the actuation of an action or a passion in time; therefore, it must necessarily be conceived as something that begins and therefore as something that ends; therefore, whatever is expressed by the verb "cannot exist without time and passion." Thus, Boethius concludes, this is evidence of one of the fundamental proofs that in fact all other parts of speech may philosophically be reduced to two classes, nouns and verbs.

From everything that we have said so far, it is clear how true the statement is that already in the Patristic period of Christian thought a tradition was formulated concerning the relationship between logic and philosophy in language, at least to the degree that that tradition was expressed at that time, so that when the Patristic period was ended a new orientation was gradually given to this tradition.

The greatest of the Church Fathers, and one of the greatest thinkers of all time, is St. Augustine (A.D. 354-430), an African. In his *Confessions* he discusses the origin of speech in himself; also he investigates the problems of memory. Elsewhere in many works he again and again discusses the relations of human thought to speech, of the human mind to space and time.

From CONFESSIONS OF ST. AUGUSTINE

Passing hence from infancy, I came to boyhood, or rather it came to me, displacing infancy. Now did that depart,—(for whither went it?)—and yet it was no more. For I was no longer a speechless infant, but a speaking boy. This I remember; and have since observed how I learned to speak. It was not that my elders taught me words (as, soon after, other learning) in any set method; but I, longing by cries and broken accents and various motions of my limbs to express my thoughts, that so I might have my will, and yet unable to express all I willed, or to whom I willed, did myself, by the understanding which Thou, my God, gavest me, practise the sounds in my memory. When they named any thing, and as they spoke turned towards it, I saw and remembered that they called what they would point out by the name they uttered. And that they meant this thing and no other was plain from the motion of their body, the natural language, as it were, of all nations, expressed by the countenance, glances of the eye, gestures of the limbs, and tones of the voice, indicating the affections of the mind, as it pursues, possesses, rejects, or shuns. And thus by constantly hearing words, as they occurred in various sentences, I collected gradually for what they stood; and having broken in my mouth to these signs, I thereby gave utterance to my will. Thus I exchanged with those about me these current signs of our wills, and so launched deeper into the stormy intercourse of human life, yet depending on parental authority and the beck of elders.

O God my God, what miseries and mockeries did I now experience, when obedience to my teachers was proposed to me, as proper in a boy, in order that in this world I might prosper, and excel in tongue-science, which should serve to the "praise of men," and to deceitful riches. Next I was put to school to get learning, in which I (poor wretch) knew not what use there was; and yet, if idle in learning, I was beaten. . . .

These things do I within, in that vast court of my memory. For there are present with me, heaven, earth, sea, and whatever I could think on therein, besides what I have forgotten. There also meet I with myself, and recall myself, and when, where, and what I have done, and under what feelings. There be all which I remember, either on my own experience, or other's credit. Out of the same store do I myself with the past continually combine fresh and fresh likenesses of things which I have experienced, or, from what I have experienced, have believed: and thence again infer future actions, events and hopes, and all these again I reflect on, as present. "I will do this or that," say I to myself, in that great receptacle of my mind, stored with the images of things so many and so great, "and this or that will follow." "O that this or that might be!" "God avert this or that!" So speak I to myself: and when I speak, the images of all I speak of are present, out of the same treasury of memory; nor would I speak of any thereof, were the images wanting.

Great is this force of memory, excessive great, O my God; a large and boundless chamber! who ever sounded the bottom thereof? yet is this a power of mine, and belongs unto my nature; nor do I myself comprehend all that I am. Therefore is the mind too strait to contain itself. And where should that be, which it containeth not of itself? Is it without it, and not within? how then doth it not comprehend itself? A wonderful admiration surprises me, amazement seizes me upon this. And men go abroad to admire the heights of mountains, the mighty billows of the sea, the broad tides of rivers, the compass of the ocean, and the circuits of the stars, and pass themselves by; nor wonder that when I spake of all these things, I did not see them with mine eyes, yet could not have spoken of them, unless I then actually saw the mountains, billows, rivers, stars which I had seen, and that ocean which I believe to be, inwardly in my memory, and that, with the same vast spaces between, as if I saw them abroad. Yet did not I by seeing draw them into myself, when with mine eyes I beheld them; nor are they themselves with me, but their images only. And I know by what sense of the body each was impressed upon me.

Yet not these alone does the unmeasurable capacity of my memory retain. Here also is all, learnt of the liberal sciences and as yet unforgotten; removed as it were to some inner place, which is yet no place: nor are they the images thereof, but the things themselves. For, what is literature, what the art of disputing, how many kinds of questions there be, whatsoever of these I know, in such manner exists in my memory, as that I have not taken in the image, and left out the thing, or that it should have sounded and passed away like a voice fixed on the ear by that impress, whereby it might be recalled, as if it sounded, when it no longer sounded; or as a smell while it passes and evaporates into air affects the sense of smell, whence it conveys into the memory an image of itself, which remembering, we renew, or as meat, which verily in the belly hath now no taste, and yet in the memory still in a manner tasteth; or as any thing which the body by touch perceiveth, and which when removed from us, the memory still conceives. For those things are not transmitted into the memory, but their images only are with an admirable swiftness caught up, and stored as it were in wondrous cabinets, and thence wonderfully by the act of remembering, brought forth.

But now when I hear that there be three kinds of questions, "Whether the thing be? what it is? of what kind it is?" I do indeed hold the images of the sounds of which those words be composed, and that those sounds, with a noise passed through the air, and now are not. But the things themselves which are signified by those sounds, I never reached with any sense of my body, nor ever discerned them otherwise than in my mind; yet in my memory have I laid up not their images, but themselves. Which how they entered into me, let them say if they can; for I have gone over all the avenues of my flesh, but cannot find by which they entered. For the eyes say, "If those images were coloured, we reported of them." The ears say, "If they sound, we gave knowledge of them." The nostrils say, "If they smell, they passed by us." The taste says, "Unless they have a savour, ask me not." The touch says, "If it have not size, I handled it not; if I handled it not, I gave no notice of it." Whence and how entered these things into my memory? I know not how. For when I learned them, I gave not credit to another man's mind, but recognised them in mine; and approving them for true, I commended them to it, laying them up as it were, whence I might bring them forth when I willed. In my heart then they were, even before I learned them, but in my memory they were not. Where then? or wherefore, when they were spoken, did I acknowledge them, and said, "So is it, it is true," unless that they were already in the memory, but so thrown back and buried as it were in deeper recesses, that had not the suggestion of another drawn them forth I had perchance been unable to conceive of them?

Wherefore we find, that to learn these things whereof we imbibe not the images by our senses, but perceive within by themselves, without images, as they are, is nothing else, but by conception, to receive, and by marking to take heed that those things which the memory did before contain at random and unarranged, be laid up at hand as it were in that same memory where before they lay unknown, scattered and neglected, and so readily occur to the mind familiarised to them. And how many things of this kind does my memory bear which have been already found out, and as I said, placed as it were at hand, which we are said to have learned and come to know which were I for some short space of time to cease to call to mind, they are again so buried, and glide back, as it were, into the deeper recesses, that they must again, as if new, be thought out thence, for other abode they have none: but they must be drawn together again, that they may be known; that is to say, they must as it were be collected together from their dispersion: whence the word "cogitation" is derived. For cogo (collect) and cogito (re-collect) have the same relation to each other as ago and agito, facio and factito. But the mind hath appropriated to itself this word (cogitation), so that, not what is "collected" any how, but what is "re-collected," i.e., brought together, in the mind, is properly said to be cogitated, or thought upon.

The memory containeth also reasons and laws innumerable of numbers and dimensions, none of which hath any bodily sense impressed; seeing they have neither colour, nor sound, nor taste, nor smell, nor touch. I have heard the sound of the words whereby when discussed they are denoted: but the sounds are other than the things. For the sounds are other in Greek than in Latin; but the things are neither Greek, nor Latin, nor any other language. I have seen the lines of architects, the very finest, like a spider's thread; but those are still different, they are not the images of those lines which the eye of flesh showed me: he knoweth them, whosoever without any conception whatsoever of a body, recognises them within himself. I have perceived also the numbers of the things with which we number all the senses of my body; but those numbers wherewith we number are different, nor are they the images of these, and therefore they indeed are. Let him who seeth them not, deride me for saying these things, and I will pity him, while he derides me.

All these things I remember, and how I learnt them I remember. Many things also most falsely objected against them have I heard, and remember; which though they be false, yet is it not false that I remember them; and I remember also that I have discerned betwixt those truths and these falsehoods objected to them. And I perceive that the present discerning of these things is different from remembering that I oftentimes discerned them, when I often thought upon them. I both remember then to have often understood these things; and what I now discern and understand, I lay up in my memory, that hereafter I may remember that I understand it now. So then I remember also to have remembered; as if hereafter I shall call to remembrance, that I have now been able to remember these things, by the force of memory shall I call it to remembrance.

The same memory contains also the affections of my mind, not in the same manner that my mind itself contains them, when it feels them; but far otherwise, according to a power of its own. For without rejoicing I remember myself to have joyed; and without sorrow do I recollect my past sorrow. And that I once feared, I review without fear; and without desire call to mind a past desire. Sometimes, on the contrary, with joy do I remember my fore-past sorrow, and with sorrow, joy. Which is not wonderful, as to the body; for mind is one thing, body another. If I therefore with joy remember some past pain of body, it is not so wonderful. But now seeing this very memory itself is mind (for when we give a thing in charge, to be kept in memory, we say, "See that you keep it in mind"; and when we forget, we say, "It did not come to my mind," and, "It slipped out of my mind," calling the memory itself the mind); this being so, how is it that when with joy I remember my past sorrow, the mind hath joy, the memory hath sorrow; the mind upon the joyfulness which is in it, is joyful, yet the memory upon the sadness which is in it, is not sad? Does the memory perchance not belong to the mind? Who will say so? The memory then is, as it were, the belly of the mind, and joy and sadness, like sweet and bitter food; which, when committed to the memory, are as it were, passed into the belly, where they may be stowed, but cannot taste. Ridiculous it is to imagine these to be alike; and yet are they not utterly unlike.

But, behold, out of my memory I bring it, when I say there be four perturbations of the mind, desire, joy, fear, sorrow; and whatsoever I can dispute thereon, by dividing each into its subordinate species, and by defining it, in my memory find I what to say, and thence do I bring it: yet am I not disturbed by any of these perturbations, when by calling them to mind, I remember them; yea, and before I recalled and brought them back, they were there; and therefore could they, by recollection, thence be brought. Perchance, then, as meat is by chewing the cud brought up out of the belly, so by recollection these out of the memory. Why then does not the disputer, thus recollecting, taste in the mouth of his musing the sweetness of joy, or the bitterness of sorrow? Is the comparison unlike in this, because not in all respects like? For who would willingly speak thereof, if so oft as we name grief or fear, we should be compelled to be sad or fearful? And yet could we not speak of them, did we not find in our memory, not only the sounds of the names according to the images impressed by the senses of the body, but notions of the very things themselves which we never received by any avenue of the body, but which the mind itself perceiving by the experience of its own passions, committed to the memory, or the memory of itself retained, without being committed unto it.

But whether by images or no, who can readily say? Thus, I name a stone, I name the sun, the things themselves not being present to my senses, but their images to my memory. I name a bodily pain, yet it is not present with me, when nothing aches: yet unless its image were present to my memory, I should not know what to say thereof, nor in discoursing discern pain from pleasure. I name bodily health; being sound in body, the thing itself is present with me; yet, unless its image also were present in my memory, I could by no means recall what the sound of this name should signify. Nor would the sick, when health were named, recognise what were spoken, unless the same image were by the force of memory retained, although the thing itself were absent from the body. I name numbers whereby we number; and not their images, but themselves are present in my memory. I name the image of the sun, and that image is present in my memory. For I recall not the image of its image, but the image itself is present to me, calling it to mind. I name memory, and I recognise what I name. And where do I recognise it, but in the memory itself? Is it also present to itself by its image, and not by itself?

What, when I name forgetfulness, and withal recognise what I name? whence should I recognise it, did I not remember it? I speak not of the sound of the name, but of the thing which it signifies: which if I had forgotten, I could not recognise what that sound signifies. When then I remember memory, memory itself is, through itself, present with itself: but when I remember forgetfulness, there are present both memory and forgetfulness; memory whereby I remember, forgetfulness which I remember. But what is forgetfulness, but the privation of memory? How then is it present that I remember it, since when present I cannot remember? But if what we remember we hold it in memory, yet, unless we did remember forgetfulness, we could never at the hearing of the name recognise the thing thereby signified, then forgetfulness is retained by memory. Present then it is, that we forget not, and being so, we forget. It is to be understood from this that forgetfulness when we remember it, is not present to the memory by itself but by its image: because if it were present by itself, it would not cause us to remember, but to forget. Who now shall search out this? who shall comprehend how it is?

Lord, I, truly, toil therein, yea and toil in myself; I am become a heavy soil requiring over much sweat of the brow. For we are not now searching out the regions of heaven, or measuring the distances of the stars, or enquiring the balancings of the earth. It is I myself who remember, I the mind. It is not so wonderful, if what I myself am not, be far from me. But what is nearer to me than myself? And lo, the force of mine own memory is not understood by me; though I cannot so much as name myself without it. For what shall I say, when it is clear to me that I remember forgetfulness? Shall I say that that is not in my memory, which I remember? or shall I say that forgetfulness is for this purpose in my memory, that I might not forget? Both were most absurd. What third way is there? How can I say that the image of forgetfulness is retained by my memory, not forgetfulness itself, when I remember it? How could I say this either, seeing that when the image of any thing is impressed on the memory, the thing itself must needs be first present, whence that image may be impressed? For thus do I remember Carthage, thus all places where I have been, thus men's faces whom I have seen, and things reported by the other senses; thus the health or sickness of the body. For when these things were present, my memory received from them images, which being present with me, I might look on and bring back in my mind, when I remembered them in their absence. If then this forgetfulness is retained in the memory through its image, not through itself, then plainly itself was once present, that its image might be taken. But when it was present, how did it write its image in the memory, seeing that forgetfulness by its presence effaces even what it finds already noted? And yet, in whatever way, although that way be past conceiving and explaining, yet certain am I that I remember forgetfulness itself also, whereby what we remember is effaced.

Great is the power of memory, a fearful thing, O my God, a deep and boundless manifoldness; and this thing is the mind, and this am I myself. What am I then, O my God? What nature am I? A life various and manifold, and exceeding immense. Behold in the plains, and caves, and caverns of my memory, innumerable and innumerably full of innumerable kinds of things, either through images, as all bodies; or by actual presence, as the arts; or by certain notions or impressions, as the affections of the mind, which, even when the mind doth not feel, the memory retaineth, while yet whatsoever is in the memory is also in the mind—over all these do I run, I fly; I dive on this side and on that, as far as I can, and there is no end. So great is the force of memory, so great the force of life, even in the mortal life of man.

Elsewhere, in his *On the Trinity* (Book XV) St. Augustine writes that "The word is nothing other than thought expressed . . . the word that issues forth is a sign of the word concealed within, which better deserves the name, for that which passes out is the word of the flesh and is said because of that which is within".

In his *The City of God* St. Augustine discusses the world language after the fall of the Tower of Babel.

BOOK XVI, CITY OF GOD

As the fact of all using one language did not secure the absence of sin-infected men from the race—for even before the deluge there was one language, and yet all but the single family of just Noah were found worthy of destruction by the flood—so when the nations, by a prouder godlessness, earned the punishment of the dispersion and of the confusion of tongues, and the city of the godless were called Confusion or Babylon, there was still the house of Heber in which the primitive language of the race survived. Because when the other races were divided by their own peculiar languages, Heber's family preserved that language which is not unreasonably believed to have been the common language of the race. It was thenceforth named Hebrew. We are induced to believe that this was the primitive and common language because the multiplication and change of languages was introduced as a punishment, and it is fit to ascribe to the people of God an immunity from this punishment. Nor is it without significance that this is the language which Abraham retained and which he could not transmit to all his descendants, but only to those of Jacob's line, who distinctively and eminently constituted God's people, received His covenants, and were Christ's progenitors according to the flesh. In the same way, Heber himself did not transmit that language to all his posterity, but only to the line from which Abraham sprang.

THE MEDIEVAL PERIOD AND AFTER

The Medieval Period and After

Although refreshed by the Muslim theologians, such as the Persian Avicenna (*ibn-Sina*) (A.D. 980-1037), who thought of the alternatives of language and silence as modes (*per modum quietis, per modum motus*) and brought this idea into the methodology of philosophy—rather as the French *Nouvelle Vague* novelists have done in the late twentieth century—the novelist's freedom "exists only in language, the sole domain of human liberty." (John Weightman, reviewing Alain-Grillet in *The New York Review*, 1 June 1972)—the medieval theologians were rather polishers of previously made points, than innovators.

Peter Abelard (1079-1142) is an exception. In his *Dialectic 1.3* he discusses the "ways of signifying": "To signify belongs not only to words but to things; the letters one makes and which are offered to our eyes, represent for us the elements of words. For this it is written in the *Peri Hermeneias*, 'Written words are pronounced words.' The marks, that is, signify them. Also often things represent another by way of resemblance, thus a statue of Achilles represents Achilles himself. It also happens that we may suggest something by signs. But we often pass from one thing to another without any expressed relationship of significance between them, merely by habit or because of their relationship, as, for example, from a father to a son. The meaning of words can thus be understood in several ways: 1) by imposition: the word *man* means a moral, rational animal, upon whom this name has been imposed; 2) by determination: one arrives at the rationality of man by naming the substances of which men are predicated, thus determining also for them rationality. That is why Aristotle says in the *Categories*, 'gender and kind determine quality.' " For Abelard, also, "Language is generated by intelligence and generates intelligence."

St. Albert the Great (A.D. 1193-1280), or Albertus Magnus, the only canonised astrologer, divided speech into three parts, like Gaul: *verbum interius* (internal speech); *verbum oris* (mouthed, or spoken words); and *verbum imaginatum* (imagined speech). Of this latter he wrote: "Some say that the concept which descends from the intellectual part into the imagination and is its organ, is in the anterior part of the head and from this reaches the air in which the voice is figured, and there it generates, by the imagination's strength, the intention given to the fact by the voice." (*De Anima*, Book II, Tract III, chap. XXII.)

Until the rise of the Universities, grammar was the most important of the seven liberal arts. The grammars used were very ancient: that of Donatus (fl. circa A.D. 350), who wrote the *Ars Minor*, a primary grammar and the *Ars grammatica*; and that of Priscian, who had taught grammar in Constantinople around A.D. 500. Priscian's first sixteen books of grammar dealt with the eight parts of speech. He discussed syntax in his final two books.

Medieval philosophy, or Scholasticism, crumbled into grammar and linguistics, much as twentieth-century philosophy has. By the mid-thirteenth century when Thomas of Erfurt wrote, the chief intellectual concern was language, much as it is in twentieth-century Oxford. The following is a *resumé* of Thomas' position.

From PHILOSOPHICAL ESSAYS FOR A. N. WHITEHEAD

The cure for wild analogy is the critical analysis of analogy and the continual watchful scrutiny of the modes of signifying which are the subject matter of speculative grammar. The work of Thomas of Erfurt presupposes a familiarity and sophistication about analogies, and the main burden of his exposition is to show the routes of signification through the terms of Latin grammar. The basic terms of his exposition are, on the strictly grammatical side, nouns and verbs, and on the logical side the transcendentals and the Aristotelian predicables, essence, genus, species, property, and accident. Nouns are divided into two kinds, substantive and adjective; the twenty-four kinds of the latter are impressive and exhaustive, showing the many kinds of dependent existences that are reflected in the Scotist use of Latin. The chief distinctions here are based on the serial nature of the modes of dependence on the substantive. The analysis of verbs follows a parallel pattern since the chief grammatical function of the verb is to compound the forms and matters which the orders of nouns have distinguished. Pronouns, adverbs, and prepositions take their interstitial places. Finally there is a discussion of grammatical construction which approaches a kind of rhetorical analysis of the larger grammatical units.

I shall not go farther into these details, important as they may be, but I shall only point out one or two general themes that run through the exposition and use them to comment farther on the nature of symbols.

In the first place it seems to me that it is clear throughout that the subject-matrix about which the various propositions in the science of grammar are made is the analogical pattern that I have been describing. As I have suggested, the modes of signifying follow lines of signification that run as if horizontally or vertically between rows and columns of rectangular arrays of terms. It is through this analogical form as through a medium, that signs move the intellect. But it is insisted throughout that these forms of signification have their bases in the properties of things; active modes of signifying are directed to passive modes of signifying, and these are properties of things. The Latin is interesting, proprietates rerum, if we recall that res is in other contexts a transcendental, meaning universal. Both property and thing are to be taken in their broadest meaning: there are essential properties, proper properties, and accidental properties; things may be composite substances, formal substances, or merely universals. In the Scotist system these make a fairly complete list of the kinds of being, and the task of the grammarian is to show how the modes of signifying not only reflect these distinctions but also connect any particular mode in however complicated a grammatical manner with the appropriate basic property of a thing. Some things and their properties may be beyond the powers of human reason, and to that extent any system of symbols must come short of adequacy, but it is in the nature of things and in the nature of human knowledge that the system of signs shall be founded in the system of the things of reason (res).

But this claim raises doubts that have embarrassed modern thought almost continuously since the time of Duns Scotus [(1265-1300)] and Thomas of Erfurt. The origin and career of the Latin language, limited as it is both in space and in time, cannot be adequate to the scientific and philosophic themes of all time and eternity. In the case of any special set of symbols it seems that there must be not only a radical incommensurability of sign and thing signified, but also a component at least of vicious arbitrariness of construction which will fool the wisest of men if they take the burden of discursive thought seriously. Descartes and Leibnitz were seriously concerned with this difficulty and set the fashion of non-conformity and doubt for the modern period. Aristotelian logic came under the shadow of this doubt as soon as it was suspected that Aristotle connived to make his categories fit the grammar of the Greek language. At the same time there were attempts to save both Latin and mathematical notations by transposing them from the human tongue and the pen to more substantial mediums such as the lever, the balance, the astrolabe, and the wheel, where at least natural things could more obviously defend the symbols against merely human doubts. Also at the same time local European vernaculars took on the responsibilities of technical discourse, and of course a similar thing happened in literature, and religion. It is interesting to recall that Roger Bacon foresaw this welter of translation and vehemently pled for the study of grammar as the only stable basis for empirical science; his plea was in effect a plea for a new study, the grammar of nature. It is interesting also to note that the only breaks in the continuous exposition of the *De Modis Significandi* are made to answer objections which claim that various modes are fictional, a theme that runs regularly through modern epistemology.

* * *

A whole new interest in language was generated by the emergence of many languages from the decomposition of Latin, and such a great writer as Dante (1265-1321) wrote at length about the origins of language in his *De Vulgo Eloquio*. He was led logically to dethrone Hebrew from its position as the original language, and in the *Paradiso* (Canto 26) he makes Adam say that at the time of the confusion of Babel there had already been a considerable degeneration of the primeval language, to such an extent that nothing now was left intact of the language of Adam, so it was impossible to reconstruct it. "And this is true, whether or not that language had been infused into him by God or whether the first man himself had discovered it for himself." Dante, in fact, suggested language to be dynamic, constantly changing.

In Spain, Ludovico Vives (1492-1540) regarded speech as much a perquisite of man as is reason: "tam naturalis est homini sermo quam ratio." (*De Anima*, II, 85.)

At the very dawn of the Renaissance lived the German Cardinal, Nicholas of Cusa (1401-1464), from whom the following is taken.

From the COMPENDIUM

Because our first parents had been created perfectly, they necessarily received from God not only natural perfection but also perfect knowledge of those signs through which they were able to disclose their thoughts to one another and hand this knowledge on to their children and posterity. And hence, because this knowledge is so basic and necessary for well-being, we see that children can acquire the art of speaking as soon as they are [physically?] able to talk. Nor does it seem absurd, if one believes that man's original speech was indeed abounding in synonyms, that all later, separate languages were contained in it. For all human languages come from that first language of our parent Adam, that is man. And just as there is no language which man may not understand, so also Adam, who is the same as man, would not be ignorant of any language he heard. For we read that he himself gave things their names. Therefore no word of any language was originally instituted by anyone but him. And we should not be surprised about Adam, since it is certain that many people, by the gift of

God, have suddenly acquired a knowledge of all languages. Furthermore, no art is more natural and easy for man than that of speaking, for no fully developed man lacks it. Nor should one doubt that our first parents also possessed the art of writing or tracing out words, since this confers many benefits on mankind. For through writing past and absent things become present.

NEW WORLDS, NEW THEORIES

New Worlds, New Theories

Gradually the full impact of the Renaissance discoveries had its effect also on language theories. In the hundred fifty years after "Columbus sailed the ocean blue" and discovered the Americas, interest in the peoples of those countries, who had no connection with Greece, Rome or Christianity—the three main influences on Western Europe—and whose languages bore no relation to European ones, and, for the most part, had no alphabets or writing, grew and spread. The impact of such peoples as the Chechuas and Topinamborus of Peru, of such individuals as Pocahontas, on European thinkers was enormous, and altered people's ideas about human nature itself, and, of course, about the origins of speech.

There were tremendous arguments in all the universities (particularly in Paris) and among individual philosophers, between those who believed that human speech is a function of human reason and those who claimed it to be an attribute of human nature.

René Descartes (1596-1650), the French philosopher, took up St. Augustine's premise that "if I err, then I am," and based on it his system with the words, "I think, therefore I am" (*je pense, donc je suis*). He naturally attached great significance to language and wrote (*Works of Descartes*, Vol. IX, p. 724.):

> Not one of our exterior actions can assure those who examine them that our body is anything other than a self-moving machine, or that there is also in it a soul which has thoughts, *except for words or other signs* made as a result of subjects which present themselves without being related to any passion.

Among those who argued for reason was Antoine Arnauld

(1612-1694), a priest of the Abbey of Port Royal in Paris. His views were condemned by the Catholic Church as Jansenist, that is to say, as deriving from a Dutch heretic called Cornelius Jansen (1585-1638). Here follows an extract from *The Port-Royal Logic*, by Antoine Arnauld, translated from the French by Thomas Spencer Baynes. (John Gordon, Edinburgh, 1861.)

From THE PORT-ROYAL LOGIC

CHAPTER ONE

Of Words in Their Relation to Propositions.
As it is our design to explain here the various reflections which men have made on their judgments, and as these judgments are propositions composed of various *parts*, it is necessary to begin with the explanation of *these parts*, which are principally nouns, pronouns, and verbs.

It is of little importance to examine whether it belongs to *grammar* or to *logic* to treat of these; it is enough to say, that everything which is of use to the end of any art, belongs to it, whether that knowledge be *special* to it, or *common* also to other arts and sciences which contribute to it.

Now, it is certainly of some use to the *end* which logic contemplates—*that of thinking well*—to understand the different uses of the sounds devoted to the expression of our ideas, and which the mind is accustomed to connect so closely with them, that it scarcely ever conceives the one without the other; so that the idea of *the thing* excites the idea of the *sound*, and the idea of the *sound*, that of the *thing*.

We may say, in general, on this subject, that WORDS are *sounds distinct and articulate, which men have taken as signs to express what passes in their mind*. And since what passes there may be reduced to *conceiving, judging, reasoning*, and *disposing* (as we have already said), words serve to indicate all these operations, and those which have been invented for this purpose are principally of *three kinds*, which are essential, and of which it will be sufficient to speak. These are nouns, pronouns, and verbs [read, *verbs and pronouns*], which take the place of nouns, but in a different way. It will be here necessary to explain this more in detail.

Of Nouns.

The *objects* of our thoughts being, as we have already said, either *things*, or *modes of things*, the words set apart to signify both things and modes are called nouns.

Those which signify things are called nouns substantive, as *earth, sun*. Those which signify modes—marking, however, at the same time, the *subject* of which they are the modes—are called nouns adjective, as *good, just, round*.

This is why—when, by mental abstraction, we conceive these modes without connecting them with any subject, since they then subsist in some sort by themselves in the mind—they are expressed by a *substantive* word, as *wisdom, whiteness, colour*.

And, on the contrary, when that which is of itself the substance of a thing comes to be conceived in *relation to another subject*, the words which express it in this relation become *adjectives, as human, carnal*; and, taking away from these adjectives formed from nouns of substance, their relation to these, they are made substantives anew. Thus, after having formed from the substantive word *homo* (*homme*), the adjective *human*, we form from the adjective *human*, the substantive *humanity*.

There are some nouns which pass for *substantives* in grammar, but are *really adjectives*, as *king, philosopher, physician*, since they denote a subject's manner or mode of being. But the reason why they pass for substantives is, that as they belong only to a *single subject*, we always understand that single subject, without its being necessary to express it. For the same reason, these words, *red, white*, &c., are *real adjectives*, because the relation is denoted; but the reason why we do not express the substantive to which they are related is, that it is a general substantive, which comprehends all the subjects of these modes, and is hence unique in that generality. Thus, *red* is *everything red; white, everything white*; or, as it is said in geometry, *any* red thing [*rubrum quodcunque*]. These adjectives have, therefore, essentially *two* significations: the one *distinct*, which is that of a *mode* or *manner*; the other *confused*, which is that of the *subject*. But though the signification of mode may be more distinct, it is nevertheless indirect; and, on the contrary, that of subject, though confused, is direct. The word *white* (*candidum*) signifies directly, but confusedly, the subject, and indirectly, though distinctly, *whiteness*.

Of Pronouns.
The use of pronouns is to occupy the place of nouns, and thus enable us to avoid a too tedious repetition; but we are not to imagine that, in taking the place of nouns, they produce entirely the same effect on the mind. This is by no means true; on the contrary, they remove the disgust felt at repetition only because they represent nouns, but in a confused manner. Nouns disclose, in some sort, the things to the mind; pronouns present them, as it were, veiled, though the mind perceives, nevertheless, that they are the same things as those signified by the nouns. This is why no inconvenience arises from the noun and the pronoun being joined together: *Tu Phaoedria, Ecce ego Joannes*.

Of Different Kinds of Pronouns.
Men perceiving that it was often useless and ungraceful to name themselves, introduced the pronoun of the first person to supply the place of him who speaks, *Ego, moi, je*. And in order that they might not be obliged to name the person to whom they spoke, they thought it good to denote him by a word, which they have called the pronoun of the second person [*tu, vos*], *thou*, or *you*; while, in order to avoid repeating the names of other persons and things of which they spoke, they invented pronouns of the third person—*ille, illa, illud*, [*he, she, it*]. Among these, there are some which point out, as with a finger, the thing spoken of, and are hence called demonstratives—*hic, iste, this, that*; there are also some which are called reciprocal, because they denote the relation of a thing to itself, as the pronoun—*sui, sibi, se* [*himself, herself, itself*]: as *Cato slew himself*.

All the pronouns have, as we already said, this in common: they mark confusedly the noun whose place they occupy. But there is this specially in the neuter of these pronouns, *illud, hoc*, when it is taken absolutely, that is to say, without a noun expressed: that whereas the other kinds, *hic, hoec, ille, illa*, are often, indeed almost always, related to distinct ideas, which they nevertheless denote only confusedly; (as, *illum expirantem flammas*, that is to say, *illum Ajacem—His ego nec metas rerum nec tempora ponam*, that is to say, *Romanis*); the neuter, on the contrary, is always related to a general and confused term (as, *hoc erat in votis*, that is to say, *hoec res, hoc negotium erat in votis—hoc erat alma parens*, &c.) Thus, there is a double confusion in the neuter; to wit, that of the pronoun, the signification of which is always confused, and that of the word *negotium, thing*, which is equally general and confused.

Of The Relative Pronoun.

There is yet another pronoun which is called relative—*qui, quoe, quod—who, which, that, that which, what*. This relative pronoun has something in common with the other pronouns, and something peculiar to itself. It has this *in common*, that it takes the place of a noun, and excites a confused idea. It has this *peculiar*, that the proposition into which it enters may be made part of the subject or predicate of a proposition, and thus form one of those added or incidental propositions, of which we shall speak more at large further on. *God* WHO *is good,—the world* WHICH *is visible*.

(We presume here that these terms, *subject* and *predicate* of propositions, are understood, though they have not as yet been formally explained, because they are so common that they are usually understood before logic is studied. Those who do not understand them, need only refer to the place where their meaning is explained [page].)

We are, hence, able to resolve this question: What is the precise meaning of the word *that* when it follows a verb, and appears to be related to nothing?—*John answered that he was not the Christ; Pilate said that he found no guilt in Jesus Christ*. There are some who would make of *that* an *adverb*, as well as of the word *quod*, which the Latins sometimes, though rarely, take in the same sense as our *that* (*que*). *Non tibi objicio quod hominem spoliâsti*, says Cicero. [In Verrem, act. II., lib. i.]

But the truth is, that the word *that* (*quod*) is nothing more than the *relative pronoun*, and it preserves its meaning; thus, in that proposition, *John answered that he was not the Christ*, the *that* retains the office of connecting another proposition, to wit, *was not the Christ*, with the attribute contained in the word *answered*, which signifies *juit respondens*. The other use, to *supply the place of the noun, and refer to it*, appears here, indeed, much less obtrusively, which has led some able men to say, that this *that* is entirely without such a use [*i.e.* has no antecedent noun] in this case. We may, however, say, that it retains it here also; for, in saying that *John answered*, we understand that he made an answer; and to this confused idea of answer the *that* refers. In the same way, when Cicero says, *Non tibi objicio quod hominem spoliâsti*, the *quod* refers to the confused idea of a *thing objected*, formed by the word *objicio*; and that thing objected, conceived before obscurely, is then particularised by the incidental proposition, connected by the *quod—quod hominem spoliâsti*.

The same thing may be remarked in these questions—*I suppose that you will be wise—I say that you are wrong. This term I SAY* causes us at once to conceive confusedly a *thing said*; and to this thing said the *that* refers. *I say that*, meaning, *I say a thing which is*. And, in the same way, he who says, *I suppose*, gives a confused idea of a thing supposed; for *I suppose* means, *I make a supposition*; and to this idea of thing supposed the *that* refers. *I suppose that* is tantamount to, *I make a supposition which is*—. . . .

CHAPTER TWO

Of the Verb.

We have borrowed thus far what we have said of nouns and pronouns, from a little book [of ours] printed some time ago, under the title of a *General Grammar*, with the exception of some points, which we have explained in a different way; but in regard to the verb, which is treated of in the 13th chapter [of that work], we shall merely transcribe what is there said, since it appears to us that nothing can be added to it.

"Men," it is there said, "have no less need to invent words which may denote affirmation, which is the principal manner of our thoughts, than to invent those which may denote the *objects of our thoughts*. And herein properly consists that which we call *verb. This is nothing else than a word, the principal use of which is to express affirmation*, that is to say, to denote that the discourse wherein the word is employed is the discourse of a man who not only *conceives* things, but who *judges* and *affirms* of them. Herein the verb is distinguished from certain nouns, which also signify affirmation, as *affirmans, affirmatio*, because these signify it only so far as through a reflection of the mind it becomes an object of our thoughts, and thus they do not denote that he who employs these words *affirms*, but only that he *conceives an affirmation*.

"I said that the *principal* use of the verb was to signify *affirmation*, because, as we shall come to see further on, it is employed also to express other movements of the mind, as those of *desiring, entreating, commanding*, &c. But this is done only by changing the inflection and the mood, and thus we shall consider the verb, through the whole of this chapter, in its principal signification alone, which is that which it has in the *indicative mood*. According to this view, we may say that the verb of itself can have no other office than that of marking the connection which we make in our mind between the two terms of a proposition. But the verb *to be*, which we call substantive, is the only one remaining in this simplicity. And even the verb substantive, properly speaking, has only remained so in the third person present, *is*, and on certain occasions; for, as men naturally come to abbreviate their expressions, there are joined almost always to the affirmation other significations in the same word.

"I. They have joined to it that of some attribute, so that then two words constitute a proposition; as when I say, *Petrus vivit, Peter lives*, because the word *vivit* contains in itself the *affirmation*, and, moreover, the *attribute* of *being alive*; thus it is the same thing to say, *Peter lives*, as it is to say, *Peter is living*. Hence has arisen the great diversity of verbs in every language; whereas, if men had been satisfied with giving to the verb the general signification of affirmation, without joining to it any particular attribute, each language would have needed only a single verb, that, to wit, which is called substantive.

"II. They have further joined to it, in certain cases, the subject of the proposition; so that then two words, and indeed a single word even, may make a complete proposition. Two words: as when I say *sum homo*; since *sum* expresses not only affirmation, but includes the signification of the pronoun *ego*, which is the subject of this proposition, and which we always express in our language (*je suis homme*), *I am a man*. A single word: as when I say *vivo, sedes*. For these verbs contain in themselves both the *affirmation* and the *attribute* (as we have already said); and being in the first person, they contain also the subject, *I am living, I am sitting*.

Hence arises the difference of persons, which is commonly found in all verbs.

"III. They have also added a relation to the time in regard to which we affirm, so that a single word, as *coenasti*, signifies that I affirm of him to whom I speak the action of supping, not in relation to the present time, but to the past. Hence arises the *diversity of times* [or *tenses*], which also is, for the most part, common to all verbs.

"The diversity of these significations united in the same word has prevented many persons, otherwise very able, from clearly understanding the nature of the verb, because they have not considered it in relation to what is essential to it, which is *affirmation*, but according to other relations, which, as verb, are *accidental to it*. Thus Aristotle, dwelling on the third of the adscititious significations, defined the verb—*vox significans, cum tempore* (a word significant, with time).

"Others, as Buxtorf, having added the second, have defined it, *vox flexilis, cum tempore, et persona* (a word with various inflections, including time and person).

"Others [as Priscian], stopping at the first of these adscititious significations, and considering that the attributes which men have joined to the affirmation in a single word, are commonly actions and passions, have held that the essence of the verb consists in *expressing actions and passions*.

"Finally, Julius Caesar Scaliger thought that he had found out a mystery, in his book on the Principles of the Latin Language, in saying that the distinction of things *in permanentes et fluentes* (into those which remain and those which pass away), was the true origin of the distinction between *nouns* and *verbs*; the office of nouns being to express what remains—of verbs, what passes away.

"But it may be easily seen, that all these definitions are false, and do not explain the true nature of the verb.

"The manner in which the two first are conceived, sufficiently proves this; since they do not say what the verb signifies, but only what its signification is connected with,—*cum tempore, cum persona*.

"The two last are still worse. They have the two great vices of a definition: namely, that they belong neither to the whole thing defined, nor to it alone—*neque omni, neque soli*. For there are verbs which signify neither actions nor passions, nor that which passes away; as *existit, quiescit, friget, alget, tepet, calet, albet, viret, claret*, &c. And there are words which are not verbs, which signify actions and passions, and even things which pass away—according to the definition of Scaliger. For it is certain that *participles* are true nouns, and that, nevertheless, those of active verbs do not signify actions less, and those of passives, passions less, than the verbs whence they are derived; and there is no reason at all for maintaining that *fluens* does not signify a thing which passes away, as well as *fluit*.

"To which we may add, against the two first definitions of the verb, that the participles also signify time, since they are of the present, of the past, and of the future, especially in Greek. And those who believe, and not without reason, that the vocative case is a true second person, especially when it has a different termination from the nominative, will maintain that there is, in this point of view, only a difference, of more or of less, between the vocative and the verb. [But, *Plus, et minus non variant, speciem*.]

"And thus the essential reason why a *participle* is not a *verb* is this, that it does not *express affirmation*; whence it happens that it cannot make a proposition, which it is the property of the verb to do, except by being joined to a verb; that is to say, by that being restored to it which had been taken away, in changing the verb into a participle. For how is it that *Petrus vivit, Peter lives*, is a proposition, and that *Petrus vivens, Peter living*, is not one, unless you add *est, is*, to it, *Petrus est vivens, Peter is living*; except, because the *affirmation* which is contained in *vivit* had been taken away, in order to make the participle *vivens*? Whence it appears, *that the presence or absence, in a word, of affirmation, is what constitutes it a verb, or not a verb*.

"On which we may farther remark, by the way, that the *infinitive*, which is very often a noun (as when we say *le boire, le manger, to drink, to eat*), is then different from the participles in this,—that the participles are nouns adjective, while the infinitive is a noun substantive, made by abstraction of that adjective, in the same way as from *candidus* is made *candor*, and from *white* comes *whiteness*. Thus the verb *rubet* expresses *is red*, including at once both the affirmation [*est*] and the attribute *rubens*; whereas the participle signifies simply red, without any affirmation; and *rubere* taken for a noun, signifies *redness*.

"It ought, therefore, to be laid down as established, that, considering simply, which is *essential* in the verb, its only true definition is,—*vox significans affirmationem* (*a word signifying affirmation*).

"For we can find no word denoting affirmation which is not a verb, and no verb which does not denote it, at least in the indicative; and it is unquestionable that if one had been invented, as *is*, always marking affirmation, without any difference of persons or of times, so that the diversity of persons were denoted only by nouns and pronouns, and diversity of times by adverbs, it would still, nevertheless, be a true verb. As, in fact, is the case in the propositions which philosophers term those of eternal truth: as, *God is infinite; all body is divisible; the whole is greater than its part*. Here the word *is* marks, simple affirmation only, without any relation to time; because these are true in relation to all times, and the attention of the mind is not arrested by any diversity of persons.

"Thus the verb, considered as to what is essential to it, is a word which denotes *affirmation*. But if we wish to include in the definition of the verb its principal accidents, we may define it thus: *Vox significans affirmationem, cum designatione personoe, numeri et temporis*,—(*A word signifying affirmation, with the designation of person, number, and time*). This agrees specially with the substantive verb.

"For in relation to the other [or adjective] verbs, in so far as they differ from the verb substantive, by the union which men have made of the affirmation with certain attributes, we may define them as follows: *Vox significans affirmationem alicujus attributi, cum designatione personoe, numeri, et temporis,—(A word denoting the affirmation of some attribute, together with the determination of person, number, and time*).

"We may remark, in passing, that since affirmation, as conceived, may also be the attribute of the verb, as in the verb *affirmo*, this verb expresses two affirmations; of which one regards the person who speaks, and the other the person who is spoken of, whether this be oneself or another. For when I say, *Petrus affirmat*, *affirmat* is the same thing as *est affirmans*; and *est* then marks my affirmation, or the judgment I make touching Peter, and *affirmans*, the affirmation which I conceive and attribute to Peter. The verb *nego*, on the contrary, contains an affirmation and a negation, for the same reason.

"It is, however, still necessary to remark, that though all our judgments are not affirmations, but some of them negations, yet, nevertheless, that verbs only signify of themselves affirmations,—the negations being expressed by the particles *non, not*, or by words involving *nullus, nemo, no, none, no one* [*nothing, no, none, no one, nobody*, &c.], which being united to verbs, change them from affirmative to negative: as, *no man is immortal; no body is indivisible*."

CHAPTER THREE

What Is Meant by a Proposition, and of Four Kinds of Propositions.

After having conceived things through ideas, we compare these ideas together; and, finding that *some agree* together, and that others *do not agree*, we unite or separate them, which is called affirming or denying, and generally, judging.

This judgment is called also a proposition, and must have, as will be easily seen, *two terms*; the one, that of which we affirm or deny something, called the subject; and the other, that [something] which we affirm or deny, called the attribute, or predicate.

It is not sufficient to *conceive* these two terms,—the mind must also *unite* or *separate* them; and this action of our mind is denoted, as we have already said, in discourse, by the verb *is*, either alone, when we affirm, or with the negative particle, when we deny. Thus, when I say, *God is just; God* is the *subject* of that proposition, *just* is the *attribute*; and the word *is* marks the operation of my mind in affirming, that is to say, in connecting together these two ideas, *God* and *just*, as agreeing with each other. And if I say, *God is not unjust; is*, being joined with the particle *not*, signifies the contrary action to that of affirming, to wit, that of *denying*, by which I regard these two ideas as repugnant to each other, since there is something contained in the idea of *unjust* which is contrary to what is contained in the idea of *God*. [The substantive verb thus employed is called the copula.]

But though every proposition contains necessarily these *three things*, yet, as we have said in the preceding chapter, it may have only *two words*, or even *one* alone. For men, wishing to abbreviate their speech, have made a multitude of words which express in themselves an affirmation—express, that is to say, what is signified by the substantive verb, and a certain attribute which is affirmed, besides. Such are all verbs except the substantive verb: as *God exists, i.e. is existing; God loves men, i.e. God is loving men*. And the substantive verb, when it is alone, ceases to be purely substantive: as when I say, *I think, therefore I am*; because there is then joined to it the most general of attributes, which is *being*; for *I am*, means *I am a being—I am something*.

There are also certain other cases in which the subject and the affirmation are contained in a single word, as in the *first* and *second persons* of the verb, especially in Latin; as when I say, *Sum Christianus*. For the *subject* of this proposition is *ego*, which is contained in *sum*. Whence it appears, that in that language a single word makes a proposition in the first and second persons of verbs, which, by their nature, already contain the affirmation with the attribute; thus, *veni, vidi, vici*, are three propositions.

We see from this that *every proposition is affirmative or negative*, and that this is denoted by the verb which is affirmed or denied.

But there is *another difference of propositions* which arises from their *subject*, which is that of being universal, or particular, or singular. For terms, as we have already said in the First Part, are either *singular*, or *common*, or *universal*.

And *universal* terms may be taken either according to their *whole extension*, by joining them to universal signs, expressed or understood: as *omnis, all* [&c.], for affirmation; *nullus, none* [&c.], for negation; as *all men, no man*.

Or according to an *indeterminate part of their extension*; which is, when there is joined to them *aliquis, some* [&c.]; as *some man, some men*; or other words, according to the custom of languages.

Whence arises a remarkable difference of propositions; for when the *subject of a proposition is a common term*, which is taken in *all its extension*, propositions are called universal, whether affirmative, as, *Every impious man is a fool*,—or negative, as, *No vicious man is happy*.

And when the common term [or subject] is taken according to an *indeterminate part only of its extension*, since it is then restricted by the indeterminate word *some*, the proposition is called particular; whether it affirms, as, *Some cruel men are cowards*,—or whether it denies, as, *Some poor men are not unhappy*.

And if the subject of a proposition be *singular*, as when I say, *Louis XIII took Rochelle*, it is called singular. But though this singular proposition may be different from the universal, in that its subject is not common, it ought nevertheless to be referred *to it*, rather than to the *particular*; for this very reason, that it is singular, since it is necessarily taken in *all its extension*, which constitutes the *essence* of a *universal proposition*, and which distinguishes it from the *particular*. For it matters little, so far as the universality of a proposition is concerned, whether its subject be great or small, provided that, whatever it may be, the whole is taken entire. And hence it is that singular propositions take the place of universals in reasoning. Thus we may reduce all propositions to *four* sorts, which, in order to assist the memory, have been denoted by these four vowels—A, E, I, O:—

A. Universal affirmative: as, *Every vicious man is a slave*.
E. Universal negative: as, *No vicious man is happy*.
I. Particular affirmative: as, *Some vicious men are rich*.
O. Particular negative: as, *Some vicious men are not rich*.

The following two verses have been made for the better remembering of those:

> Asserit A, negat E, verum generaliter ambo;
> Asserit I, negat O, sed particulariter ambo.

It is customary to call the *universality* or *particularity* of propositions their quantity. By quality is meant the *affirmation* or *negation*, which depends on the verb; and this is regarded as the *form* of a proposition.

Thus A and E agree in *quantity*, and differ according to *quality*; and so also I and O.

But A and I *agree* according to *quality*, and *differ* according to *quantity*; and in the same way, E and O.

Propositions are divided, again, according to *their matter*, into true and false. And it is clear that there are none which are not either true or false, since every proposition denoting the judgment which we form of things is true when that judgment is conformed to truth, and false when it is not so conformed.

But since we are often in want of light to recognise true and false, besides those propositions which appear to us certainly true, and those which appear certainly false, there are others which appear to us true, but whose truth is not so evident as to free us from all apprehension that they may be false, or which appear to us false, but of whose falsity we are not certainly sure. These are the propositions which we call probable, of which the first are more probable and the last less probable. We shall say something in the Fourth Part of what enables us to judge with certainty whether a proposition is true.

CHAPTER FOUR

Of the Opposition Between Propositions Having the Same Subject and Attribute.

We have said there are four sorts of propositions—A, E, I, O. We inquire now what agreement or disagreement they have together, when we make from the *same subject*, and the *same attribute*, different kinds of propositions. This is what is called opposition.

And it is easy to see that this opposition can be only of *three kinds*, though one of the three is subdivided into two others.

For if propositions are opposed, both in *quantity and quality*, they are called contradictories, as A O, and E I. *Every man is an animal, Some man is no animal,—No man is sinless, Some man is sinless.*

If they differ in *quantity alone*, and agree in *quality*, they are called subalterns, as A I, and E O, *Every man is an animal, Some man is an animal,—No man is sinless, Some man is not sinless.*

And if they differ *in quality*, and agree in *quantity*, they are then called contraries, or sub-contraries. Contraries when they are universal, as *Every man is an animal, No man is an animal.* Sub-contraries when they are particular, as *Some man is an animal, Some man is not an animal.* In considering these opposed propositions, according to their truth or falsehood, we may easily determine—

1. *That* contradictories *are never both either true or false together*, but if one is true the other is false; and if one is false the other is true. For if it be true that every man is an animal, it cannot be true that some man is not an animal; and if, on the contrary,

it be true that some man is not an animal, it is consequently not true that every man is an animal. This is so clear that it would only be obscured by further explanation.

2. Contraries *can never be both true, but they may be often both false*. They cannot be true because the contradictories would be true. For if it be true that *Every man is an animal*, it is false that *Some man is not an animal*, which is the contradictory; and, by consequence, still more false that *No man is an animal,* which is the contrary. But the falsehood of one does not imply the truth of the other, for it may be false that all men are just, without its being true, on that account, that no man is just, since there may be just men, though all are not just.

3. Sub-contraries, *by a rule directly opposed to that of contraries, may be both true*, as these, *Some man is just, Some man is not just*, because justice may belong to one part of men, and not to another; and thus the affirmation and negation do not regard the same subject, since *some men* is taken for one part of men, in one of the propositions, and for another in the other. But they *cannot be both false*, since otherwise the contradictories would be both false; for if it were false that *Some men were just*, it would therefore be true that *No man was just*, which is the contradictory, and with much more reason that *Some man is not just*, which is the sub-contrary.

4. With regard to the Subalterns, *there is no true opposition*, since the particulars are consequents of the general, for if *All men are animals, Some man is an animal*; if *No man is an ape, Some man is not an ape*. Hence the truth of the universals involves that of the particulars; but the truth of the particulars does not involve that of the universals, for it does not follow, because it is true that some man is just, that it should be also true that every man is just; and, on the contrary, the falsehood of particulars involves the falsehood of universals, for if it be false that some man is sinless, it is still more false that every man is sinless. But the falsity of the universals does not involve the falsity of the particulars, for although it may be false that every man is just, it does not follow that it is false to say that some man is just. Hence it follows that there are many cases in which these subalternate propositions are both true, and others in which they are both false. . . .

* * *

CHAPTER SEVEN

Of the Falsity That May Be Met with in Complex Terms and Incidental Propositions.

What we have said may enable us to resolve a celebrated question, which is, *Whether falsehood is to be found only in propositions*, or whether it does not also enter into *ideas* and *simple terms*?

I speak of falsehood rather than of truth, because there is a truth which is in things in relation to the mind of God, whether men think it, or whether they do not; but falsehood can only be in relation to the *mind of man*, or to some mind subject to error, which judges falsely that a thing is that which it is not.

It is asked, then, whether this falseness is only found in *propositions* and *judgments*? We commonly reply, *no*; which is true in a sense. But this does not secure that there shall not be sometimes falsehood, not in *simple ideas* but in *complex terms*, since it is enough for this that there be some judgment and affirmation, either expressed or understood.

We shall understand this better by considering in detail *two sorts of complex terms*, in one of which the *who* is explicative—in the other, determinative.

We need not wonder that falsehood is to be found in the first kind of complex terms, since here the attribute of the incidental proposition is affirmed of the subject to which the relative pertains. *Alexander, who is the son of Philip*. I affirm of Alexander, although incidentally, that he is the son of Philip; and, consequently, if it be not so, there is falsehood in this.

But two or three things, which are important, must be remarked here:—

1. That the *falsehood of the incidental proposition* does not commonly *affect the truth of the principal proposition*; for example,—*Alexander, who was the son of Philip, conquered the Persians*. This proposition ought to be considered true, though Alexander be not the son of Philip; since the affirmation of the principal proposition falls only on Alexander, and that which is incidentally connected with it, though false, does not prevent it being true that Alexander conquered the Persians. If, however, the attribute of the principal proposition be related to the incidental proposition, as if I were to say,—*Alexander, the son of Philip, was the grandson*

of Amyntas; in this case only would the falsehood of the incidental proposition make the principal proposition false.

2. The titles which are commonly given to certain dignitaries may be given to all those who possess these dignities, though that which is signified by the title may not belong to them at all. Thus, because formerly the title of *holy*, and of *very holy*, was given to all bishops, we see that the Catholic bishops, in the Council of Carthage, did not hesitate to bestow that name on Donatist bishops. (*Sanctissimus Petillianus dixit*), although they knew well that true holiness could not belong to a schismatical bishop. We see also that Paul, in the Acts, gives the title of *very good*, or *very excellent*, to Festus, governor of Judaea, because that was the title commonly given to these governors.

3. The case is different when a man is the author of the title which he gives to another, and which he gives to him, not according to the opinion of others, or according to popular error, but for himself alone; for we may then, with justice, impute to him the falsehood of these propositions. Thus, when a man says, —*Aristotle, who is the prince of philosophers* (or simply,—*the prince of philosophers*), *believed that the origin of the nerves is in the heart*; we ought not to tell him that this is false, because Aristotle is not the best of philosophers, for it is enough that he follows in this the common opinion, though false. But if any one said,—*Gassendi, who is the most able of philosophers, believes that there is a void in nature*; we might dispute with such a man the quality which he wished to bestow on Gassendi, and make him responsible for the falsehood which we might maintain was to be found in that incidental proposition. He may, therefore, be accused of falsehood in giving to the same person a title which does not belong to him, and we cannot be accused of it in giving to him another which belongs to him still less in truth. For example,—*Pope John XII. was neither holy, nor chaste, nor pious*, as Baronius allows; and yet those who should call him *very holy* could not be accused of falsehood, while those who called him *very chaste*, or *very pious*, would be great liars, although they may only have done this by incidental propositions, as if they were to say,—*John XII., a very chaste pontiff, ordained such a thing*.

So much touching the first kinds of incidental propositions, in which the relative (*who, which*) is *explicative*.

In relation to the *others*, where the relative is determinative, as—*A man who is pious,—Kings who love their people*—it is certain that, in general, they are not susceptible of falsehood, since the attribute of the incidental proposition is not affirmed of the subject to which the relative refers. For if we say, for example,—*Judges who never do anything by request or favour are worthy of praise*; we do not say, on that account, that there is any judge in the world who has attained to that perfection. Nevertheless I believe that there is always in these propositions a *tacit* or *virtual affirmation*, not of the *actual* agreement of the attribute with the subject to which the *who* refers, but of its *possible* agreement. And if an error be committed here, I believe we shall have reason to hold that there may be falsehood in these incidental propositions; as if, for example, it were said,—*Minds which are square are more solid than those which are round*. Here the idea of *square* and *round* being incompatible with the idea of *mind*, taken for the principle of thought, I hold that such incidental propositions ought to be reckoned false.

We may even say that the greater number of our errors spring from this. For, having the idea of a *thing*, we often join to it another idea which is incompatible with it, although, through error, we believed it compatible, which leads us to attribute to this idea that which never belonged to it.

Thus, finding in ourselves two ideas, that of a *substance thinking*, and that of a *substance extended*, it often happens, that when we consider our soul, which is a substance which thinks, we mingle insensibly with it something of the idea of a substance extended. As when, for instance, we imagine that our soul must fill a space as the body does, and that it could not exist if it had no parts,—things which belong exclusively to the body; and hence has arisen the impious error of those who believe the soul to be mortal. We may see an excellent discourse on this subject by St. Augustine, in the Tenth Book "Of the Trinity." There he shows that there is nothing which may be known more easily than the nature of the soul; but that which perplexes men is this, that, wishing to know it, they are not satisfied with that which they may know without difficulty, that it is a substance which thinks, wills, doubts, knows, but they join to what *it is*, that which *it is not*, striving to imagine it under some of those forms through which they are accustomed to conceive of corporeal things.

When, on the other hand, we consider *body*, it is very difficult to restrain ourselves from mingling with it something of the idea of that which thinks, which leads us to say of heavy bodies that they *tend* towards a centre; of plants that they *seek* the nourishment which is proper for them; of the crisis of a malady, that it is nature which is *striving* to get rid of that which offends it; and of a thousand other things, especially in our body, that nature *wishes* to do this or that, though we are well assured that we have not willed it, nor thought anything about it: and it is ridiculous to imagine that there is *in us* anything else beside *ourselves* which knows what is suitable or hurtful, which seeks the one and avoids the other.

I believe that it is to this mixture of incompatible ideas we must attribute all the complaints which men make against God; for it would be impossible to murmur against God if we conceived of him truly as he is—all powerful all-wise, and all-good. But wicked men, conceiving of him as all-powerful, and as the sovereign ruler of all the world, attribute to him all the evils which happen to them, wherein they are right. And since at the same time, they conceive him to be cruel and unjust, which is incompatible with his goodness, they rail against him, as though he had done them wrong in laying upon them the evils which they suffer.

CHAPTER EIGHT

Of Complex Propositions in Relation to Affirmation and Negation, and of a Species of These Kinds of Propositions which Philosophers Call Modals.

Beside the propositions of which the subject or the attribute is a complex term, there are others which are complex, because they have incidental terms or propositions, which regard only the form of the proposition, that is to say, the affirmation, or negation, which is expressed by the verb: as, if I say,—*I maintain that the earth is round; I maintain* is only an incidental proposition, which must be a part of something in the principal proposition. Yet, it is clear that it makes no part either of the subject or the attribute, for it makes no change in them at all; and they would be conceived in precisely the same way, if I said, simply, *the earth is round*. And thus it can belong only to the affirmation, which is expressed in two ways, the one, which is the usual, by the verb *is,—The earth is round*, and the other more expressly by the verb *I maintain*.

In the same way, when it is said, *I deny that it is true*, [or] *it is not true*; or when we add in a proposition that which supports its truth: as when I say—*The reasons of astronomy convince us that the sun is much larger than the earth*; for that first part is only a support of the affirmation. . . .

CHAPTER EIGHTEEN

Of the Conversion of Affirmative Propositions.
We call the conversion of a proposition *the changing of the subject into the attribute, and of the attribute into the subject, without affecting the truth of the proposition*, or rather, so that it necessarily follows from the conversion that it is true, supposing that it was so before.

Now, by what we have just said, it will be easily understood how this conversion must be effected. For as it is impossible that one thing can be joined to another, without that second thing being also joined to the first; it follows very clearly that if A be joined to B, B is joined to A, and it is clearly impossible that two things can be conceived as identified, which is the most perfect of all unions, unless that union be reciprocal,—that is to say, that we be able mutually to affirm the two united terms, in the manner in which they are united, which is called conversion.

Thus, for example, in particular affirmative propositions, as when we say *Some man is just*, the subject and the attribute are both particular (the subject, man, being particular by the mark of particularity which is added to it—and the attribute, *just*, being so also, inasmuch as its extension being restricted by that of the subject, signifies only the justice which is in *some man*). Here it is evident that if *some man* is identified with *some just, some just* is also identified with *some man*, and that thus we need only change the attribute into the subject, preserving the same particularity, in order to convert such propositions.

The same thing cannot be said of universal affirmative propositions, because in these propositions the subject alone is universal, that is to say, taken according to its whole extension. The attribute, on the contrary, is limited and restrained, and consequently, when we make it the subject by conversion, it must preserve the same restriction, and have added to it a mark which determines it, that it may not be taken generally. Thus, when I say that *man is animal*, I unite the idea of *man* with that of *animal*, restraining and confining it to men alone. Therefore, when I wish to look at that union under another aspect, beginning with animal, and then affirming man, it is necessary to preserve to this term the same restriction, and in order that no mistake may be made, to add to it some mark of determination.

So that, although universal affirmative propositions can only be converted into particular affirmatives, we must not conclude that they are converted less properly than the others; for since they are made up of a general subject and a restricted attribute, it is clear that when they are converted by changing the attribute into the subject, they ought to have a subject restricted and confined, that is to say, particular: whence we obtain these two rules.

Rule 1.

Universal affirmative propositions may be converted by adding a mark of particularity to the attribute when changed into the subject.

Rule 2.

Particular affirmative propositions are to be converted without any addition or change; that is to say, by retaining for the attribute, when changed into the subject, the *mark of particularity* which belonged to the first subject. But it is easily perceived that these two rules may be reduced to one, which includes them both:

The attribute being restrained by the subject in all affirmative propositions, if we wish to change it into the subject, we must preserve that restriction and give it a mark of particularity, whether the first subject be universal or particular.

Nevertheless, it often happens that universal affirmative propositions may be converted into other universals. But this happens exclusively, when the attribute is not in itself of wider extension than the subject, as when we affirm the *difference*, or the *property* of the *species*, or the *definition* of the *thing defined*; for, then, the attribute not being restricted, may be taken as generally in conversion as the subject was—*all man is rational, all rational is man*.

But these conversions, being true only under particular circumstances, are not reckoned true conversions, which ought to be certain and infallible, by the simple transposition of the terms.

CHAPTER NINETEEN

Of the Nature of Negative Propositions.

The nature of negative propositions cannot be expressed more clearly than by saying, that it is *the conceiving that one thing is not another*; but, in order that one thing be not another, it is not necessary that it should have nothing in common with it; it is enough that it has not all which the other has, as it is enough, in order that a *beast* be not a *man*, that it should not have all that a man has, and it is not necessary that it should have nothing of what is in man. Whence we may obtain this axiom:—

Axiom v.

The negative proposition does not separate from the subject all the parts contained in the comprehension of the attribute, but it separates only the total and complete idea composed of all these attributes united.

If I say that matter is not a substance that thinks, I should not, therefore, say that it is not a *substance*, but I say that it is not a *thinking substance*, which is the total and complete idea that I deny of matter.

It is quite the reverse with the *extension* of an idea; for the negative proposition separates from the subject the idea of the attribute, according to the *whole of its extension*. And the reason of this is clear; for, to be the *subject of an idea*, and to be *contained in* [*under*] *its extension*, is nothing else but to comprehend that idea; and, consequently, when we say that one idea does not comprehend another, which is termed denying, we say that it is not one of the subjects of that idea.

Thus, if I say that *man is not an insensible being*, I mean to say that he is not among the number of insensible beings, and I, therefore, separate them all from him. Whence we may obtain this other axiom:—

Axiom vi.

The attribute of a negative proposition is always taken generally. This may also be expressed more distinctly thus: *All the subjects of the one idea, which is denied of the other, are also denied of that other idea*; that is to say, that an idea is always denied according to its *whole extension*. If triangle is denied of square, all that is contained under triangle will be denied of square. This rule is commonly expressed in the schools in these terms, which mean the same thing: *If the genus is denied, the species also is denied*; for the species is a subject of the genus. Man is a subject of animal, because he is contained under its extension.

Not only do negative propositions separate the attribute from the subject, according to the whole extension of the attribute, but they separate also this attribute from the subject, according to the whole extension which the subject has in the proposition; that is to say, they separate it universally, if the subject is universal,—and particularly, if the subject is particular. If I say that *no vicious man is happy*, I separate all the happy persons from all the vicious persons; and if I say that *some doctor is not learned*, I separate learned from some doctor. And hence we may obtain this axiom:—

Axiom vii.

Every attribute denied of a subject, is denied of everything that is contained under the extension which that subject has in the proposition.

CHAPTER TWENTY

Of the Conversion of Negative Propositions.

Since it is impossible totally to separate two things, except the separation be mutual and reciprocal, it is clear that if I say, *No man is a stone*, I can say also that *no stone is a man*: for if any stone were a man, that man would be a stone; and, consequently, it would not be true that no man was a stone. And thus,

Rule 3.

Negative universal propositions may be converted, by simply changing the attribute into the subject, and preserving to the attribute, when it has become the subject, the same universality which the first subject had.

For the attribute, in negative universal propositions, is always taken universally, since it is denied according to the whole of its extension, as we have already shown above.

But for this very reason we cannot convert particular negative propositions;—we cannot say, for example, that *some physician is not a man*, because we said that *some man is not a physician*. This arises, as I said, from the very nature of the negation, according to the explanation just given; which is, that in negative propositions the attribute is always taken universally, and according to the whole of its extension; so that, when a particular subject becomes the attribute, by conversion, in a particular negative proposition, it becomes universal, and changes its nature contrary to the rules of true conversion, which ought not to change the extension or limitation of the terms. Thus, in this proposition, *Some man is not a physician*, the term, man, is taken particularly; but in this false conversion, *Some physician is not a man*, the word man is taken universally. Now, because the quality of physician is separated from *some man* in this proposition, *Some man is not a physician*, and because the idea of triangle is separated from that of *some* figure in the other proposition, it by no means follows that there are *physicians who are not men* and *triangles which are not figures*.

Among Antoine Arnauld's opponents was the German philosopher Gottfried Wilhelm Leibniz (1646-1716), whose concern with language, the forms of speech and their origins, is still studied and commented on by contemporary linguists. He and Arnauld exchanged letters.

Some extracts from various works by Leibniz follow.

From PREFACE TO AN EDITION OF NIZOLIUS, 1670

Clearness in speech applies not merely to the words but also to constructions. For if a construction is not clear, one may indeed know what the words mean simply and taken singly but not what they mean in this particular place and related to the others. But in the matter of obscurity of construction, speakers and poets are more apt to sin than are our philosophers. Therefore we shall speak of the clarity of words taken by themselves. . . . The clarity of a word arises from two factors—either from the *word in itself* or from its *context in speech*. The clarity of a word in itself, again, has two sources—*origin* and *usage*. The origin of a word, finally, can be resolved into two factors—the *use* of the root and the *analogy* of the derivation made from the root. *Usage* is the meaning of a word known in common by all who use the same language. *Analogy* is a meaning reached by shifting, or by derivation, which is likewise known to all who use the same language. For example, the usage or meaning of the word *fate* is the necessity of events. In origin it is compounded from the usage of the root and from analogy. The root is *for* or *fari*, the meaning of the root is "to say" (*dicere*); the analogy of fate is *fatum*, the perfect passive participle of the designated verb in Latin, so that the origin of *fate* and *dictum* is the same. Mostly, too, usage has arisen from origin by a certain figure of speech. This appears in the given example, since *fatum* is originally the same as *dictum* but means in usage what will happen necessarily. Let us see, therefore, whose *dictum* will happen necessarily; it is manifest that God's commands alone fit this description. Thus by origin fate is dictum, then by *antonomasia* or par excellence, the dictum of God, then by *synecdoche* the dictum of God concerning the future, or the decree of God, and finally by the *metonymy* of cause, what will happen necessarily, which is the present usage of the word. Thus the good grammarian, and the philosopher as well, must deduce the usage of a word from its origin by a continuous sorites of figures of speech, so to speak. I consider Julius Caesar Scaliger the great master in this work. His books on origins are now lost, to the great detriment of philosophy, except as his son has perhaps used them in his notes on Varro, but these differ for the most part from what his father had already published and scattered through his own writings. So, although we have greater erudition in the thought of the son, we have lost the greater acumen and philosophy in the book of origins of the father.

This rule must be adhered to in applying words—if the origin disagrees with the usage, we should follow the usage in speech rather than the origin; but if the usage is either doubtful or does not forbid it, we should rather cling to the origin. If the word has multiple usages, one must either be careful to abstract some so-called formal meaning, that is, the meaning which includes all usages in it, . . . or if this cannot be done, one must at least establish some one usage which may be called original, i.e., from which the others follow in the same way in which it itself follows from the origin, namely, through a series of figures of speech. . . . In either case, whether selecting the more original usage or the formal meaning, one must make sure above all else to choose among the many usages offered that one which is nearest the origin of the word. Once chosen, however, the meaning must be reduced, if there is place, to a definition and submitted to the reader or listener. For a definition is nothing but the expressed meaning of a word or, more briefly, the meaning signified. In a definition care must be taken not only that the definition be reciprocally true but also that it be clear. Technical terms are therefore to be shunned as worse than dog or snake, and one must abstain particularly from those words for categories which are far removed from Latin usage. Once set up, the definition is to be adhered to consistently, so that, wherever you substitute the definition for the term defined, there results no absurd statement. Even if no definition is given beforehand, the use of a word should be uniform so that the same definition could be substituted anywhere. Thus, *for any given word, we should see what meaning is attached to it and, conversely, what word should be attached to a given meaning*. . . .

From A LETTER TO WALTER VON TSCHIRNHAUS, May, 1678

Meanwhile I admit that no more beautiful example of the art of combinations can be found anywhere than in algebra and that therefore he who masters algebra will the more easily establish the general art of combinations, because it is always easier to arrive at a general science a posteriori from particular instances than a priori. But there can be no doubt that the general art of combinations or characteristics contains much greater things than algebra has given, for by its use all our thoughts can be pictured and, as it were, fixed, abridged, and ordered; pictured to *others* in teaching them, *fixed* for ourselves in order to remember them; *abridged* so that they may be reduced to a few; *ordered* so that all of them can be present in our thinking. And though I know you are prejudiced, by reasons which I do not know, to look rather adversely upon these meditations of mine, I believe that, when you examine the matter more seriously, you will agree that this general characteristic will be of unbelievable value, since a spoken and written language can also be developed with its aid which can be learned in a few days and will be adequate to express everything that occurs in everyday practice, and of astonishing value in criticism and discovery, after the model of the numeral characters. We certainly calculate much more easily with the characters of arithmetic than the Romans did, either with pens or in their heads, and this is undoubtedly because the Arabic characters are more convenient, that is, because they better express the genesis of numbers.

No one should fear that the contemplation of characters will lead us away from the things themselves; on the contrary, it leads us into the interior of things. For we often have confused notions today because the characters we use are badly arranged; but then, with the aid of characters, we will easily have the most distinct notions, for we will have at hand a mechanical thread of meditation, as it were, with whose aid we can very easily resolve any idea whatever into those of which it is composed. In fact, if the character expressing any concept is considered attentively, the simpler concepts into which it is resolvable will at once come to mind. Since the analysis of concepts thus corresponds exactly to the analysis of a character, we need merely to see the characters in order to have adequate notions brought to our mind freely and without effort. We can hope for no greater aid than this in the perfection of the mind. I wanted to write this to you a little more fully, my friend, to find out whether reasons do not carry more weight with you than prejudiced opinions. If you reply that the matter is clear but difficult, this is all I ask of you, for the difficulties do not frighten me, since I see certain, and unless I am mistaken, very appropriate means for overcoming them.

From PAPERS ON GRAMMATICAL ANALYSIS

From an untitled paper

. . . . . . Before we may proceed in our logical inquiries, and make something out of these, we need grammatical inquiries first. In particular, reference must be made to Vossius's *Aristarchus*.

A noun substantive and an adjective are distinguished in that an adjective has its gender governed by another. But as one can do without genders in a rational language, the distinction between substantive and adjective can be neglected.

Abstract terms [*abstracta*] are substantives made either from other substantives or from adjectives, such as "humanity" and "beauty"; "human being" [*homo*] is "that which has humanity", "beautiful" is "having beauty". But we must see whether we cannot do without abstract terms in a rational language, at any rate as far as possible.

"Masculine" is an adjective, "man" [*vir*] is a substantive, since for "man" one can substitute "masculine human being"; that is, it can be analysed into a substantive together with an epithet.

An epithet is an adjective joined to a substantive to make one term, i.e. without a copula, and governed in the same way.

Adverbs. "Peter writes beautifully"; i.e. Peter writes something beautiful, or, Peter writes, and what Peter writes is beautiful. "Peter stands beautifully": i.e. Peter is beautiful in so far as he is a stander [*quatenus est stans*].

Plural. "Men write": i.e. Titius is a writer, Caius is a writer; Titius is a man, Caius is a man. Or, "Men write": i.e. one man writes, another man writes.

A "pronoun" is a noun put in place of another noun, i.e. designating another noun, though not explaining any attribute of it, but only an extrinsic denomination relative to the discourse itself. An example is "this", i.e. "shown", "said", "present". "That" and "this" differ as the nearer and the farther. "I": that is, the one now speaking. "You": that is, the one now listening to hear what is said.

All oblique inferences—e.g. "Peter is similar to Paul, therefore Paul is similar to Peter"—are to be explained by explanations of words. Such may be seen from the logic of Jungius. It is reduced to the propositions "Peter is A now" and "Paul is A now".

All inflexions and particles are to be explained, and all are to be reduced to the simplest explanations, which can always be put in their place without affecting the sense. From these, definitions of everything are to be formed. . . . . .

[There follows a list of authors from whom Leibniz proposes to borrow the definitions of various sciences. The last completed part of the paper (it is followed by uncompleted definitions of "equal to", "like" and "given to") is an analysis of the genitive case:]

The	hand		hand		part
	son		son		effect
	horse	of a man, that is, the	horse	which is a	possession
	heat		heat		accident
	title		title		predicate

	whole
	cause
in so far as a man is a	master
	substance
	subject

From Grammatical Thoughts

. . . . . . Distinction of gender is not relevant to a rational grammar; neither do distinctions of declensions and conjugations have any use in a philosophical grammar. For we vary genders, declensions and conjugations without any benefit, without any gain in brevity—unless perhaps the variation pleases the ear; and this consideration does not concern philosophy, especially as we can give beauty to a rational language by another method, in such a way that it will not be necessary to think up useless rules. Certainly it is clear that the most difficult part of grammar is learning the different genders, declensions and conjugations. Yet a man who speaks a language and neglects these differences, as I heard a Dominican from Persia do in Paris, is understood none the less.

One needs a catalogue of derivations, i.e. of terminations which make derivations, such as

—ble	—tive	—titude
lovable	active	rectitude

. . . . . . To some, a noun is what expresses a thing without time. By this definition, pronouns will be nouns, and participles will not.

A noun expresses a certain idea, but no truth, i.e. no proposition. In this sense, a pronoun and a participle are nouns. . . . . .

Every verb indicates time. A noun also can indicate time, like the participle "about to act", "about to love".

It can be disputed whether there are verbs which are not active, such as "I am", "I live", "I run", or whether an accusative must always be understood, as "to live one's life", "to run one's course". Scioppius says that it must, but it does not seem to me to be at all necessary. For by joining with some noun the verb "I am" (which Scioppius himself admits not to have an accusative) a verb can at once be made, such as "I am a sick man" ("I ail"), "I am a healthy man" ("I flourish").

Particles which are clearly of a different nature are badly confused under the name of "adverb". For example, what has "whether" [*an*], the adverb of interrogation, in common with the adverb "bravely", i.e. "with bravery"? Consequently, what are called adverbs of interrogation I would rather count as conjunctions. This, however, must be considered more carefully . . . . . .

Every adjective has a similar substantive, either explicit or implicit.

The genitive is the addition of a substantive to a substantive, by which that to which it is added is distinguished from another. For example, "the sword of Evander", that is, "the sword which Evander has"; "a part of a house", that is, "a part which a house has"; "a reading of the poets", that is, "an action by which a poet is read". This will be the best way of explaining "Paris is the lover of Helen", that is, "Paris loves, *and by that very fact* [*et eo ipso*] Helen is loved". Here, therefore, two propositions have been brought together and abbreviated into one. Or, "Paris is a lover, and by that very fact Helen is a loved one". "The sword is the sword of Evander", that is, "The sword is an article of property in so far as Evander is an owner". A poet is read in so far as this or that person is a reader. For unless you analyse the oblique cases into several propositions, you will never escape without being compelled, with Jungius, to invent new ways of reasoning . . . . . .

In a rational grammar, oblique cases and other inflexions are not necessary. Similarly, one can dispense with abstract nouns. To avoid inflexions, one must take a roundabout way; but it is worth the price to reason in a concise way, even if you do not express yourself concisely.

From An Untitled Paper

Vocables [*vocabula*] are either words [*voces*] or particles. Words constitute the matter, particles the form of discourse . . . . . .

In a philosophical language, cases are unnecessary when prepositions are used, and when cases are used one can do without prepositions . . . . . .

Just as prepositions govern the cases of nouns [*nominum*], so conjunctions govern the moods of verbs . . . . . .

There is a difficulty as to whether there ought to be as many moods of verbs as there are purely formal conjunctions, just as we wanted there to be as many cases of nouns as there are purely formal prepositions. It seems that, in the same way, a governing conjunction is unnecessary when a mood is used, and conversely that a mood is unnecessary when a governing conjunction is used, just as we said about preposition and case. However, I think that men have used these for the sake of greater effectiveness, to teach by saying the same thing twice. Conjunctions which connect periods to periods are non-governing. Moods affect the copula of the verb, i.e. the mode of affirmation . . . . . .

Not only verbs, but also nouns can have tense and place—just as we have seen in the case of participles, which are simply nouns derived from verbs by removing the copula and keeping the tense. Indeed, adverbs also can have a tense—e.g. if I were to coin the adverb "amusingly-to-be" [*ridiculurè*], that is, that which is not immediately amusing, but which will be amusing at some time. Such was the badge of the tailors; a facetious painter had produced a splendid and elegant one, but in water-colours, and when these vanished there appeared an oil-painting of a goat, which in Germany is regarded as an insult. You could say that this man had painted something which was going to be amusing, or would be amusing in future; that is, that he had painted amusingly-to-be, i.e. amusingly with respect to future time . . . . . .

In a rational language, the distinction between adjective and substantive is not of great importance . . . . . .

"Man" is the same as "human entity" . . . . . .

If a verb is made from a noun substantive, an adverb is made from an adjective . . . . . .

Everything in discourse can be analysed into the noun substantive "entity" or "thing", the copula, i.e. the substantive verb "is", adjectives and formal particles . . . . . .

The tenses of nouns: just as one speaks of "loving", the act of one who loves, so there might be the "has-been-loving" or "about-to-be-loving" [*amavitio vel amaturitio*] of one who has loved, or is about to love. Just as the infinite has a preterite in Latin, so it should also have an imperfect . . . . . .

In Hebrew the root is a verb, but I would prefer it to be a noun, such as "life" . . . . . .

The multitude of declensions and conjugations is superfluous. It is superfluous to have inflexions in adjectives, for it is enough to have them in the substantive to which the adjective is attached. In the same way, number is unnecessary in the verb, for this is sufficiently understood from the noun to which it is attached. In Hebrew, Syriac, Chaldaic, Arabic and Ethiopian, verbs also have genders, which is incongruous enough. Also, the person of verbs can be invariable, as it is sufficient for "I", "you", "he" &c. to be varied . . . . . .

* * *

Jean le Rond D'Alembert, philosopher and mathematician (1717-1783) was one of the moving spirit of the great French *Encyclopedie*. Sceptical in religion, a member of the French Academy of sciences, secretary of the Academie Française, his major work is on the differential calculus. The following is taken from his article on Elements of Science in the *Encyclopedie*.

From the ENCYCLOPEDIE

I call *vulgar terms* those used in ordinary speech or even in other sciences, elsewhere than in a specific science. For example, the words *space, Movement*, in Mechanics; *body*, in geometry; *sound* in Music; and many others. I call *scientific terms* those particular to science, which it was necessary to invent in order to designate certain objects, and which are unknown to those quite unfamiliar with science.

It would seem at first that vulgar terms need no definition, since, being as might be supposed, of frequent usage, the idea that is attached to these words must have been clearly spelled out and familiar to everyone. But the language of the sciences cannot be too precise, while that of vulgar usage is often vague and obscure: therefore one cannot be too careful to establish the meaning of the words one uses, if only in order to avoid errors. But in order to establish the meaning of words, or, which comes to the same thing, to define them, it is first necessary to examine which are the simple ideas that the word includes: I call simple idea one which cannot be broken down into others and thus made easier to grasp: such, for example, is the idea of *existence*, that of *sensation*, and many others. This needs further explanation. Correctly speaking, we have no idea which is not simple, for, however complex an object may be, the operation by which our intelligence conceives it as complex is instantaneous and unique: thus it is by a single simple operation that we conceive of a body as a substance at the same time elongated, opaque, moulded and colored.

Thus it is not by the nature of the operations of the intelligence that one must judge the degrees of simplicity of ideas; it is the greater or less simplicity of the object which determines this. Moreover, this greater or less simplicity, is not that which is determined by the greater or less number of parts of an object, but by the greater or less number of properties which one considers at the same time. Thus, although space and time are composed of parts, and consequently are not simple things, yet the idea we have of them is a simple idea. Because all the parts of time and of space are exactly similar, the idea which we have of them is always exactly the same, and, finally, this idea cannot be divided, since one could not simplify the idea of the extent of space or of time without destroying them: on the contrary, by taking from the idea of body, for example, the idea of opaqueness, of shape, and of color, there still remains the idea of extent.

Simple ideas in the sense we understand them can be reduced to two kinds: the one is abstract ideas; abstraction indeed is nothing else than the operation by which we consider in an object a particular quality, without paying any attention to those which join with it in order to constitute its essence. The second kind of simple ideas is contained in those primitive notions that we obtain from our sensations, like those of specific color, cold, heat, and several others like them: also there can be no circumlocution that more correctly makes such things comprehensible, other than the single term which expresses them.

When all the simple ideas that a term contains have been discovered, it will be defined by expressing these ideas in as clear, as brief, and as precise a manner as possible. It follows from these principles that every vulgar term that only expresses a simple idea cannot, and should not, be used in any scientific field, because no definition will make the sense more clear. As to vulgar terms which contain several simple ideas it is good to define them, however current their usage, in order to develop clearly the simple ideas which they contain.

Thus in Mechanics, or the science of the movement of bodies, neither time nor space should be defined, because these words only contain one simple idea, but one can, and indeed one should, define movement, although the idea of it is pretty familiar to everyone, because the idea of movement is a complex idea which contains two simple ones, that of the space traversed, and that of the time taken to traverse it. It follows, further, from these same principles, that simple ideas which enter into a definition, must be so distinguished one from another that not one can be dispensed with. Thus in the ordinary definition of a rectilineal triangle, it is a mistake to bring in the three sides and the three angles. It is enough to bring in the three sides, for a figure bounded by three straight lines necessarily has three angles. One cannot be too careful of this, so as not unnecessarily to multiply words, any more than things, and in order not to take for two distinct ideas what is one only.

One can thus say not only that a definition should be short, but that the shorter it is, the clearer it will be: for brevity consists in employing only necessary ideas, and in disposing them in the most natural order. One is often obscure because one goes on too long: obscurity come principally from the fact that ideas are not clearly distinguished one from another and are not arranged in their proper places. Finally, brevity being necessary in definitions, one can and should employ terms which contain more complex ideas, just so long as these terms have previously been defined and that therefore the simple ideas which are contained within them have been developed. Thus one can say that a rectilineal triangle is a figure bounded by three straight lines, provided that one has already defined what is meant by *figure*: this contains three ideas: those of extent, of limits, and of limits in all directions.

These are the general rules of a definition, and this is the idea which one should have of a definition, and according to which a definition is nothing else but the development of the simple ideas which a term includes. After this has been done, it is quite useless to examine whether the definitions are of a name or a thing, or whether they explain the nature of the object indicated by this term. In fact, what is the nature of a thing? In what does it really consist, and do we know it? If one wishes to reply clearly to these questions, one will see how the distinction in question is futile and absurd, for ignorant as we are about what things are in themselves, the knowledge of the nature of a thing (at all events in relation to ourselves) can only consist in the clear and uncomplicated idea of it, not in the real and absolute principles of this thing but of those which it *seems* to us to possess. Every definition must be viewed from this last point of view: in such a case it will be more than a simple definition of a name, since it will not be limited to the explanation of the sense of a term, but also will analyse its object. And it will thus also be less than the definition of a thing, because the true nature of the object, although thus analysed, can remain still unknown.

So much for the definition of vulgar terms.

Michael Cesarotti (1730-1808) discusses other aspects of the problem of language in his *"Essay on the Philosophy of Language Applied to the Italian Language"**

From ESSAY ON THE PHILOSOPHY OF LANGUAGE

As for words, I shall first note generally that they can all be divided into two classes: memorative words and representative words. The former recall the object, the latter in some way illustrate it. Thus, the first can be called symbolic terms, and the others figure terms. The former, in the manner of Chinese keys**, have only a conventional and arbitrary relationship with the idea, while the latter have a directly or indirectly natural relationship with the idea. And in the manner of the writings of the early centuries, these can be subdivided into two other species: the hieroglyphic which represents the object itself first as a whole and then summarized or suggested, and the symbolic which represents one object with the image of another, or gives visible form to an intellectual idea.

To make my intentions more easily understood, I shall explain

*From *Discussioni Linguistiche del Settecento*, edited by Mario Puppo. Torino. Unione Tipografico Editrice Torinese. 1966.

**Chinese keys: the radical monosyllables of the Chinese language. (Bigi)

something of the natural development of language, and of the universal sources of words. It is certain that man in his creative capacity extracted from Nature an inchoate and in a certain sense uniform language, which serves as a common base for the immense family of all the languages in the universe. And men of learning have found clearly defined traces of this common base in every one of these languages. When man was pressed by an immediate need to fix with some name the objects that interested him, and to make them known to others with equal readiness, and with a minimum of ambiguity, he had two means, two spontaneous gifts of Nature, with which to help himself: his tendency to imitate and the primitive disposition of his vocal organ. Man's first linguistic act must necessarily have been that of gathering and imitating the relationships which Nature had placed between the sound of certain objects and that of the voice, and of giving to the objects themselves a name analogous to the sound that they convey. The Greeks knew this well and taught it as the first natural origin of words, and they called this method par excellence *Onomatopea*, or the invention of names . . .

It was not difficult to understand these two direct and intrinsic relationships between sound and things; but how does one name the visible objects that have no analogy to the voice? This is where ingenuity helped nature. Everything is connected in the universe, and everything is connected either well or poorly in our mind. The exact correspondence between the idea and the object constitutes truth. The exact correspondence between the connection of our ideas with the natural connection of beings forms science. But because these two series correspond exactly, a third is needed which establishes the exchange, and fixes them reciprocally. Words are like the transversal chain that reunites that of the objects with that of the ideas. A primitive word drawn from the sound rouses directly only the idea of the sounding object as such, but indirectly awakens even the idea of the entire substance with all its intrinsic properties. This substance has many and various relationships more or less close or evident with other infinite substances, since the first word has, by means of its primitive elements multiple relationships with other terms that result from their mixture. Therefore the first born word formed by the procreating sound is like the last link to which the chain of objects and the other chain of the analogous words are laterally connected; and so any derivation from this first word will correspond with the derivation of the first object, and will awaken in the mind some image of it.* We should however observe four things of great consequence. First, the relationship between the sound and the derived objects, which does not exist if not indirectly and mediately. The relationship between the words and the objects of this species will be less noticeable and less vivacious than that between the words and the sounding object. Second, the relationship between the sound of the voice and that of the sounding object is one, precise, and distinct; that between the word and the visible object is vague, confused and multiple, since an object has many appearances for which it can belong to another. Nor

*In the metaphysical doctrines which form the preamble of my discourse, I have held largely to the system of the wise and erudite philosopher De Brosses in his renowned work on the mechanical formation of languages. Since this was not however the object of my book, I have only touched lightly that bit of his doctrine which was sufficient for my intentions, only to use it as a basis for my theory of the beauty of terms. Therefore to be brief and to pass to my true thesis, I shall perhaps be less clear to some. Condillac wisely observes that the idea of an object, chosen from among the most eminent, does not awaken or arrest itself in the memory, if not fixed by a sign, of which none is more secure, more distinct, more dependent on our arbitrary judgment than the vocal signs; but to rouse quickly the idea it is best that the vocal sign have some relationship with the object itself, and this in the beginning cannot be other than the sound. Therefore, among the physical objects, those which are sounding objects, and those that have a quality relative to sound were the first to be named. With the name of an object fixed in this way by its sound relationship, the first word, by means of the rather diversified sound itself, became the root of another name to indicate a second object, which had some relationship with the first, even though the relationship was no longer one of sound, but of some other diverse quality. Imagine that the object that fixes the attention of a man, who is beginning a language, is the sea which I will call A. He would like to name it, but does not know how. He hears that the sea with waves makes a sound similar to B. He imitates that sound and calls precisely BA that unknown object. In this way saying BA, the similarity of the sound B awakens in him the idea of the object A. But the sea has a relationship with ships, not however in the quality of sound, but of navigation. Our man sees a ship, and observes its relationship with the sea and having called this BA, calls the ship BARC; thus the new articulation BARC, derived from the primitive sound BA, serves to indicate an object which certainly had a relationship with the first A, but not before with the sound B which served to name it. See the following note.

can one who listens have a way of knowing of what this relationship should consist. Third, an object has infinitely more relationships with the other objects even of the same species, than a sound has with the sounds of the same class; therefore the derivations of the ideas have to be superior without comparison in number to the vocal derivations. Thus a sole articulation will include many varied meanings of the objects derived in ways different from the first. Hence, at length each one is able to observe simultaneously various and diverse relationships between an object itself and many others of the same or of very different species, and each one can even denote these different relationships with the same and with very similar vocal derivations. The result is that the person listening either will not easily come to understand which substance is indicated with which derived word, or he will willingly substitute his own ideas for those of others, supposing that the person speaking means to indicate with that term the same relationship by which he himself was much more taken. Fourth, each object derived through the previously mentioned relationships being able to become the center of many, and these successively of others ad infinitum, it follows that the more the words stray from the first radical term, the more they deviate from its meaning, and proceed at intervals and transversely from idea to idea, in such a way that they can not arrive again at the first if not by a labyrinth of obliquity, for which it is difficult enough to find the thread.**

**It would be desireable to have in hand an example drawn from a sounding object that could render fully understandable the reflections of the text, but the immense deviation of languages from their origin, and the infinite mixing and encumbrances of the same does not permit us to find in them any of this class which is completely exact. Fortunately however I find one in De Brosses which is well enough suited, although drawn not from sounding objects, but from a quality analogous to sound. This is fixedness and arrestment, the representation of which seems indicated by Nature to be the articulation *St* formed by the dental *T*, more stable than every other letter, to which the *S* joins an impulse of force. Here then is that multiplicity of analogous and disparate objects and ideas which might be included under one sole though slightly varied articulation of sound.

St radical articulation

The Latins with this sound intimated arrest and silence.

Statore, the name of Jove that stopped the enemies.

Sto, from which come *Stanza, Exto, Resto, Adsto*, and *Constare* and *Constantia*;

Notwithstanding the imperfections of this method, it is certain to be more natural than any other, so that not only in primitive times, but in every time, men made constant use of this method to name new objects and new combinations of ideas.

---

and *Praesto* and *Praestantia*, and *Substantia*, in which names the idea of material stability is nearly lost from view.

Stabilis, Statuo, Constituo, and hence *Statuto*, and *Constituzione*, indicating a moral stability, and *Destituo* and *Substituo* and *Prostituo* from which comes *Prostituzione*, in which the trace of the first sense is nearly drowned by the accessories.

Statua, Staffa, Stabulum, or *Stalla*; and *Stallone* and *Stabbio*, manure, for its sole relationship of belonging in the stall.

Stella, Stellione, Stellionato, very disparate objects.

Stereos in Greek (*solid*), *Sternon* the breast.

Stipite, stock of a tree, and *Stipite*, stock of a family.

Stipula, Stipulazione, Stili in Greek *Pillar*.

Stirps root and stock.

Stupore, Stupido.

We see that while the idea of the word went rambling through an infinity of objects, the word itself always holds to the first radical articulation *St* placed next to only the five vowel sounds.

Sta, Ste, Sti, Sto, Stu.

Applying now to this example the reflections given above it will be easy to observe the irregular course of the mind in the association and derivation of ideas, and the more natural tendency of men in the naming of the objects, and the inevitable inconveniences of this method.

FROM ROMANTICS TO NATURALISTS

From Romantics to Naturalists

The eighteenth century was full of philosophers talking about talking. There were two main groups: the French Romantics and the German. The Romantics generally took a mystical view of language. From exterior language romantic idealism proceeded to interior, and then confounded the problem of language with that of art and poetry, as Mariano Campo wrote of the German Romantics:

> What is the central focus which is at the base of the various romantic speculations about language? For the Romantics language is essential in order to express the ineffable, to live the infinite. Without this continuous thread through the anthropological, cosmological and theological aspect of traditional metaphysical thought, it is not possible to understand the various dimensions of the problem of languages in the German Romantics. The Word is a colloquy between man and nature, man and himself, man and the community, man and God. Through language man can take possession of himself, speak to himself, relate memories and histories and smile at his condition with an irony which preludes his ascending liberty.

The German Romantics, to complicate matters, were very much influenced by the "French Father of Romanticism," Jean-Jacques Rousseau (1712-1778), who wrote a prize essay on *The Origin of Language*.

From THE ORIGIN OF LANGUAGE[10]

On the Various Means of Communicating Our Thoughts

Speech distinguishes man among the animals; language distinguishes nations from each other; one does not know where a man comes from until he has spoken. Out of usage and necessity, each learns the language of his own country. But what determines that this language is that of his country and not of another? In order to tell, it is necessary to go back to some principle that belongs to the locality itself and antedates its customs, for speech, being the first social institution, owes its form to natural causes alone.

As soon as one man was recognized by another as a sentient, thinking being similar to himself, the desire or need to communicate his feelings and thoughts made him seek the means to do so. Such means can be derived only from the senses, the only instruments through which one man can act upon another. Hence the institution of sensate signs for the expression of thought. The inventors of language did not proceed rationally in this way; rather their instinct suggested the consequence to them.

Generally, the means by which we can act on the senses of others are restricted to two: that is, movement and voice. The action of movement is immediate through touching, or mediate through gesture. The first can function only within arm's length, while the other extends as far as the visual ray. Thus vision and hearing are the only passive organs of language among distinct individuals.

Although the language of gesture and spoken language are equally natural, still the first is easier and depends less upon conventions. For more things affect our eyes than our ears. Also, visual forms are more varied than sounds, and more expressive, saying more in less time. Love, it is said, was the inventor of drawing. It might also have invented speech, though less happily. Not being very well pleased with it, it disdains it; it has livelier ways of expressing itself. How she could say things to her beloved, who traced his shadow with such pleasure! What sounds might she use to work such magic?

Our gestures merely indicate our natural unrest. It is not of those that I wish to speak. Only Europeans gesticulate when speaking; one might say that all their power of speech is in their arms. Their lungs are powerful too, but to nearly no avail. Where a Frenchman would strain and torture his body, emitting a great verbal torrent, a Turk will momentarily remove his pipe from his mouth to utter a few words softly, crushing one with a single sentence.

Since learning to gesticulate, we have forgotten the art of pantomime, for the same reason that with all our beautiful systems of grammar we no longer understand the symbols of the Egyptians. What the ancients said in the liveliest way, they did not express in words but by means of signs. They did not say it, they showed it. . . .

Pantomime without discourse will leave you nearly tranquil; discourse without gestures will wring tears from you. The passions have their gestures, but they also have their accents; and these accents, which thrill us, these tones of voice that cannot fail to be heard, penetrate to the very depths of the heart, carrying there the emotions they wring from us, forcing us in spite of ourselves to feel what we hear. We conclude that while visible signs can render a more exact imitation, sounds more effectively arouse interest.

This leads me to think that if the only needs we ever experienced were physical, we should most likely never have been able to speak; we would fully express our meanings by the language of gesture alone. We would have been able to establish societies little different from those we have, or such as would have been better able to achieve their goals. We would have been able to institute laws, to choose leaders, to invent arts, to establish commerce, and to do, in a word, almost as many things as we do with the help of speech. Without fear of jealousy, the secrets of oriental gallantry are passed across the more strictly guarded harems in the epistolary language of salaams. The mutes of great nobles understand each other, and understand everything that is said to them by means of signs, just as well as one can understand anything said in discourse. M. Pereyra and those like him who not only consider that mutes speak, but claim to understand what they are saying, had to learn another language, as complicated as our own, in order to understand them.

Chardin says that in India, traders would take each other by the hand, varying their grip in a way that no one could see, thus transacting all their business publicly yet secretly. . . .

Animals have a more than adequate structure for such communication, but none of them has ever made use of it. This seems to me a quite characteristic difference. That those animals which live and work in common, such as beavers, ants, bees, have some natural language for communicating among themselves, I would not question. Still, the speech of beavers and ants is apparently by gesture; i.e., it is only visual. If so, such languages are natural, not acquired. The animals that speak them possess them a-borning: they all have them, and they are everywhere the same. They are entirely unchanging and make not the slightest progress. Conventional language is characteristic of man alone. That is why man makes progress, whether for good or ill, and animals do not. That single distinction would seem to be far-reaching. It is said to be explicable by organic differences. I would be curious to witness this explanation.

On the Distinctive Characteristics of the First Language and the Changes It Had to Undergo

Simple sounds emerge naturally from the throat; and the mouth is naturally more or less open. But the modifications of the tongue and palate, which produce articulation, require attention and practice. One does not make them at all without willing to make them. All children need to learn them, and some do not succeed easily. In all tongues, the liveliest exclamations are inarticulate. Cries and groans are simple sounds. Mutes, which is to say the deaf, can make only inarticulate sounds. Father Lamy thinks that if God had not taught men to speak, they would never have learned by themselves. There are only a small number of articulations; there are infinitely many sounds, and the accents that distinguish them can be equally numerous. All the musical notes are just so many accents. True, we have only three or four in speech. The Chinese have many more; but on the other hand, they have fewer consonants. To these possible combinations, add those of tense and number, and you have not only more words, but more distinct syllables than even the richest tongue requires.

I do not doubt that independent of vocabulary and syntax, the first tongue, if it still existed, would retain the original characteristics that would distinguish it from all others. Not only would all the forms of this tongue have to be in images, feelings, and figures, but even in its mechanical part it would have to correspond to its initial object, presenting to the senses as well as to the understanding the almost inevitable impression of the feeling that it seeks to communicate.

Since natural sounds are inarticulate, words have few articulations. Interposing some consonants to fill the gaps between vowels would suffice to make them fluid and easy to pronounce. On the other hand, the sounds would be very varied, and the diversity of accents for each sound would further multiply them. Quantity and rhythm would account for still further combinations. Since sounds, accents, and number, which are natural, would leave little to articulation, which is conventional, it would be sung rather than spoken. Most of the root words would be imitative sounds or accents of passion, or effects of sense objects. It would contain many onomatopoeic expressions.

This language would have many synonyms for expressing the same thing according to various relationships. It would have few adverbs and abstract names for expressing these same relationships. It would have many augmentatives, diminutives, composite words, expletive particles to indicate the cadence of sentences and fullness of phrases. It would have many irregularities and anomalies. It would deemphasize grammatical analogy for euphony, number, harmony, and beauty of sounds. Instead of arguments, it would have aphorisms. It would persuade without convincing, and would represent without reasoning. It would resemble Chinese in certain respects, Greek and Arabic in others. . . .

On Script

Anyone who studies the history and progress of the tongues will see that the more the words become monotonous, the more the consonants multiply; that, as accents fall into disuse and quantities are neutralized, they are replaced by grammatical combinations and new articulations. But only the pressure of time brings these changes about. To the degree that needs multiply, that affairs become complicated, that light is shed, language changes its character. It becomes more regular and less passionate. It substitutes ideas for feelings. It no longer speaks to the heart but to reason. Similarly, accent diminishes, articulation increases. Language becomes more exact and clearer, but more prolix, duller and colder. This progression seems to me entirely natural.

Another way of comparing languages and determining their relative antiquity is to consider their script, and reason inversely from the degree of perfection of this art. The cruder the writing, the more ancient the language. The primitive way of writing was not to represent sounds, but objects themselves whether directly, as with the Mexicans, or by allegorical imagery, or as the Egyptians did in still other ways. This stage corresponds to passionate language, and already supposes some society and some needs to which the passions have given birth.

The second way is to represent words and propositions by conventional characters. That can be done only when the language is completely formed and an entire people is united by common laws; for this already presupposes a twofold convention. Such is the writing of Chinese; it truly represents sounds and speaks to the eyes.

The third is to break down the speaking voice into a given number of elementary parts, either vocal or articulate, with which one can form all the words and syllables imaginable. This way of writing, which is ours, must have been invented by commercial peoples who, in traveling to various countries, had to speak various languages, which would have impelled them to invent characters that could be common to all of them. This is not exactly to represent speech, but to analyze it.

These three ways of writing correspond almost exactly to three different stages according to which one can consider men gathered into a nation. The depicting of objects is appropriate to a savage people; signs of words and of propositions, to a barbaric people, and the alphabet to civilized peoples [*peuples policés*]. One need not think that this latter device is proof of the great antiquity of the people who invented it. On the contrary, those who invented it probably did so in order to facilitate communication with other people who spoke other languages as old as their own, if not older. The same cannot be said of the two other methods. I grant, however, that if one sticks to history and to known facts, alphabetical writing appears to go back as far as any other. . . .

French, English, German: each is a language private to a group of men who help each other, or who become angry. But the ministers of the gods proclaiming sacred mysteries, sages giving laws to their people, leaders swaying the multitude, have to speak Arabic or Persian. Our tongues are better suited to writing than speaking, and there is more pleasure in reading us than in listening to us. Oriental tongues, on the other hand, lose their life and warmth when they are written. The words do not convey half the meaning; all the effectiveness is in the tone of voice. Judging the Orientals from their books is like painting a man's portrait from his corpse.

For a proper appreciation of their actions, men must be considered in all their relationships: which we simply are not capable of doing. When we put ourselves in the position of others, we do not become what they must be, but remain ourselves, modified. And, when we think we are judging them rationally, we merely compare their prejudices to ours. Thus, if one who read a little Arabic and enjoyed leafing through the Koran were to hear Mohammed personally proclaim in that eloquent, rhythmic tongue, with that sonorous and persuasive voice, seducing first the ears, then the heart, every sentence alive with enthusiasm, he would prostrate himself, crying: Great prophet, messenger of God, lead us to glory, to martyrdom. We will conquer or die for you. Fanaticism always seems ridiculous to us, because there is no voice among us to make it understood. . . .

* * *

Relationship of Languages to Government

These developments are neither fortuitous nor arbitrary. They belong to the vicissitudes of things. The languages develop naturally on the basis of men's needs, changing and varying as those needs change. In ancient times, when persuasion played the role of public force, eloquence was necessary. Of what use would it be today, when public force has replaced persuasion. One needs neither art nor metaphor to say *such is my pleasure*. What sort of public discourses remain then? Sermons. And why should those who preach them be concerned to persuade the people, since it is not they who dispose of benefices. Our popular tongues have become just as completely useless as eloquence. Societies have assumed their final form: no longer is anything changed except by arms and cash. And since there is nothing to say to people besides *give money*, it is said with placards on street corners or by soldiers in their homes. It is not necessary to assemble anyone for that. On the contrary, the subjects must be kept apart. That is the first maxim of modern politics.

There are some tongues favorable to liberty. They are the sonorous, prosodic, harmonious tongues in which discourse can be understood from a great distance. Ours are made for murmuring on couches. Our preachers torment themselves, work themselves into a sweat in the pulpit without anyone knowing anything of what they have said. After exhausting themselves shouting for an hour, they collapse in a chair, half dead. Surely it would not be work that fatigues them so.

It was easy for the ancients to make themselves understood by people in public. They could speak all day with no discomfort. Generals could address their troops and be understood, with no exhaustion at all. Modern historians who wanted to include harangues in their account would be able to do no more than caricature them. If a man were to harangue the people of Paris in the Place Vendôme in French, if he shouted at the top of his voice, people would hear him shouting, but they would not be able to distinguish a word. Herodotus would recite his history to Greek audiences in the open air, and everyone would restrain himself from applauding. Today, the people in the rear of the room strain to hear an academician read a memorandum at a public assembly. If charlatans are less common in the public squares of France than in those of Italy, it is not because they would receive less attention in France, but only because they would not be as well understood. M. d'Alembert thought that French recitative could be sold to the Italians. Then it would have to be sold to the ear, or it would not be understood at all. But I say that any tongue with which one cannot make oneself understood to the people assembled is a slavish tongue. It is impossible for a people to remain free and speak that tongue.

It was in the eighteenth century that the various positions taken by linguists today began to emerge. While Leibniz had declared that "nothing exists in the intellect that was not before in the tongue—except intelligence itself," John George Hamann (1730-1788) declared, "All philosophy is grammar"—a theory later elaborated by the Logical Positivists. Johann Gottfried Herder (1744-1803), the Father of German Romanticism, took issue with Rousseau and was influenced by Leibniz and Hamann.

From ESSAY ON THE ORIGIN OF LANGUAGE[11]

While still an animal, man already has language. All violent sensations of his body, and among the violent the most violent, those which cause him pain, and all strong passions of his soul express themselves directly in screams, in sounds, in wild inarticulate tones. A suffering animal, no less than the hero Philoctetus, will whine, will moan when pain befalls it, even though it be abandoned on a desert island, without sight or trace or hope of a helpful fellow creature. It is as though it could breathe more freely as it vents its burning, frightened spirit. It is as though it could sigh out part of its pain and at least draw in from the empty air space new strength of endurance as it fills the unhearing winds with its moans. So little did nature create us as severed blocks of rock, as egotistic monads! Even the most delicate chords of animal feeling—I must use this image because I know none better for the mechanics of sentient bodies—even the chords whose sound and strain do not arise from choice and slow deliberation, whose very nature the probing of reason has not as yet been able to fathom, even they—though there be no awareness of sympathy from outside—are aligned in their entire performance for a going out toward other creatures. The plucked chord performs its natural duty: it sounds! It calls for an echo from one that feels alike, even if none is there, even if it does not hope or expect that such another might answer.

Should physiology ever progress to a point where it can demonstrate psychology—which I greatly doubt—it would derive many a ray of light for this phenomenon, though it might also divide it in individual, excessively small, and obtuse filaments. Let us accept it at present as a whole, as a shining law of nature: "Here is a sentient being which can enclose within itself none of its vivid sensations; which must, in the very first moment of surprise, utter each one aloud, apart from all choice and purpose." It was, as it were, the last motherly touch of the formative hand of nature that it gave to all, to take out into the world, the law, "Feel not for yourself alone. But rather: your feeling resound!" And since this last creative touch was, for all of one species, of one kind, this law became a blessing: "The sound of your feeling be of one kind to your species and be thus perceived by all in compassion as by one!" Do not now touch this weak, this sentient being. However lonesome and alone it may seem to be, however exposed to every hostile storm of the universe, yet is it not alone: It stands allied with all nature! Strung with delicate chords; but nature hid sounds in these chords which, when called forth and encouraged, can arouse other beings of equally delicate build, can communicate, as though along an invisible chain, to a distant heart a spark that makes it feel for this unseen being. These sighs, these sounds are language. There is, then, a language of feeling which is—underived—a law of nature.

That man has such a language, has it originally and in common with the animals, is nowadays evident, to be sure, more through certain remains than through full-fledged manifestations. But these remains, too, are incontrovertible. However much we may want to insist that our artful language has displaced the language of nature, that our civilized way of life and our social urbanity have dammed in, dried out, and channeled off the torrent and the ocean of our passions, the most violent moment of feeling —wherever, however rarely, it may occur—still time and again reclaims its right, sounding in its maternal language, without mediation, through accents. The surging storm of a passion, the sudden onslaught of joy or pleasure, pain or distress, which cut deep furrows into the soul, an overpowering feeling of revenge, despair, rage, horror, fright, and so forth, they all announce themselves, each differently after its kind. As many modes of sensitivity as are slumbering in our nature, so many tonal modes too.—And thus I note that the less human nature is akin to an animal species, the more the two differ in their nervous structures, the less shall we find the natural language of that animal species comprehensible to us. We, as animals of the earth, understand the animal of the earth better than the creature of the waters; and on the earth, the herd animal better than the creature of the forest; and among the herd animals, those best that stand closest to us. Though in the case of these latter, contact and custom too contribute their greater or lesser share. It is natural that the Arab, who is of one piece with his horse, understands it better than a man who mounts a horse for the first time—almost as well as Hector in the Iliad was able to speak with the ones that were his. The Arab in the desert, who sees no life about except his camel and perhaps a flight of erring birds, can more easily understand the camel's nature and imagine that he understands the cry of the birds than we in our dwellings. The son of the forest, the hunter, understands the voice of the hart, and the Lapp that of his reindeer—. But all that follows logically or is an exception. The rule remains that this language of nature is a group language for the members of each species among themselves. And thus man too has a language of nature all his own.

Now, to be sure, these tones are very simple, and when they are articulated and spelled out on paper as interjections, the most contrary sensations may have almost a single expression. A dull "ah!" is as much the sound of languid love as of sinking despair;

the fiery "oh!" as much the outburst of sudden joy as of boiling rage, of rising awe as of surging commiseration. But are these sounds meant to be marked down on paper as interjections? The tear which moistens this lusterless and extinguished, this solace-starved eye—how moving is it not in the total picture of a face of sorrow. Take it by itself and it is a cold drop of water. Place it under the microscope, and—I do not care to learn what it may be there. This weary breath—half a sigh—which dies away so movingly on pain-distorted lips, isolate it from its living help-meets, and it is an empty draft of air. Can it be otherwise with the sounds of feeling? In their living contexts, in the total picture of pulsating nature, accompanied by so many other phenomena, they are moving and sufficient unto themselves. Severed from everything else, torn away, deprived of their life, they are, to be sure, no more than ciphers, and the voice of nature turns into an arbitrarily penciled symbol. Few in number are, it is true, the sounds of this language. But sentient nature, in so far as it suffers only mechanically, has likewise fewer chief varieties of feeling than our psychologies chalk up or invent as passions of the soul. But in that state every feeling is the more a mightily attracting bond, the less it is divided in separate threads. These sounds do not speak much, but what they speak is strong. Whether a plaintive sound bewails the wounds of the soul or of his body, whether it was fear or pain that forced out this scream, whether this soft "ah" clings to the bosom of the beloved in a kiss or in a tear—to establish all such distinctions was not the task of this language. It was to call attention to the picture as a whole. Leave it to that picture to speak for itself. That language was meant to sound, not to depict. Indeed, as the fable of Socrates has it, pain and pleasure touch. In feeling, nature shows its extremes interlinked, and what then can the language of feeling do but show such points of contact?—Now I may proceed with the application.

In all aboriginal languages, vestiges of these sounds of nature are still to be heard, though, to be sure, they are not the principal fiber of human speech. They are not the roots as such; they are the sap that enlivens the roots of language.

A refined, late-invented metaphysical language, a variant—perhaps four times removed—of the original wild mother of the human race, after thousands of years of variation again in its turn refined, civilized, and humanized for hundreds of years of its life: such a language, the child of reason and of society, cannot know much or anything of the childhood of its earliest forebear. But the old, the wild languages, the nearer they are to their origin, the more they retain of it. Here I cannot yet speak of a formation of language that might to any extent be regarded as human. I can only consider the raw materials going into it. Not a single word exists for me as yet, only the sounds fit for a word of feeling. But behold! in the languages I mentioned, in their interjections, in the roots of their nouns and verbs, how much has not been retained of these sounds! . . .

The explanation of most of these phenomena must wait for a later context. Here I note only this: One of the upholders of the divine origin of language discerns and admires divine order in the fact that all the sounds of all the languages known to us can be reduced to some twenty odd letters. Unfortunately the fact is wrong, and the conclusion still wronger. There is no language whose living tones can be totally reduced to letters, let alone to twenty. All languages—one and all—bear witness to this fact. The modes of articulation of our speech organs are so numerous. Every sound can be pronounced in so many ways that for instance Lambert in the second part of his Organon has been able to demonstrate, and rightly so, how we have far fewer letters than sounds and how imprecise therefore the latter's expression by the former must needs remain. And that demonstration was done only for German—a language that has not even begun to accept into its written form the differences and multiplicity of tones of its dialects. What then, when the whole language is nothing but such a living dialect? What explains all the peculiarities, all of the idiosyncrasies of orthography if not the awkward difficulty of writing as one speaks? What living language can be learned in its tones from bookish letters? And hence what dead language can be called to life? The more alive a language is—the less one has thought of reducing it to letters, the more spontaneously it rises to the full unsorted sounds of nature—the less, too, is it writeable, the less writeable in twenty letters; and for outsiders, indeed, often quite unpronounceable.

Father Rasles, who spent ten years among the Abnaki in North America, complained bitterly that with the greatest care he would often not manage to repeat more than one half of a word and was laughed at. How much more laughable would it have been for him to spell out such an expression with his French letters? Father Chaumont, who spent fifty years among the Hurons and who took on the task of writing a grammar of their language, still complained about their guttural letters and their unpronounceable accents: "Often two words consisting entirely of the same letters had the most different meanings." Garcilaso de la Vega complained that the Spaniards distorted, mutilated, and falsified the Peruvian language in the sounds of its words, attributing to the Peruvians the most dreadful things in consequence of nothing but errors of rendition. De la Condamine says of a small nation living on the Amazon River: "Some of their words could not be written, not even most imperfectly. One would need at least nine or ten syllables where in their pronunciation they appear to utter hardly three." And la Loubere of the language of Siam: "Of ten words pronounced by a European, a native Siamese understands perhaps no single one, try as one may to express their language in our letters."

But why go to peoples in such remote corners of the world? What little we have left of savage peoples of Europe, the Estonians and the Lapps and their like have sounds which in many cases are just as half articulated and unwriteable as those of the Hurons and the Peruvians. The Russians and the Poles—however long their languages may have been written and molded by writing—still aspirate to such an extent that the true tone of their sounds cannot be depicted by letters. And the Englishman, how he struggles to write his sounds, and how little is one a speaking Englishman when one understands written English! The Frenchman, who draws up less from the throat, and that half Greek, the Italian, who speaks as it were in a higher region of the mouth, in a more refined ether, still retains a living tone. His sounds must remain within the organs where they are formed: As drawn characters they are—however convenient and uniform long usage in writing has made them—no more than mere shadows!

Thus the fact is wrong and the conclusion wronger: It does not lead to a divine but—quite on the contrary—to an animal origin. Take the so-called divine, the first language, Hebrew, of which the greater part of the world has inherited its letters: That in its beginnings it was so full of living sounds that it could be written only most imperfectly, is made quite evident by the entire structure of its grammar, its frequent confusion of similar letters, and especially the total lack of vowels in it. What explains this peculiarity that its letters are exclusively consonants and that precisely those elements of the words on which everything depends, the self-sounding vowels, were originally not written at all? This manner of writing is so contrary to the course of sound reason—of writing the nonessential and omitting the essential—that it would be incomprehensible to the grammarians, if the grammarians were accustomed to comprehend. With us, vowels are the first, the most vital things, the hinges of language, as it were. With the Hebrews, they are not written. Why? Because they could not be written. Their pronunciation was so alive and finely articulated, their breath so spiritual and etherlike that it evaporated and eluded containment in letters. It was only with the Greeks that these living aspirations were pinned down in formal vowels, though these still required a seconding by the spiritus signs and the like, whereas with the Orientals speech as it were was a continuous breath, nothing but spiritus, the spirit of the mouth—as they so often call it in their depictive poems. What the ear caught was the breath of God, was wafting air; and the dead characters they drew out were only the inanimate body which the act of reading had to animate with the spirit of life.

This is not the place to speak about the tremendous importance of such facts for an understanding of their language, but that this wafting reveals the origin of their language is evident. What is more unwriteable than the inarticulate sounds of nature? And if it is true that language is the more inarticulate the nearer it is to its origins, it follows—does it not?—that it was surely not invented by some superior being to fit the twenty-four letters which were invented together with it, that these letters were a much later and only imperfect attempt to provide memory with a few markers, and that language did not arise from the letters of a grammar of God but from the untutored sounds of free organs. Otherwise it would be strange that precisely the letters from which and for which God invented language, by means of which he taught language to the earliest of men, are the most imperfect in the world, that they reveal nothing of the spirit of language but admit through their entire structure that they are not trying to reveal anything of it.

Judged by its worth, this hypothesis of letters would merit no more than a hint, but because of its ubiquity and the numerous attempts to cover up its shortcomings I had to unmask its baselessness and simultaneously show therein a peculiarity for which I for one know no explanation. But let us resume our course:

Since our sounds are destined to serve nature in the expression of passion, it is natural that they appear as the elements of all emotion. Who is he who—in the presence of a convulsive whimpering victim of torment, at the bedside of a moaning fellow in the throes of death, or even before a wheezing beast—when the entire machinery of the body suffers—does not feel how this Ah touches his heart? Who is so unfeeling a barbarian? The more, even in animals, the sensitive chords are strung in harmony with those of others, the more do even they feel with one another. Their nerves are tense in unison, their souls vibrate in unison, they really share with one another the mechanics of suffering. And what fibers of steel, what power to plug all inlets of sensibility are needed for a man to be deaf and hard against this!—Diderot thinks that those born blind must be less receptive to the plaints of a suffering animal than those who can see. But I believe that in certain cases the very opposite is true. To be sure, the entire moving spectacle of this wretched convulsing creature is hidden from the blind, but all examples indicate that precisely through this concealment the sense of hearing becomes less diffuse, more pointed, and more powerfully penetrating. So there the blind man listens in darkness, in the quiet of his eternal night, and every plaintive tone, like an arrow, goes the more keenly, the more penetratingly to his heart. And now let him use the help of his slowly scanning tactile sense, let him touch the convulsions, experience in direct contact the collapse of the suffering machinery—horror and pain cut through the organs of his body; his inner nerve structure senses in resonance the collapse and the destruction; the tone of death sounds. Such is the bond of this language of nature! . . .

But I cannot conceal my amazement that philosophers—people, that is, who look for clear concepts—ever conceived of the idea that the origin of human language might be explained from these outcries of the emotions: for is not this obviously something quite different? All animals, down to the mute fish, sound their sensations. But this does not change the fact that no animal, not even the most perfect, has so much as the faintest beginning of a truly human language. Mold and refine and organize those outcries as much as you wish; if no reason is added, permitting the purposeful use of that tone, I do not see how after the foregoing law of nature there can ever be human language—a language of volitional speech. Children, like animals, utter sounds of sensation. But is not the language they learn from other humans a totally different language?

The Abbé Condillac belongs in this group. Either he supposes the whole thing called language to have been invented prior to the first page of his book, or I find things on every page that could not possibly have occurred in the orderly continuity of a language in formation. He assumes as the basis for his hypothesis "two children in a desert before they know the use of any sign." Why now he assumes all this, "two children," who must perish or turn into animals; "in a desert," where the difficulties opposing their survival and their inventiveness are greatly increased; "before the use of every natural sign"; and, to boot, "before any knowledge thereof," with which no infant dispenses just a few weeks after its birth; the reason—I say—that such unnatural and mutually contradictory conditions must be assumed in an hypothesis meant to trace the natural development of human knowledge, the author of that hypothesis may or may not know; but that what is built on it is no explanation of the origin of language I believe I am able to prove. Condillac's two children get together without the knowledge of any sign, and—lo!—from the first moment on we find them engaged in a mutual exchange. And yet it is only through this mutual exchange that they learn "to associate with the outcry of emotions the thoughts whose natural signs they are." Learning natural signs of the emotions through a mutual exchange? Learning what thoughts are associated with them? And yet being involved in an exchange from the first moment of contact on, even before the acquisition of a knowledge of what the dumbest animal knows, and being able to learn—under such conditions—what thoughts are to be associated with certain signs? Of all this I understand nothing. "Through the recurrence of similar circumstances they become accustomed to associate thoughts with the sounds of the emotions and the various signs of the body. Already their memory is exercised. Already they have dominion over their imagination—have advanced far enough to do by reflection what heretofore they did only by instinct" (yet, as we just saw, did not know how to do before their exchange). Of all this I understand nothing. "The use of these signs extends the soul's range of action, and the extended range of action of it perfects the signs: outcries of their emotions were thus what evolved the powers of their souls; outcries of their emotions what gave them the habit of associating ideas with arbitrary signs; outcries of their emotions what served them as models in making for themselves a new language, in articulating new sounds, in becoming accustomed to designate things with names." I repeat all these repetitions, and I do not understand the first thing about them. Finally—after the author has built on this childish origin of language the prosody, declamation, music, dance, and poetry of the ancient languages, making from time to time sound observations (which, however, have nothing to do with our objective), he again takes up the thread: "In order to understand how men agreed amongst themselves on the meaning of the first words they intended to use, it suffices to remember that they uttered them under circumstances where everyone was obliged to associate them with the same ideas, etc." In short, words arose because words had arisen before they arose. Methinks it will not pay to follow further the thread of our guide for it appears to be tied—to nothing.

Condillac, with his hollow explanation of the origin of language, provided Rousseau, as we all know, with the occasion to get the question in our century off the ground again in his own peculiar way, that is, to doubt it. Actually, to cast doubt on Condillac's explanation, no Rousseau was needed; but to deny straightway—because of it—all human possibility of the invention of language, that to be sure did require a little Rousseauesque verve or nerve or whatever one may wish to call it. Because Condillac had explained the thing badly, could it therefore not be explained at all? Because sounds of emotion will never turn into a human language, does it follow that nothing else could ever have turned into it?

And since men are for us the only creatures endowed with language that we know and since it is precisely through language that they distinguish themselves from all animals, from where could one set out more safely on the road of this investigation than from the experiences we have about the difference between the animals and men?—Condillac and Rousseau had to err in regard to the origin of language because they erred, in so well known a way and yet so differently, in regard to this difference: in that the former turned animals into men and the latter men into animals. . . .

The ape may forever be aping, but never did he emulate. He never reflected, saying to himself, "That I will emulate in order to perfect my kind!" For had he ever said so, had he ever made a single act of emulation his own, giving it permanence in his kind through choice and intent, had he been able, just one single time, to think one single such reflection—that very moment he ceased to be an ape! With all his apish appearance, without a sound from his tongue, he was an inwardly speaking human, who sooner or later had to invent for himself an utterable language. But what orangutan, though equipped with all human organs of speech, ever spoke a single human word? . . .

There still are in Europe some good-natured primitivists who say, "Well yes perhaps—if the ape just wanted to speak!—or if the ape had the occasion!—or if the ape could!"—Could! That would be the most fitting, for the preceding two ifs are sufficiently ruled out through the natural history of the animal kingdom, and it is not for the lack of organs, as I have stated, that the "if it could" is stopped in its tracks. The orangutan has a head, outside and inside, like ours; but did it ever speak? Parrots and starlings have learned enough human sounds; but have they ever thought a human word?—But anyway, it is not as yet the external sounds of words that concern us here; we are here concerned with the inner, the necessary genesis of a word as the characteristic mark of a distinct reflection—and when ever has an animal species, in whatever way it may have been, manifested that? Such a thread of thoughts, such a discourse of the soul, no matter what type of utterance it might use, would have to be subject to observation; but who has ever observed it? The fox has acted a thousand times as Aesop had him act, but he has never acted in Aesop's sense, and the first time that he can do that, Master Fox will invent his own language for himself and be able to fabulate about Aesop the way Aesop, as things are, did about him. The dog has learned to understand many words and commands, but not as words, only as signs associated with gestures and actions. Were he ever to understand a single word in the human sense, he would no longer serve, he would create for himself his art, his society, and his language. It is easy to see, if once the precise point of genesis has been missed, the field of error is immeasurably vast in all directions! Down one way, language appears to be so superhuman that God had to invent it; down the other, it is so unhuman that every animal could invent it if it were but to take the trouble. The goal of truth is just one point! With our course set for it, we perceive to the right and the left why no animal can invent language, why no God need invent language, and why man, as man, can and must invent language.

I do not wish, on metaphysical grounds, to pursue further the hypothesis of the divine origin of language, for psychologically its baselessness has been shown in the fact that, in order to understand the language of the gods on Olympus, man must come endowed with reason and hence endowed with language. Still less can I pursue in greater detail the pleasant matter of the animal languages, for all—as we have seen—stand totally and incommensurably apart from the language of man. What I am most loathe to renounce are the diverse perspectives which, from this genetic point of language in the human soul, open out into the wide fields of logic, aesthetics, and psychology, especially with regard to the question, how far can one think without and what must one think with language, a question whose subsequent applications would spread out into practically all branches of knowledge. Here it must suffice to observe that language, from without, is the true differential character of our species as reason is from within.

In more than one language, word and reason, concept and word, language and cause have hence one designation, and this synonomy comprises their full genetic origin. Amongst the Orientals it has come to be a common turn of expression to call the recognition of a thing the naming of it: for deep in the soul the two actions are one. They call man the speaking animal and the unreasoning animals the mutes: The expression is palpably characteristic, and the Greek term *alogos* comprises both. Thus language appears as a natural organ of reason, a sense of the human soul, as the power of vision—in the story of the sensitive soul of the Ancients—built for itself the eye and the instinct of the bee builds its cell.

Excellent how this new, self-made sense of the mind is in its very origin again a means of contact!—I cannot think the first human thought, I cannot align the first reflective argument without dialoguing in my soul or without striving to dialogue. The first human thought is hence in its very essence a preparation for the possibility of dialoguing with others! The first characteristic mark which I conceive is a characteristic word for me and a word of communication for others!

. . . All difficulties are reduced to the following two postulates which have clearly been demonstrated.

1. Since all senses are nothing but forms of perception of the soul: assume only that it have distinct perception and hence distinguishing marks—with the distinguishing marks it does have inner language.

2. Since all the senses, especially in the state of human childhood, are nothing but forms of feeling of one soul, and since further—in accordance with a law of sensation of animal nature—all feeling has its sound directly, it is but necessary that this feeling be raised to the clarity of a distinguishing mark, and the word for the external language is there. Here we touch upon numerous remarkable observations regarding nature's wisdom in organizing man for the task of inventing language for himself. The principal point is this:

"Since man receives the language of teaching nature only through the sense of hearing and could not invent language without it, hearing has in a certain sense come to be the middle one of his senses, the gateway to his soul, and the connecting link among the remaining senses." I shall explain.

1. Hearing is the middle one of the human senses in its range

of receptivity from outside. The sense of touch senses only within itself and within its organ, while vision casts us by great distances outside of ourselves. Hearing stands in between in its degree of communicability. What that means for language? Assume a creature—even a rational creature—to whom the sense of touch would be (if it were possible) the major sense. How narrow is its world! And since it cannot perceive this world through the sense of hearing, it may possibly—without sounds—build for itself a language as an insect builds a web. Now assume a creature, all eye—how inexhaustible is the world of its beholdings! How immeasurably far is it cast outside itself! In what infinite multiplicity is it dispersed! Its language—we cannot form an idea of it—would be a kind of infinitely refined pantomime; its script an algebra built on colors and strokes—but sounding language, never! We creatures of hearing stand in the middle: We see, we feel; but the nature we see, the nature we feel, sounds! It teaches us language through sounds! We turn, as it were, into hearing through all our senses!

Let us appreciate the convenience of our position—through it every sense becomes language-apt. To be sure, only hearing really yields sounds, and man can invent nothing, can only find and emulate. But on the one side the sense of touch lies close by and on the other vision is the adjacent sense. The sensations unite and all converge in the area where distinguishing traits turn into sounds. Thus, what man sees with his eye and feels by touch can also become soundable. The sense for language has become our central and unifying sense; we are creatures of language.

2. Hearing is the middle one among the senses in distinctness and clarity and thus once again the sense for language. How vague is the sense of touch! It can be overridden! It perceives all things merged. It would be difficult to sort out a characteristic mark for recognition: it would not be utterable!

Again, the sense of vision is so bright and overly brilliant, it supplies such a wealth of characteristic marks that the soul appears crushed under their multiplicity and can sort out one from among them only so weakly that recognition by it becomes difficult. The sense of hearing is in the middle. All the darkly commingled characteristic marks of the sense of touch it lets lie and so, too, the excessively fine characteristic marks of the sense of vision. But now there erupts from the touched and seen object a sound. Into it are gathered the characteristic marks of the other two senses, and it becomes the distinguishing word! Hearing thus reaches out and takes in on both sides: makes clear the excessively dark and more pleasing the excessively bright; carries into the dark many-sidedness of touch more unity and into the excessively bright many-sidedness of vision likewise. And as this recognition of many-sidedness turns, by means of one thing, by means of one characteristic mark, into language, it is the organ of language.

3. Hearing is the middle sense with respect to its vividness and hence is the sense of language. Touch overwhelms; vision is too cold and aloof. The former cuts into us too deeply to be qualified for becoming language; the latter remains too quiet before us. The tone of the sense of hearing goes into our soul so intimately that it must become a distinguishing mark, yet not so overpoweringly that, as a distinguishing mark, it loses its clarity—it is the sense of language.

How short, how tiring and unbearable would be the language of any coarser sense for us! How confusing and mind-voiding the language of the excessively refined sense of vision! Who could forever taste, touch, and smell without soon dying—as Pope has it—an aromatic death? And who could forever gape attentively at a color organ without soon going blind? But the experience of hearing—of thinking words, as it were, while hearing—is one we can endure longer and at almost any time. Hearing is to the soul what the green, the intermediate color is to the sense of vision. Man is organized to be a creature of language.

4. Hearing is the middle sense with respect to the time interval of its effect and hence is the sense of language. The sense of touch throws all things into us at once: it strongly plucks the chords but does so briefly and abruptly. The sense of vision presents to us all things at once and frightens the apprentice by its boundless array of juxtaposed displays. Through the sense of hearing, note how gently our teacher of language deals with us! It counts out the tones and pours them into the soul one at a time, it keeps giving and does not tire, keeps giving and has forever more to give. It practices the art of method: it teaches progressively! Who could not thus grasp language? Invent language?

5. The sense of hearing is the middle sense in regard to the needs of expression and is hence the sense of language. The impression of the sense of touch is ineffably dark; the less therefore can it be uttered. It is of such direct concern to us! It is so centered and so submerged in itself!—The impression of the sense of vision is unutterable for the inventor of language. But then what need is there to utter at once? The objects remain. They can be shown by gestures. The objects of hearing, however, are associated with movement. They pass by, and through that, they sound. They become utterable because they must be uttered, and through the need to be uttered, through their movement, they become utterable.—What qualification for language!

6. The sense of hearing is the middle sense in regard to its development and thus the sense of language. Man is tactile feeling in his entirety: The embryo, in the first moment of life, feels as the newborn does. That is the trunk of nature from which sprout the more delicate branches of sensuousness, the wound-up ball of yarn from which unroll all the finer forces of the soul. How do they do this? As we have seen, through the sense of hearing, for it is through sounds that nature awakens the soul to a first distinct sensation, awakens it, as it were, from the dark sleep of tactile feeling to have it mature to a still finer sensuousness. If, for example, the sense of vision were developed before it or if it were possible that it be awakened from tactile feeling by means other than the intermediate sense of hearing—what poverty in wisdom! What stupidity in clairvoyance! How difficult would it be for such an all-eyed creature, if it were still to be human, to name what it sees, to bind into one the coldness of vision with the warmth of touch, with the entire continuity of mankind. But the assumption itself is contradictory: The road of human development which nature has chosen is better and is unique. Since all the senses work together, we are, through the sense of hearing, at all times, so to speak, in the school of nature, learning how to abstract, and simultaneously how to speak. The sense of vision is refined with reason: reason with the gift of naming. And thus, as man achieves the finest characterization of visible phenomena—what a treasury of language and of language similitudes lies ready for use. He took the road from feelings of touch into the sense of his imaginings via the sense of language

and learned thus to sound what he perceives by vision as well as what he perceives by touch.

If now at this point I could gather up all the loose ends and make at once visible the woven texture called human nature—in all its parts a texture for language! For that, we have seen, space and sphere were assigned to this positive power of thought: for that its substance and its matter were meted out; for that its shape and its form were created; for that its senses organized and aligned—for language! That is why man thinks neither more brightly nor more darkly; why he sees not and feels not more keenly, more lastingly, more vividly; why he has these and not more and not other senses. All things are balanced against one another. In economy and substitution! Laid out and distributed with a purpose! Unity and coherence! Proportion and order! A whole! A system! A creature of reflection and language, of the power to reflect and to create language! If anyone, after all these observations, were still ready to deny man's being destined to be a creature of language, he first would have to turn from being an observer of nature into being its destroyer! Would have to break into dissonance all the harmonies shown; lay waste the whole splendid structure of human forces, corrupt his sensuousness, and sense instead of nature's masterpiece a creature full of wants and lacunae, full of weaknesses and convulsions! And if now, on the other hand, language is precisely as it arose of necessity and in accordance with the plan and the might of the creature described?

I shall proceed to prove this last point, although I might take this occasion for a most pleasant excursus and calculate according to the rules of Sulzer's theory of pleasure what advantages and conveniences a language through the sense of hearing has for us in comparison with the language of the other senses.—But the excursus would take me too far afield and I must forsake it, while the main road still needs to be secured and rectified.—So then firstly

I. "The older and the more original languages are, the more is this analogy of the senses noticeable in their roots."

Where with later languages we characterize wrath in its roots as a phenomenon of the face or as an abstract concept—for instance through the sparkle of the eyes or a glowing of the cheeks and the like—and hence merely see or think it, the Oriental hears it, hears it roar, hears it burst out in burning smoke and storming sparks! That became the stem of the word: the nostrils the seat of wrath; the whole family of words and metaphors of wrath snort out their origin.

If to us life manifests itself through the pulse beat, through surging blood and delicate marks of characterization also in language, to him it revealed itself through audible breathing. Man lived while he respired; he died as he expired. And the root of the word could be heard as the first animated Adam was heard to respire.

While we characterize child-bearing in our way, he again hears in the corresponding designations the screams of the frightened mother or again in animals the emptying of the amniotic sac. All his images revolve about this central idea.

Where in the word dawn we faintly hear an element of beauty, brilliance, and freshness, a lingering wanderer in the Orient feels in the very root of the word the first quick delightful ray of light which the like of us has never seen or at least has never felt with full feeling.—Examples from old and unsophisticated languages, showing how warmly and with what strong emotion they characterize from hearing and feeling, are numberless. And a work of the kind that would thoroughly trace the basic feeling of such ideas in various peoples, would be a full demonstration of my postulate and of the human invention of language.

II. "The older and the more original languages are, the more the feelings intertwine in the roots of the words!"

Open at random an Oriental dictionary, and you will see the urge to express! How these inventors tore ideas away from one feeling to use them in the expression of another! How they did this borrowing most extensively from the heaviest, coldest, keenest senses! How everything had to turn into feeling and sound before it could turn into expression! Hence those powerful bold metaphors in the roots of the words! Hence the transpositions from feeling to feeling until the significations of a stem word, and still more of its branches seen side by side, form a most colorful, motley array. The genetic cause of this lies in the poverty of the human soul and in the convergence of all sensations in the unrefined individual. We see clearly his need to express himself:

We see it the more, the more remote the idea was from the feeling and the tone of sensation, so that it is no longer possible to doubt the human origin of language. For how would the protagonists of another genesis explain this intertwining of ideas in the roots of the words? Was God so lacking in ideas and words that he had to have recourse to that kind of confusing word usage? Or was he so enamored of hyperbole, of far-fetched metaphors that he impressed this spirit upon the very roots of his language?

The so-called language of God, Hebrew, is totally imbued with such boldnesses, and rightly does the Orient claim the honor of designating it with its name. But beware of calling this spirit of metaphors Asian, as though it were not to be found anywhere else! It is alive in all unpolished languages, though, to be sure, according to the degree of each nation's culture and the specific character of its way of thinking. A people not wont to subject its feelings to thorough and keen differentiation, a people not endowed with the ardor to express itself and to take hold with sovereign unconcern of expressions wherever they might be found—such a people will not worry much about fine shades of feeling and will make do with slow-paced half-expressions. A fiery people reveals its boldness in its metaphors, whether it inhabits the Orient or North America. But where in the deepest depths such transplantations are to be found in the greatest numbers, there the language was by far the least endowed, was the oldest and most original, and that—without doubt—takes us to the Orient. . . .

The upholders of the divine origin, who manage to discover divine order in everything, are hard put to it to find it here, and they deny that there are synonyms. They deny? Well now, let it be assumed that among the fifty words which the Arabs have for the lion, among the two hundred which they have for the snake, or the eighty for honey and the more than a thousand which they have for the sword, nice differences can be found, that is, were once present and have since vanished—why if they had to vanish were they present? Why did God invent an unnecessary wealth of words which, as the Arabs claim, only a divine prophet could grasp in its entire range? Was he inventing into a vacuum of oblivion? Relatively speaking, these words are still synonyms, considering the numerous other ideas for which words are totally missing. Now trace, if you can, divine order in the fact that a god, who saw the plan of language as a whole, invented seventy words for the stone and none for all the indispensable ideas, innermost feelings, and abstractions, that in one case he drowned us in unnecessary abundance while leaving us in the other in the direst need which obliged us to steal and usurp metaphors and talk half nonsense, etc.

In human terms the thing is easily explained. While difficult and rare ideas had to be expressed indirectly, those that were at hand and easy could find frequent expression. The more unfamiliar man was with nature, that is, the more numerous the angles under which in his inexperience he looked at it, hardly able to recognize it again, and the less he invented *a priori* but instead in accordance with sensuous circumstances, the more synonyms had to arise! The more numerous the individuals who did the inventing and the more they did so roaming by themselves and in isolation, inventing in general terms only within their own circle for identical things; when later on they foregathered, when their languages streamed out into an ocean of vocabulary, the more synonyms there were. None could be rejected, for which should have been? They were in use with this tribe, this clan, this singer. And so, as the Arab compiler of a dictionary put it when he had enumerated four hundred words for misery, it was a four hundred first misery to be obliged to list the words for misery. Such a language is rich because it is poor, because its inventors did not have plan enough to grow poor. And we are to believe that the idle inventor of such an outstandingly imperfect language was God?

The analogies of all languages still in the state of nature confirm my thesis: Each in its own way is both lavish and lacking, but, to be sure, each in its own way. If the Arabs have so many words for stone, camel, sword, snake (things amongst which they live), the language of Ceylon, in accordance with the inclination of its people, is rich in flatteries, titles, and verbal décor. For the term "woman" it has, according to rank and class, twelve different names, while we discourteous Germans, for example, are forced in this to borrow from our neighbors. According to class, rank, and number, you is rendered in sixteen different ways, and this as well in the language of the journeyman as in that of the courtier. Profusion is the style of the language. In Siam there are eight different ways of saying I and we, depending on whether the master speaks to the servant or the servant to the master. The language of the savage Caribs is virtually divided in two, one for women and one for men, and the most common objects—bed, moon, sun, bow—are named differently in the two. What a superfluity of synonyms! And yet these same Caribs have only four words for colors, to which they must refer all others. What paucity!—The Hurons have consistently double verbs for animate and inanimate things, so that to see, when it is "to see a stone" and to see, when it is "to see a man" are two different terms. Pursue this through all of nature. What wealth! To make use of a thing one owns or to make use of a thing owned by him to whom one is speaking is always expressed by two different words. What wealth!—In the main language of Peru, blood relations are termed in such remarkable segmentation that the sister of the brother and the sister of the sister, the child of the father and the child of the mother have quite different designations, and yet this same language has not really a plural.—Each one of these synonymies is linked to custom, character, and origin of the people; and everywhere the inventive human spirit reveals itself. . . .

1. Declensions and conjugations are merely shortcuts and identifications in the use of nouns and verbs according to number, tense, mode, and person. Therefore, the less refined a language is, the less regular is it in these determinations, reflecting at every turn the course of human reason. In fine, without the art of usage, it is a simple dictionary.

2. As the verbs of a language are earlier than the nouns roundly abstracted from them, so also were there originally the more conjugations the less numerous the concepts one had learned to place in subordination to one another. How numerous are those the Orientals have! And yet there are really none, for how numerous everywhere are not the transpositions and translocations of verbs from one conjugation to another! The thing is quite natural. Since nothing concerns man or, at least, since nothing affects him in terms of language as deeply as what he is about to relate, deeds and acts and events, there must be gathered together, in the beginning, such a mass of deeds and

events that a new verb arises for almost every state. "In the language of the Hurons everything is conjugated. An art which cannot be explained permits in it the distinction of verbs, nouns, pronouns, and adjectives. The simple verbs have a double conjugation, one for themselves and one relating to other things. The third persons have forms for the two sexes. As for the tenses, the same nice distinctions exist that are to be noted for instance in Greek. Indeed, in relating a journey, the expression differs depending on whether it was by land or by water. The active forms are multiplied as often as there are things to be covered by the doing. The term for to eat changes from one edible substance to another. Acts performed by an animate being are expressed differently from those done by an inanimate thing. Making use of one's own property and of that of the person with whom one speaks has two forms of expression, etc."

Imagine this multiplicity of verbs, modes, tenses, persons, states, genders, etc.—What trouble and what art to keep all that somehow straightened out, to evolve somehow a grammar from what was no more than a vocabulary!—The grammar of Father Leri of the Topinambuans in Brazil shows just that.—For as the first vocabulary of the human soul was a living epic of sounding and acting nature, so the first grammar was almost nothing but a philosophical attempt to develop that epic into a more regularized history. Thus it works itself down with verbs and more verbs and keeps working in a chaos which is inexhaustible for poetry, which is very rich—when subjected to a little more order—for the fixing of history, and which becomes usable only much later for axioms and demonstrations.

3. The word which in imitation followed directly upon a sound of nature followed a thing that was past. Preterits are therefore the roots of verbs, but these are preterits which are still almost valid for the present. This fact must, *a priori*, seem strange and inexplicable, since the present time ought to be the first, as indeed it came to be in all languages of later development. According to the history of the invention of language it could not be otherwise. The present is something one shows; the past is something one must relate. And since it could be related in so many ways, and since—in the beginning, in the need to find words—it had to be done in many ways, there came into being, in all the old

languages, many preterits but only one present or none at all. This then, in more civilized ages, was greatly to the advantage of poetry and history but very little to that of philosophy, for philosophy has no love of confusingly rich supplies.—Here again the Hurons, the Brazilians, the Orientals, and the Greeks are alike: Everywhere traces of the development of the human mind.

4. All the more recent philosophical languages have modified the noun in greater refinement, the verb less so but more regularly, for these languages adapted themselves more and more to the needs of a detached contemplation of what is and in fact has been and ceased to be irregularly stammering mixtures of things that possibly were and perhaps persist. The habit arose to state one after the other the things that are and in fact have been and hence to define them through numbers and articles and cases, etc. The early inventors wanted to say everything at once, not just what appeared to have been done but also who did it and when and how and where it happened. They thus carried into the noun the state; into every form of the verb the gender; they distinguished—by pre- and adformatives, by affixes and suffixes—the verb and the adverb, the verb and the noun, and all things flowed together. But later there came to be more and more differentiation, more and more enumerations: From breaths evolved articles, from starting clicks persons, from prestatements modes or adverbs. The parts of speech separated. Gradually grammar evolved. Thus the art of speech, this philosophy of language, evolved but slowly and gradually down through the centuries and ages, and the mind that was the first to think of a true philosophy of grammar, of "the art of speech," must of necessity have begun by thinking over, down through the generations and down its stages, its history. If only we had such a history! It would be, with all its deviations and excursuses, a charter of the humanity of language. . . .

The genesis of language in the human soul is as conclusively evident as any philosophical demonstration could be, and the external analogy of all ages, languages, and peoples imparts to it as high a degree of probability as is possible with the most certain events in history.

Among other eighteenth century writers who were much concerned with language and wrote about it were Denis Diderot (1713-1784), Adam Smith (1723-1790), Johann Wolfgang von Goethe (1749-1832), Destutt de Tracy (1754-1836), Maine de Biran (1766-1824), Wilhelm von Humboldt (1767-1859), Friedrich Schleiermacher (1768-1834), Frederick Hegel (1770-1831), and Friedrich Schlegel (1772-1829). Schleiermacher wrote that "thinking and speaking are so entirely one that we can only distinguish them as internal and external. Even when internal every thought is already a word." And Schlegel said that "Without language it is impossible to conceive of philosophy, nay, even of human consciousness."

By the end of the eighteenth century there were three main theories about the origin of languages.

1. The traditional, as exemplified by Joseph de Maistre (1753-1821) and Louis de Bonald (1754-1840), for whom "language is the necessary instrument of every intellectual operation" (de Bonald) and "thought and language are the two major signs of our intelligence which cannot think or know that it thinks without speaking" (de Maistre). The latter also declared that "Every day the word draws man from the void as on the first day the word drew the universe out of chaos; the word is the most profound mystery of our being; far from being able to invent it, man can't even explain it." Or, as de Bonald put it, "Man thinks his speech before speaking his thought—man cannot speak his thought without thinking his speech."

2. The inventionist, who believed man invented language.

3. The scientist. This based the origin of language on the constitution of the vocal cords; declared reason preceeded concepts, and impressions proceeded from social life.

This last view is well exemplified by Charles de Brosses (1709-1778); an exerpt from his "Traité de la Formation mechanique des Langues"[13] (Charles de Brosses, Paris, 1775, pp. 6-7, 96-111) follows.

* * *

From TRAITE DE LA FORMATION MECANIQUE DES LANGUES*

. . . We shall first of all see that every part of the mouth, printing on the air a certain movement determined by the nature of its construction, produces a noise equally determined and one which is susceptible only of a slight variation; that these noises are few in number; that, once the construction and the movement proper to each organ is known, the ear which hears the noises recognises without difficulty from which organ each has issued; that the ear can easily distinguish between what is only a variation of the same movement from essentially different noises, as those arising from another organ, and can thus set in their order all the movements impressed on the air by the human voice, each one classified under the organ which had modulated them. Each of these sounds or articulated movements is the first germination of a certain number of roots. The number of roots thus produced is not great; but that of the branches or derivatives which arise from these roots is almost infinite.

We shall see further, that when man wishes to represent some real object by his voice and make the idea of this object that is present to his own mind pass into the ear of another, he cannot use any method that is more natural, more efficacious, or more prompt, than to make with his voice the same noise that the object he wishes to name makes, for there are few objects which make no noise, and it is this noise above all that is used when one wishes to impose original names. Nothing is easier than to adopt this method, for speech is addressed to the hearing. A savage who wishes to name a gun, will not fail to call it *pouh*. One wishes to name a certain bird, one says "cuckoo" because the bird made such a sound he heard. This is the first mechanical and natural method of the formation of words.

Generally a vowel is nothing other than the voice, that is to say the simple and permanent sound of the mouth, which can be sustained, without any movement of any organ, as long as the chest can furnish air. Consonants are the articulations of this same

*N.B. All examples of pronunciation of letters as pronounced in French, in which language this *Traité* is written.

sound that are passed through a certain organ, as through a draw-plate, which gives the sound a form. This form is given in a single second, and cannot be permanent. If it seems to be so in some strong articulations which are called *rough spirits* it is no longer a clear and distinct sound. It is only a dead whistle which one is obliged to call by the contradictory name of *silent vowel*. Thus the voice and the consonant are like matter and form, substance and mode. The general instrument of the voice must be envisaged as like a long tube which stretches from the bottom of the throat to the outside of the lips. This tube can be contracted into a larger or smaller diameter or can be stretched or shortened to a greater or lesser length. Thus, the simple sound which emerges from it represents to the ear the state in which one has held the tube while filling it with air. The differences in simple sounds are like the difference in this state, from which it follows that they are infinite, since a flexible tube can be conducted by insensible degradations from its widest diameter and its longest length to its tightest and shortest state. Commonly noted are seven more obvious divisions of simple sound, or seven states of tube which are called vowels: a, e, i, o, ó, u. But it is evident that a line, having as many parts as it has individual points which make up its whole length, there are as many vowels as there can be intermediate divisions between the seven enumerated above, from which it follows that there are an infinity. It can easily be seen indeed that one nation does not divide the diapason or scale of its voice precisely like another, and that the vowels of the English, for example, are not those of the French. So that one does not even recognise the sound of the vowels in the same word pronounced in two different languages.

The consonant is the manner in which sound is affected by the organ and the form which it receives.

I say that therefore it is convenient, in order to avoid the embarrassment of these infinite varieties, to consider the vowel, or the simple sound, as unique, whatever may be the state in which each person holds the tube of his voice, and to observe only, in order to establish an alphabet, the particular state in which each of the parts which compose the tube or instrument; for this canal is formed by several parts or organs, each of which has a movement which is particular to it, an articulation of its own, and which serves to distinguish how the simple sound, by passing through the tube has been affected by this organ and not by one of the others. There are thus as many ways of affecting the sound, and of giving it, as it were, a shape, as there are organs along the length of the tube, and there is not a single one more. It is these movements imprinted on the sound which are called *letters* or *consonants*. Of themselves, they are merely forms which would not exist without the *voice*, which is their material and their subject. Thus the whole mechanism of speech can be, albeit imperfectly, compared to a flute. The air, set in motion in the tube of this flute, is its simple sound or *voice*. The holes by which the sound exits, are the divisions of this simple voice, and these divisions can just as well be in one part of the tube as another. The position in which the fingers touch these holes are the *letters* or *consonants* which give form to the sound, a form which by itself would have no existence for the sense of hearing without the air or the voice which are its matter and subject.

Of the Infinite Varieties of the Vowel.

The thing would not be less evident if we compared the voice, or the simple sound of the vowel, with that which a cord stretched on an instrument emits, where the divisions are marked by notes along its whole length. There is no one who has not noticed that in order to form in their order the five common vowels, one merely shortens the cord successively. "A" is the full and entire voice, where the cord is stretched out in its full length, from the throat to the lips. "I" is the cord shortened to half, stretched from the palate to the lips; "O" is the end of the cord at the lips extremity. We lengthen the lips outwardly, and pull, as it were, the end of the cord from above to make "U" with it (a vowel peculiar to the French, that other nations do not have) whilst the Orientals lengthen it as much as they can from the bottom, to make from it a profoundly guttural sound, "h". Thus, the two most marked extremities of the cord, the *complementum acuti* and the *complementum imi*, are the whistled u, and the aspiration, h; they make the overtone and the contre-bass sounded on the cord of the word.

As the cord, in its whole length, is infinitely divisible, there are an infinity of points in the line where one can put a division, so that the different vowels of all the people in the universe, though infinitely varied, only differ in that one people divides its cord at one place, and another. Also, the Orientals of the olden days, in their writing, neglected to mark the voice, which they inserted when reading at intervals between the real letters, which are the consonants. Moreover, it is only to be more easily understood, that I compared the vowel to a simple straight line, divisible along its whole length. The true image of the voice, like that of the open mouth, is that of a flexible funnel both of whose diameters can be diminished at will in order to lower the vowel sound, so that "a" is the widest funnel, and "u" the smallest. But I shall content myself here with showing the size of each of these concentric funnels by a line which is part of the axis which traverses them all.

Of the Six Consonants Produced by the Six Organs of the Vocal Canal.

I have just declared that each organ that is in the mouth possesses its own shape and movement which form a letter peculiar to it; that there are as many letters or consonants as there are organs, and that there are no more. These are: 1) the lips; 2) the throat; 3) the teeth; 4) the palate; 5) the tongue. There is a sixth, that is the nose, which must be regarded as a second tube added to the instrument; for, just as one moves the air from the bottom of the throat to the tips of the lips, so one can move it from the bottom of the throat to the tips of the nostrils. This organ has its consonant; it has even, as we shall soon see, its vowel an, in, on, etc., or its simple sound peculiar to it, and in this sense it should really be said that there are two vowels, that of the mouth and that of the nose; however, although the vowel is susceptible to an effective difference according to the tube by which the air is conducted, I will not cease to regard it as unique, so long as I only regard it as the air coming out of an instrument. One can name each letter or consonant by the name of its own organ, which would render it recognisable by all the nations of the earth, whatever character one may figure it by. We figure it thus: lip, "Be"; throat, "Ke"; teeth, "De"; palate "Je"; tongue, "Le"; nose, "Se". I add to the letters, to make them ring a bit, the mute vowel we call the "e" mute. Of these six letters, the first three are completely mute; the other three are somewhat liquid and permanent, in that being flowing or whistled, the form of the movement of the organ can continue a trifle longer by a kind of deaf voice, whereas, in the three preceding ones, the form is purely instantaneous.

THE MULTIPLICATION OF LETTERS IS NOTHING MORE THAN THE EFFECT OF THE STRONGER OR WEAKER MOVEMENT OF EACH ORGAN. Each organ can make its special movement in a gentle, medium or harsh manner, more or less gentle, more or less harsh. Those modifications are harsh which push the sound outwards: je;te; re;ke;che;se. The gentle, those which seem to hold it back: ve; the;ne;ghe;ze. These changes produce in each letter variations which make one think that there is a greater number of them than is indeed the case. And if one wished to distinguish by its particular *character* each of the degrees of these differences, one would have an infinite number of letters, consonants, for the same reason that I have already mentioned when discussing the infinite number of vowels. But just to take only the three movements gentle, medium and harsh, three differences are found in each primitive letter, and these are called *permutable* letters or *of the same organ*. They are very often used to substitute for one another in the same word and in the same language; even more so, when the word passes from one language to another. This observation, which as is well known applies to Greek, is equally true of other languages. Soft lip, "Be"; medium, "Pe"; harsh, "Fe"; soft throat, "Gue" (or Greek gamma); medium, "Ce", "Ke"; harsh, "Que" (GkXi). Soft tooth, "THe" (English) or Gk Theta); medium, "De"; rough, "Te". Soft palate, "Ze"; medium, "Je"; harsh, "CHe". Soft tongue, "Ne"; medium, "Le"; harsh, "Re". In the tongue letter, Le, Ne, Re; the medium "Le" works from the tip of the tongue; the soft "Ne" from the middle of the tongue, lifted slightly toward the palate, by ejecting the air through the tube of the nose; the harsh "Re" proceeds from the root of the swollen up tongue puffed by ejecting the air initially out of the throat. As for the nose, since it is a less flexible organ, it does not vary its nasal whistle, "Se".

The palate, which is even more inflexible than the nose, could not operate at all without the help of the tongue, so that one can almost consider the palatal letter and the letters of the *tongue* as having the same cause.

The teeth set into the jaws, whose movement has so little variety, help each other greatly in forming the letter which is proper to them, with the help of the tongue, which is correctly regarded as the general agent of speech.* It is, of course, the most flexible of all and the one placed at the centre of the instrument. Only the throat and the lips at the two extremities can do without its help. But none, not even the tongue, can do without the lungs, which are the bellows of this type of vocal organ which impel the air compressed and rendered more powerful into the narrow canal of the larynx. From the larynx and the lungs comes the intensity and volume of the voice, the strength or weakness of

*Recently (Dec. 1768) the newspapers carried an account of an extraordinary phenomenon, if accurately related, a girl who spoke without a tongue. "In this town (Nantes) there is a girl of 19 who speaks without a tongue. Following upon smallpox, which she contracted when she was 8, her tongue rotted and fell out. For two years following this occurrence, she remained without speaking having only a cry, like the dumb; after this, she started to talk, and clearly asked her mother for bread; from that time on, she has preserved the use of her speech, and even sings easily. This girl, called Marie Greslar, was born in the parish of St. Hilaire near Mortagne in Poictou. It cannot be doubted that the tongue is the principal agent of speech, and one would not have believed that it was possible to talk when one lacked this organ. However, one can prove, and I had already made the experiment, that the organ of the lip, and even that of the throat, situated at the two extremities of the instrument can, speaking absolutely, effect their articulations without the help of the tongue, or, at any event, making little use of its help. And perhaps with exercise, one could arrive at doing without it entirely. But the intermediate letters which are articulated in the middle of the vocal instrument, such as those of the tongue, palate, and even teeth, are impossible to pronounce without the tongue. Thus without having seen Marie Greslar one can be sure that, although she can indeed speak a little, after having completely lost her tongue, it is only very imperfectly that her faculty is reduced to pronouncing the labial or guttural letters B, P, F, V, M, G, Q, K and the words formed from them; but that she cannot pronounce l, n, r, j, CH, Z, D, T though the people around her being used to hearing her may supplement them in the words she tries to say. As to vowels, there is less difficulty. As no articulation is needed, but only a simple sound, the vocal trumpet can suffice. Thus it is less surprising that this girl sings with a certain facility. But one must suppose that she hums the air of a tune without using the words, which she would probably find it impossible to do."

intonation, which should not be confused with the strength and weakness of articulation. Strong or weak intonation is a function only of the vowel, strong or weak; the tongue would make movements and shapes in free air in vain. Nothing perceptible to the ear would result if that air were at the same time forced out by the exhalation of the lungs, and compressed into the passage of the larynx. It is this compression which gives a voice its sound and which distinguishes it from simply non-sonorous exhalation.

THE NINETEENTH CENTURY

The Nineteenth Century

The discovery of Sanskrit is the turning point in the history of linguistics. Sir William Jones wrote on the importance of Sanskrit in 1786. He was followed by the brothers Jacob (1785-1863) and William Grimm (1786-1859), who postulated a law by which Sanskrit letters were modified in words used currently in most European languages. Franz Bopp (1791-1867) published, in 1816, an analytical comparison of the Sanskrit, Greek, Latin and Teutonic languages.

Sanskrit and Chinese were seen to be the two opposed poles of linguistic structure, each "perfect in the consistent following of one principle." The astonishing thing about Sanskrit is that it contains only one hundred and twenty-one concepts and eight hundred roots and "every thought that has ever passed through the mind of India so far as it is known to us in its literature, has been expressed in these."

Antoine Meillet (1866-1936), the master of modern linguistics, said that concordances between two or many languages arise frequently after the dissolution of the mother language and arise from parallel developments. Meillet claims there is on one side unity within plurality, on the other plurality in unity. At its beginning, no community had complete identity of language.

Ferdinand de Saussure (1857-1913) showed the antithesis between language and word. Russians and Norwegians living close to each other speak Russenork, a conglomerate of both tongues; the Siberians speak a Russo-Chinese dialect; the Savoyards, a French-Italian one.

It was not until 1870 that scholars began seriously to seek out the principles that govern the life of languages. An important book here is Whitney, *Life and Growth of Language*.

In England a shoemaker's son, George Boole (1815-1864), in

his *Laws of Thought*, made, Bertrand Russell (1872-1967) declared, the "first advance in logic since Euclid." Boole is regarded as the founder of Logical Positivism. An excerpt from his *Studies in Logic and Probability* follows.

From STUDIES IN LOGIC AND PROBABILITY[12]

. . . It is a doctrine contained in the symbolism of my treatise of the *Laws of Thought* that the three fundamental operations of Conception, Judgment and Reasoning are subject to certain primary formal laws.

By a formal law, I mean a law determining the permitted variety of form in the expression of thought. I regard such laws as founded in the nature of thought, and as governing its outward manifestation. Suppose for instance, that an object of thought is regarded as possessing two independent attributes. We cannot give expression to our thought of it as such without expressing one of these attributes first. We think of a flower as white in colour and as fragrant in scent, and if we think of it only as such, i.e. if we add no idea of priority or of connexion, we express our thought either in the form, "white, fragrant flower", or, "fragrant, white flower". That we must think of these attributes in order, is a condition, I will not say of thought itself, but of thought as capable of expression,—that we may think of and express them in either of the orders which are possible is a law of such expression and in this sense, a formal law of thought. This particular law, indeed, belongs to that operation of thought which is called conception, and there exist other such laws, the entire system both determining the forms of possible conceptions and excluding forms which would represent impossible ones. Thus the so-called Principle of Contradiction forbids the formal combination of any attribute with its contradictory attribute, as of white with not-white, in the expression of a Conception. The laws of thought include, however, formal laws of judgment and formal laws of reasoning. Of these, the formal laws of judgment determine the forms of necessary propositions, i.e. of propositions true in consequence of their form alone. For instance, the proposition, "A man is a man", is a necessary proposition, and the law of thought which it and all propositions of the same form manifest is that which Logicians term the principle of "identity". The propositions, "A man is either a negro or not a negro",—"A man is either a tree or not a tree",—are likewise necessary propositions. Their truth is involved in their very form and is quite independent of any information we may possess as to the nature of the classes of things represented by, "man", "negro", "tree". By logicians, the law of thought involved in such propositions as "A man is a negro or not a negro", is called the law of Excluded Middle. The idea expressed by this term is that no middle supposition exists between the two which are specified. Of course, this supposes the conception expressed by the term "negro" to be definite and fixed. Lastly, the formal laws of thought include formal laws of reasoning by which, from the forms of propositions given as true, the forms of other inferred as true, may be determined. Before proceeding further, I will briefly compare the above with received doctrines. As yet, there is not much difference to notice.

Logicians recognise that tripartite division of thought into Conception, Judgment and Reasoning, and they do, for the most part, recognize the subjection of these operations to laws. The chief difference which exists would have respect to the question: What are we to consider as the ultimate laws of thought? And the answer which those in modern days who have felt the importance of the question have most generally given is, that they are the Laws of Identity of Contradiction and of the Excluded Middle. Comparing this view with that really involved in the symbolism of my work, I should say that the laws specified belong to, but do not of themselves constitute, the formal laws of thought, and that the system which regards them as alone fundamental errs by defect. They have their formal equivalents in the system of laws upon which the rules and methods of my treatise are founded, but they form only a part of that system.

2ndly. It is a doctrine also contained in the symbolism of my work that the Laws of Thought constitute together a system; that the ground of this system consists in a certain relation of dependence in which all our conceptions of things stand to two fundamental conceptions, viz. those of the existence and non-existence;

and lastly, that the actual procedure of thought is governed partly by formal laws, partly by the above mentioned relation of dependence in our conceptions of things.

I do not know that there exists any doctrine of the ordinary Logic which can be directly compared with this. But there are familiar considerations which, if they do not lead to it, seem to me at least to point to it, and on these I will say a few words.

It is a familiar truth that the validity of reasoning, and of the formal processes of thought generally, does not depend upon the particular meaning of the general terms or names employed. Thus the validity of the syllogism

Men are mortal,
Caius is a man,
Therefore Caius is mortal,

does not depend upon what class of things is represented by "men", what individual by "Caius", what attribute by "mortal". The question then arises: If the validity of the inference does not depend upon the particular or distinctive meaning of these terms, does it depend upon some general meaning which they possess in common, or is it altogether independent of their meaning? Now the answer given to this question is that the terms must be contemplated as representing that which exists or does not exist; in other words, that of whatsoever else we may make abstraction, not of this. I think that attentive consideration will probably confirm this view. I think it will tend to show that as it is the essence of a proposition to be true or false, so it is the essence of the terms or names between which propositions express relations to represent something which we must regard as existent or nonexistent. But I am not sure that this is the view which, upon general considerations like these, will be most likely to commend itself. I think I should myself have been at first disposed to conjecture that the validity of inference depends upon the formal laws of operations alone. I would add that it is not upon considerations such as these the proposition as involved in the symbolism of my treatise rests. It is upon the fact which is established: that the formal laws of all conceptions of class are those which are common to the two limiting conceptions of Universe and Nothing, i.e. to the two conceptions which express simply the ideas of existence and non-existence.

How this common relation, in which all our conceptions of things stand to the two ideas of existence and non-existence, comes to be applied in the actual processes of Logic, I shall endeavour to explain in the next section.

3rdly. The symbolism of the *Laws of Thought* leads to a definite answer to the old question: What is the Universal type of Inference?

As I think this the most remarkable result of the entire investigation, I shall, before stating it, make one or two preliminary observations.

Every process of reasoning consists in deducing a legitimate conclusion from given premises. In the Logic of Class, which alone we are now considering, each premise is a proposition, connecting terms by means of the copula "is", or "are", and these terms are either simple or complex,—in the latter case being formed by that mental process by which different conceptions are combined together into a single conception. Thus the premises consist of express logical relations among conceptions, and any legitimate conclusion will express a deduced relation among those conceptions or among some of those conceptions. In the case of the syllogism, for instance, we have two premises expressing relations between three conceptions, two only of which are retained in the conclusions, the remaining one (middle term) having been got rid of, or to speak technically, eliminated. The most general idea of logical inference here suggested is that of a process of thought enabling us, 1st., to eliminate from any given system of premises, however complicated and however numerous, any of the conceptions which they may involve; 2ndly., to express the whole of the logical relation connecting the remaining conceptions according to any legitimate order. Now the formal laws of thought, and chiefly those known as the principles of contradiction and excluded middle, enable us to form a necessary proposition connecting any proposed conceptions whatever in perfect independence of any relation established between them by premises. Taking for instance, the two conceptions "men" and "rational beings", we may at once say:—Men are either rational or not-rational, meaning thereby that every individual man belongs necessarily to one or other of two alternative classes composing the predicate term. If we introduce another conception, "animal", we have the necessary proposition—

Men are either rational animals,
or rational but not animal,
or not rational but animal,
or not rational, not animal;

expressing that every individual man belongs of necessity to some one of the four alternative classes forming the predicate term. If we introduce another conception, we should be able to construct a necessary proposition involving 8 alternative classes in its predicate term, and so on. Speaking generally, we see that in these necessary propositions, the subject term expresses some given conception, and the predicate term the possible alternatives which can be formed from certain given conceptions and predicated of that subject, each individual thing in the class represented by the subject being referred to some one of the alternative classes composing the predicate. We see further, that each of the alternative classes composing the predicate is in respect of what is called its logical quantity *indefinite*. Thus is the necessary proposition,

Men are either rational or irrational,

while the subject term "men" is universal, since *all* men are referred to one or other of the classes, "rational beings", or "irrational beings", each of those class terms is indefinite, since it is undetermined of the class of "rational beings", for instance, whether the whole or some of that class, or none, is contained in the class "men". As I shall have to speak of other relations of quantity beside the universal and the indefinite, I will designate all such by the general term *category*.

Now the consequences deduced from the symbolism of the *Laws of Thought* with reference to the general type of logical inference are the following:

1st. A logical conclusion is always in the form of a necessary proposition modified by means of the premises.

2nd. The nature of the modification is the following: The alternative classes which in the predicate term of the unmodified necessary proposition were all in the category of the indefinite, are each determined under some one of the following four categories, viz.:—

1st. The universal. When one of the alternative classes of the predicate is in this category, it is implied that all its members are contained in the class denoted by the subject.

2nd. The indefinite. This has been already explained.

3rd. The non-existent. When one of the alternative classes of the predicate is in this class, it is implied that none of its members are contained in the subject.

4th. The impossible. When one of the alternative classes of the predicate term is in this category, two things are implied in the symbolism, first, that it is impossible that any of that class should exist in the class denoted by the subject; second, the absolute non-existence of the class itself. I suppose we may connect these two things and confine ourselves to the larger inference, viz. that the class is absolutely non-existent; for this implies the impossibility of finding any members of it in any other class. But the two interpretations are separately involved in the symbolism, and it is therefore my business to state them both.

Before I proceed to illustrate this doctrine of inference, I will say a few words about the genesis of the categories of the *indefinite* and the *impossible*. And I will do this because I think that the question very naturally arises: How can symbolic forms lead us to new ideas?

We postulate as the very basis of our symbolism the existence of the general conception of class and of those fundamental operations of thought by which, from conceptions given, others are formed. These, as I have stated, are primarily the operation of composition, exemplified in the derivation of the conception "red flower" from the component conceptions "red" and "flower",—and the operation of addition, exemplified in the derivation of the conception "men and women" from the conception of "men", and the conception "women". To these operations there exist two others which are respectively *inverse*, viz. as inverse to aggregation, that process by which, from the conception of a whole by the subtraction of one of its parts we form the conception of the remainder, and as inverse to composition, that by which from a given conception, we ascend to some higher conception, from which by a given act of composition, the conception given may be formed. The operation commonly called abstraction is in its formal character a particular case of this. When from the conception "red flowers", we ascend to that of "flowers", we arrive at a conception which, by composition with "red", gives "red flowers". We premise lastly, that the conception of class has two limiting forms, viz.: the conception of the Universe as the most comprehensive, the conception of Nothing as the least comprehensive, of all possible classes.

THE TWENTIETH CENTURY

The Twentieth Century

Subsequent to the discovery of Sanskrit, the three theories as to the origin of speech prevalent at the beginning of the nineteenth century were somewhat modified. The imitative theory, by which man was supposed to copy animals, was called the *bow-wow* theory; a second theory declared language to come from instinctive ejaculations aroused by pain or other sensations. This was called the *pooh-pooh*, or *ow-ow* theory. The third theory was called the *ding-dong*. It declared there was a dialectic between sound and sense from which language arose. A fourth theory, the *yo-heave-ho*, was based on the different vibrations taken by the vocal cords under the impact of breath. All the propounders of these theories turned to studies of:

a) children's language
b) primitive languages
c) the history of language.

Joseph Stalin (1879-1953), a dialectician and a naturalist, discussed the relation of Marxism to linguistics.

From CONCERNING MARXISM IN LINGUISTICS

A group of younger comrades have asked me to give my opinion in the press on questions relating to the science of language, particularly in reference to Marxism in linguistics. I am not a philologist and cannot of course satisfy the request of the comrades fully. As to Marxism in linguistics, as in other social sciences, this is something directly in my field. I have therefore consented to answer a number of questions put by the comrades.

Question: Is it true that language is a superstructure on the basis?

Answer: No, it is not true.

The basis is the economic structure of society at the given stage of its development. The superstructure is the political, legal, religious, artistic, philosophical views of society and the political, legal and other institutions corresponding to them.

Every basis has its own corresponding superstructure. The basis of the feudal system has its superstructure, its political, legal and other views, and the corresponding institutions; the capitalist basis has its own superstructure, so has the socialist basis. If the basis changes or is eliminated, then following after this its superstructure changes or is eliminated; if a new basis arises, then following after this a superstructure arises corresponding to it.

In this respect language radically differs from the superstructure. Take, for example, Russian society and the Russian language. In the past thirty years the old, capitalist basis has been eliminated in Russia and a new, socialist basis has been built. Correspondingly the superstructure on the capitalist basis has been eliminated and a new superstructure created conforming to the Socialist basis. The old political, legal and other institutions have been consequently supplanted by new, socialist institutions. But in spite of this the Russian language has remained basically what it was before the October Revolution.

What has changed in the Russian language in this period? To a certain extent the vocabulary of the Russian language has changed, in the sense that it has been replenished with many new words and expressions, which have arisen in connection with the rise of new socialist production, the appearance of a new state, a new socialist culture, a new social milieu and ethics, and, lastly, in connection with the development of technology and science; a number of words and expressions have changed their meaning, have acquired a new significance; a number of obsolete words have dropped out of the vocabulary. As to the basic stock of words and grammatical system of the Russian language, which constitute the foundation of a language, they, after the elimination of the capitalist basis, far from having been eliminated and supplanted by a new basic word stock and a new grammatical system of the language, have been preserved in their entirety and have not undergone any serious changes—have been preserved precisely as the foundation of modern Russian.

Further, the superstructure is a product of the basis, but this does not mean that it merely reflects the basis, that it is passive, neutral, indifferent to the fate of its basis, to the fate of classes, to the character of the system. On the contrary, having come into being, it becomes an exceedingly active force, actively assisting its basis to take shape and consolidate itself, and doing everything it can to help the new system finish off and eliminate the old basis and the old classes.

It cannot be otherwise. The superstructure is created by the basis precisely in order to serve it, to actively help it take shape and consolidate itself, to actively strive for the elimination of the old, moribund basis together with its old superstructure. The superstructure has only to renounce this role of auxiliary, it has only to pass from a position of active defence of its basis to one of indifference towards it, to adopt an equal attitude to all classes, and it loses its virtue and ceases to be a superstructure.

In this respect language radically differs from the superstructure. Language is not a product of one or another basis, old or new, within the given society, but of the whole course of the history of the society and of the history of the bases for many centuries. It was created not by any one class, but by the whole of the society, by all the classes of the society, by the efforts of hundreds of generations. It was created for the satisfaction of the needs not of one class, but of the whole of the society, of all the classes of the society. Precisely for this reason it was created as a single language for the society, common to all members of that society, as the common language of the whole people. Hence the functional role of language, as a means of intercourse between people, consists not in serving one class to the detriment of other classes, but in equally serving the whole of society, all the classes of society. This in fact explains why a language may equally serve both the old, moribund system and the new, rising system; both the old basis and the new basis; both the exploiters and the exploited.

It is no secret to anyone that the Russian language served Russian capitalism and Russian bourgeois culture before the October Revolution just as well as it now serves the socialist system and socialist culture of Russian society.

The same must be said of Ukrainian, Byelorussian, Uzbek, Kazakh, Georgian, Armenian, Estonian, Latvian, Lithuanian, Moldavian, Tatar, Azerbaijan, Bashkir, Turkmen and the languages of the other Soviet nations; they served the old, bourgeois system of these nations just as well as they serve the new, socialist system.

It cannot be otherwise. Language exists, language has been created precisely in order to serve society as a whole, as a means of intercourse between people, in order to be common to the members of society and constitute the single language of society, serving members of society equally irrespective of their class status. A language has only to depart from this position of being the common language of the whole people, it has only to give preference and support to some one social group to the detriment of other social groups of the society, and it loses its virtue, ceases to be a means of intercourse between the people of that society, and becomes the jargon of some social group, degenerates and is doomed to disappear.

In this respect, while it differs in principle from the superstructure, language does not differ from implements of production, from machines, let us say, which are as indifferent to classes as is language and may, like it, equally serve a capitalist system and a socialist system.

Further, the superstructure is the product of one epoch, the epoch in which the given economic basis exists and operates. The superstructure is therefore short-lived; it is eliminated and disappears with the elimination and disappearance of the given basis.

Language on the contrary is the product of a whole number of epochs, in the course of which it takes shape, is enriched, develops and is polished. A language therefore exists immeasurably longer than any basis or any superstructure. This in fact explains why the rise and elimination not only of one basis and its superstructure, but of several bases and their corresponding superstructures, have not led in history to the elimination of a given language, to the elimination of its structure and the rise of a new language with a new stock of words and a new grammatical system.

It is more than a hundred years since Pushkin died. In this period the feudal system and the capitalist system were eliminated in Russia, and a third, a socialist system has arisen. Hence two bases, with their superstructures, were eliminated, and a new, socialist basis has arisen, with its new superstructure. Yet if we take the Russian language, for example, it has not in this long span of time undergone any fundamental change, and the modern Russian language differs very little in structure from the language of Pushkin.

What has changed in the Russian language in this period? The Russian vocabulary has in this period been greatly replenished; a large number of obsolete words have dropped out of the vocabulary; the meaning of a great many words has changed; the grammatical system of the language has improved. As to the structure of Pushkin's language, with its grammatical system and its basic stock of words, in all essentials it has remained as the basis of modern Russian.

And this is quite understandable. Indeed, what necessity is there, after every revolution, for the existing structure of the language, its grammatical system and basic stock of words to be destroyed and supplanted by new ones, as is usually the case with the superstructure? What object would there be in calling "water", "earth", "mountain", "forest", "fish", "man", "to walk", "to do", "to produce", "to trade", etc., not water, earth, mountain, etc., but something else? What object would there be in having the modification of words in a language and the combination of words in sentences follow not the existing grammar but some entirely different grammar? What would the revolution gain from such an upheaval in language? History in general never does anything of any moment without some particular necessity. What, one asks, can be the necessity for such a language revolution, if it has been demonstrated that the existing language and its structure are fundamentally quite suited to the needs of the new system? The old superstructure can and should be destroyed and replaced by a new one in the course of a few years, in order to give free scope for the development of the productive forces of society; but how can an existing language be destroyed and a new one built in its place in the course of a few years without causing anarchy in social life and without creating the threat of the disintegration of society? Who but a Don Quixote could set himself such a task?

Lastly, one other radical distinction between the superstructure and language. The superstructure is not directly connected with production, with man's productive activity. It is connected with production only indirectly, through the economy, through the basis. The superstructure therefore reflects changes in the level of development of the productive forces not immediately and not directly, but only after changes in the basis, through the prism of the changes wrought in the basis by the changes in production. This means that the sphere of action of the superstructure is narrow and restricted.

Language, on the contrary, is connected with man's productive activity directly, and not only with man's productive activity, but with all his other activity in all his spheres of work, from production to the basis, and from the basis to the superstructure. For this reason language reflects changes in production immediately and directly, without waiting for changes in the basis. For this reason the sphere of action of language, which embraces all fields of man's activity, is far broader and more comprehensive than the sphere of action of the superstructure. More, it is practically unlimited.

It is this that primarily explains why language, or rather its vocabulary, is in an almost constant state of change. The continuous development of industry and agriculture, of trade and transport, of technology and science, demands that language should replenish its vocabulary with new words and expressions needed for their functioning. And language, directly reflecting these needs, does replenish its vocabulary with new words, and perfects its grammatical system.

Hence:

a) A Marxist cannot regard language as a superstructure on the basis;

b) To confuse language and superstructure is to commit a serious error.

Question: Is it true that language always was and is class language, that there is no such thing as language which is the single and common language of a society, a non-class language of its entire people?

Answer: No, it is not true.

It is not difficult to understand that in a society which has no classes there can be no such thing as a class language. There were no classes in the primitive communal clan system, and consequently there could be no class language—the language was then the single and common language of the whole community. The objection that the concept class should be taken as covering every human community, including the primitive communal community, is not an objection but a playing with words that is not worth refuting.

As to the subsequent development from clan languages to tribal languages, from tribal languages to the languages of nationalities, and from the languages of nationalities to national languages —everywhere and at all stages of development, language, as a means of intercourse between the people of a society, was the single and common language of that society, serving its members equally irrespective of their social status.

I am not referring here to the empires of the slave and medieval periods, the empires of Cyrus or Alexander the Great, let us say, or of Caesar or Charles the Great, which had no economic base of their own and were transient and unstable military and administrative associations. Not only did these empires not have, they could not have a single language common to the whole empire and understood by all the members of the empire. They were conglomerations of tribes and nationalities, each of which lived its own life and had its own language. Consequently, it is not these or similar empires I have in mind, but the tribes and nationalities composing them, which had their own economic base and their own languages, evolved in the distant past. History tells us that the languages of these tribes and nationalities were not class languages, but languages common to the whole of a tribe or nationality, and understood by all its people.

Side by side with this, there were, of course, dialects, local vernaculars, but they were dominated over by and subordinated to the single and common language of the tribe or nationality.

Later, with the appearance of capitalism, the elimination of feudal division and the formation of national markets, nationalities developed into nations, and the languages of nationalities into national languages. History shows that national languages are not class, but common languages, common to the members of each nation and constituting the single language of that nation.

It has been said above that, as a means of intercourse between the people of a society, language serves all classes of that society equally, and in this respect displays what may be called an indifference to classes. But people, the various social groups, the classes, are far from being indifferent to language. They strive to utilise the language in their own interests, to impose their own special vocabulary, special terms, special expressions upon it. The upper strata of the propertied classes, who have divorced themselves from and detest the people—the aristocratic nobility, the upper strata of the bourgeoisie—particularly distinguish themselves in this respect. "Class" dialects, jargons, high-society "languages" are created. These dialects and jargons are often incorrectly referred to in literature as languages—the "aristocratic language" or the "bourgeois language" in contradistinction to the "proletarian language" or the "peasant language". For this reason, strange as it may seem, some of our comrades have come to the conclusion that national language is a fiction, and that only class languages exist in reality.

There is nothing, I think, more erroneous than this conclusion. Can these dialects and jargons be regarded as languages? Certainly not. They cannot, firstly, because these dialects and jargons have no grammatical systems or basic word stocks of their own—they borrow them from the national language. They cannot, secondly, because these dialects and jargons are confined to a narrow sphere, are current only among the upper strata of a given class and are entirely unsuitable as a means of intercourse for society as a whole. What, then, have they? They have a collection of specific words reflecting the specific tastes of the aristocracy or the upper strata of the bourgeoisie; a certain number of expressions and locutions distinguished by refinement and gallantry and free of the "coarse" expressions and locutions of the national language; lastly, a certain number of foreign words. But all the fundamentals, that is, the overwhelming majority of the words and the grammatical system, are borrowed from the common, national language. Dialects and jargons are therefore offshoots of the common national language, devoid of all linguistic independence and doomed to stagnation. To believe that dialects and jargons can develop into independent languages capable of ousting and supplanting the national language means losing one's sense of historical perspective and abandoning the Marxist position.

References are made to Marx, and the passage from his article "St. Max" is quoted which says that the bourgeois have "their own language", that this language "is a product of the bourgeoisie", that it is permeated with the spirit of mercantilism and huckstering. Certain comrades cite this passage with the idea of proving that Marx believed in the "class character" of language and denied the existence of a single national language. If these comrades were impartial, they should have cited another passage from this same article "St. Max", where Marx, touching on the way single national languages arose, speaks of "the concentration of dialects into a single national language as the result of economic and political concentration".

Marx, consequently, did recognise the necessity of a *single* national language, as the highest form, to which dialects, as lower forms, are subordinate.

What, then, can this bourgeois language be which Marx says is "a product of the bourgeoisie"? Did Marx consider it as much a language as the national language, with a specific linguistic structure of its own? Could he have considered it such a language? Of course not. Marx merely wanted to say that the bourgeois had polluted the common national language with their hucksters' vocabulary, that the bourgeois, in other words, have their hucksters' jargon.

It thus appears that these comrades have misrepresented Marx. And they misrepresented him because they quoted Marx not like Marxists but like dogmatists, without delving into the essence of the matter.

References are made to Engels, and the words from his *Condition of the Working Class in England* are cited where he says that ". . . the English working class has gradually become a race wholly apart from the English bourgeoisie", and "the workers speak other dialects, have other thoughts and ideals, other customs and moral principles, a different religion and other politics than those of the bourgeoisie". Certain comrades conclude from this passage that Engels denied the necessity of a common, national language, that he believed, consequently, in the "class character" of language. True, Engels speaks here of dialects, not language, fully realising that, being an offshoot of the national language, a dialect cannot supplant the national language. But these comrades, apparently, do not regard the existence of a difference between language and dialect with any great sympathy.

It is obvious that the quotation is inappropriate, because Engels here speaks not of "class languages" but chiefly of class thoughts, ideals, customs, moral principles, religion, politics. It is perfectly true that the thoughts, ideals, customs, moral principles, religion and politics of bourgeois and proletarians are directly antithetical. But what has this to do with national language, or the "class character" of language? Can the existence of class contradictions in society serve as an argument in favour of the "class character" of language, or against the necessity of a common national language? Marxism says that a common language is one of the cardinal earmarks of a nation, although knowing very well that there are class contradictions within the nation. Do the comrades referred to recognize this Marxist thesis?

References are made to Lafargue, and it is said that in his pamphlet *Language and Revolution* he recognises the "class character" of language, and denies the necessity of a common, national language. This is not true. Lafargue does indeed speak of a "noble" or "aristocratic language" and of the "jargons" of various strata of society. But these comrades forget that Lafargue, who is not interested in the difference between languages and jargons and refers to dialects now as "artificial languages," now as "jargons," definitely says in this pamphlet that "the artificial language which distinguished the aristocracy . . . arose out of the language common to the whole people, which was spoken by bourgeois and artisan, by town and country."

Consequently, Lafargue recognizes the existence and necessity of a common language of the whole people, and fully realises that the "aristocratic language" and other dialects and jargons are subordinate to and dependent on the language common to the whole people.

It follows that the reference to Lafargue misses the mark.

References are made to the fact that at one time in England the feudal lords spoke "for centuries" in French, while the English people spoke English, and this is alleged to be an argument in favour of the "class character" of language and against the necessity of a common language of the whole people. But this is not an argument, it is more like a joke. Firstly, not all the feudal lords spoke French at that time, but only a small upper stratum of English feudal barons attached to the court and in the counties. Secondly, it was not some "class language" they spoke, but the ordinary common language of the French. Thirdly, we know that in the course of time this French language fad disappeared without a trace, yielding place to the common language of all the English people. Do these comrades think that the English feudal lords "for centuries" held intercourse with the English people through interpreters, that they did not use the English language, that there was no language common to all the English at that time, and that the French language in England was then anything more than the language of high society, current only in the restricted circle of the upper English aristocracy? How can one possibly deny the existence and the necessity of a common language of the whole people on the basis of laughable "arguments" like these?

There was a time when Russian aristocrats at the tsar's court and in high society also made a fad of the French language. They prided themselves on the fact that when they spoke Russian they lisped in French, that they could only speak Russian with a French accent. Does this mean that there was no common Russian language, no language of the whole people, at that time in Russia, that a common language of the whole population was a fiction, and "class languages" a reality?

Our comrades are here committing at least two mistakes.

The first mistake is that they confuse language with superstructure. They think that since the superstructure has a class character, language too must be a class language, and not a common language of the whole people. But I have already said above that language and superstructure are two different concepts, and that a Marxist must not confuse them.

The second mistake of these comrades is that they conceive the opposition of interests of the bourgeoisie and the proletariat, the fierce class struggle between them, as meaning the disintegration of society, as a break of all ties between the hostile classes. They believe that, since society has disintegrated and there is no longer a single society, but only classes, a common language of society, a national language, is unnecessary. If society has disintegrated and there is no longer a language common to the whole people, a national language, what remains? There remain classes and "class languages". Naturally, every "class language" will have its "class" grammar—a "proletarian" grammar or a "bourgeois" grammar. True, such grammars do not exist in nature. But that does not worry these comrades: they believe that such grammars will appear in due course.

At one time there were "Marxists" in our country who asserted that the railways left to us after the October Revolution were bourgeois railways, that it would be unseemly for us Marxists to utilise them, that they should be torn up and new, "proletarian" railways built. For this they were nicknamed "troglodytes". . . .

It goes without saying that such a primitive-anarchist view of society, of classes, of language has nothing in common with Marxism. But it undoubtedly exists and continues to prevail in the minds of certain of our muddled comrades.

It is of course wrong to say that, because of the existence of a fierce class struggle, society has disintegrated into classes which are no longer economically connected one with another in one society. On the contrary, as long as capitalism exists, the bourgeois and the proletarians will be bound together by every economic thread as parts of one capitalist society. The bourgeois cannot live and grow rich unless they have wage labourers at their command; the proletarians cannot exist unless they hire themselves to the capitalists. If all economic ties between them were to cease, it would mean the cessation of all production, and the cessation of all production would mean the doom of society, the doom of the classes themselves. Naturally, no class wants to incur self-destruction. Consequently, however sharp the class struggle may be, it cannot lead to the disintegration of society. Only ignorance of Marxism and complete failure to understand the nature of language could have suggested to some of our comrades the fairy tale about the disintegration of society, about "class" languages, and "class" grammars.

Reference is further made to Lenin, and it is pointed out that Lenin recognised the existence of two cultures under capitalism —bourgeois and proletarian—and that the slogan of national culture under capitalism is a nationalist slogan. All this is true and Lenin is absolutely right here. But what has this to do with the "class character" of language? When these comrades refer to what Lenin said about two cultures under capitalism, it is evidently with the idea of suggesting to the reader that the existence of two cultures, bourgeois and proletarian, in society means that there must also be two languages, inasmuch as language is linked with culture—and, consequently, that Lenin denies the necessity of a common national language, and, consequently, that Lenin believes in "class" languages. The mistake these comrades make here is that they identify and confuse language with culture. But culture and language are two different things. Culture may be bourgeois or socialist, but language, as a means of intercourse, is always a language common to the whole people and can serve both bourgeois and socialist culture. Is it not a fact that the Russian, the Ukrainian, the Uzbek languages are now serving the socialist culture of these nations just as well as they served their bourgeois cultures before the October Revolution? Consequently, these comrades are profoundly mistaken when they assert that the existence of two different cultures leads to the formation of two different languages and to the negation of a common language.

When Lenin spoke of two cultures, he proceeded precisely from the precept that the existence of two cultures cannot lead to the negation of a common language and the formation of two languages, that the language must be a common one. When the Bundists accused Lenin of denying the necessity of a national language and of regarding culture as "non-national", Lenin as we know vigorously protested and declared that he was fighting against bourgeois culture, and not against national languages, the necessity of which he regarded as indisputable. It is strange that some of our comrades should be trailing in the footsteps of the Bundists.

As to a common language, the necessity of which Lenin allegedly denies, it would be well to pay heed to the following words of Lenin:

"Language is the most important means of human intercourse, unity of language and its unimpeded development are most important conditions for genuinely free and extensive commercial intercourse on a scale commensurate with modern capitalism, for a free and broad grouping of the population in all its separate classes."

It follows that our highly respected comrades have misrepresented the views of Lenin.

Reference, lastly, is made to Stalin. The passage from Stalin is quoted which says that "the bourgeoisie and its nationalist parties were and remain in this period the chief directing force of such nations". This is all true. The bourgeoisie and its nationalist party really do direct bourgeois culture, just as the proletariat and its internationalist party direct proletarian culture. But what has this to do with the "class character" of language? Do not these comrades know that national language is a form of national culture, that a national language may serve both bourgeois and socialist culture? Are our comrades unaware of the well-known formula of the Marxists that the present Russian, Ukrainian, Byelorussian and other cultures are socialist in content and national in form, i.e., in language? Do they agree with this Marxist formula?

The mistake our comrades commit here is that they do not see the difference between culture and language, and do not understand that culture changes in content with every new period in the development of society, whereas language remains basically the same through a number of periods, equally serving both the new culture and the old.

Hence:

a) Language, as a means of intercourse, always was and remains the single language of a society, common to all its members;

b) The existence of dialects and jargons does not negate but confirms the existence of a language common to the whole of the given people, of which they are offshoots and to which they are subordinate;

c) The Russian language was enlarged from the vocabularies of the other languages, but far from weakening, this enriched and strengthened the Russian language.

As to the specific national individuality of the Russian language, it did not suffer in the slightest, because the Russian language preserved its grammatical system and basic word stock and continued to advance and perfect itself in accordance with its inherent laws of development.

There can be no doubt that Soviet linguistics has nothing of any value to gain from the crossing theory. If it is true that the chief task of linguistics is to study the inherent laws of language development, it has to be admitted that the crossing theory does not even set itself this task, let alone accomplish it—it simply does not notice it, or does not understand it.

Question: Did *Pravda* act rightly in inaugurating an open discussion on linguistics?

Answer: It did.

Along what lines the problems of linguistics will be settled, will become clear at the conclusion of the discussion. But it may be said already that the discussion has been very useful.

It has brought out, in the first place, that in linguistic bodies both in the centre and in the Republics, a regime has prevailed which is alien to science and men of science. The slightest criticism of the state of affairs in Soviet linguistics, even the most timid attempt to criticise the so-called "new doctrine" in linguistics was persecuted and suppressed by the leading linguistic circles. Valuable workers and researchers in linguistics were dismissed from their posts or demoted for being critical of N. Y. Marr's heritage or expressing the slightest disapproval of his teachings. Linguistic scholars were appointed to leading posts not on their merits, but because of their unqualified acceptance of N. Y. Marr's theories.

It is generally recognised that no science can develop and flourish without a battle of opinions, without freedom of criticism. But this generally recognised rule was ignored and flouted in the most unceremonious fashion. There arose a close group of infallible leaders, who, having secured themselves against any possible criticism, became a law unto themselves and did whatever they pleased.

To give an example: the so-called "Baku Course" (lectures delivered by N. Y. Marr in Baku), which the author himself had rejected and forbidden to be republished, was republished nevertheless by order of this leading caste (Comrade Meshchaninov calls them "disciples" of N. Y. Marr) and included without any qualification in the list of manuals recommended to students. This means that the students were deceived, a rejected "Course" being represented to them as a sound textbook. If I were not convinced of the integrity of Comrade Meshchaninov and the other linguistic leaders, I would say that such conduct is tantamount to sabotage.

How could this have happened? It happened because the Arakcheyev regime established in linguistics cultivates irresponsibility and encourages such arbitrary actions.

The discussion has been very useful first of all because it brought this Arakcheyev regime into the light of day and smashed it to smithereens.

But the usefulness of the discussion does not end there. It not only smashed the old regime in linguistics but also brought out the incredible confusion of ideas on cardinal questions of linguistics which prevails among the leading circles in this branch of science. Until the discussion began they hushed up and glossed over the unsatisfactory state of affairs in linguistics. But when the discussion started silence became impossible, and they were compelled to come out in the pages of the press. And what did we find? It turned out that in N. Y. Marr's teachings there are a whole number of defects, errors, ill-digested problems and vague propositions. Why, one asks, have N. Y. Marr's "disciples" begun to talk about this only now, after the discussion opened? Why did they not see to it before? Why did they not speak about it in due time openly and honestly, as befits scientists?

Having admitted "some" errors of N. Y. Marr, his "disciples", it appears, think that Soviet linguistics can only be advanced on the basis of a "rectified" version of N. Y. Marr's theory, which they consider a Marxist one. No, save us from N. Y. Marr's "Marxism"! N. Y. Marr did indeed want to be and endeavoured to be a Marxist, but he failed to become one.

* * *

Lezcek Kolakowski (1930-) replied to Stalin as follows:

From TOWARDS A MARXIST HUMANISM

A few days after the Greatest Philologist in the World (Stalin) published in a daily newspaper his opus announcing that Marr's theory was false, I had the opportunity to attend a congress of philologists on this very subject. In the course of the discussion one of the participants made a most tactless step. He produced a pamphlet issued several weeks earlier by one of his colleagues who was present and read an extract that ran roughly as follows: "It is quite obvious that in linguistics Marr's theory is the only genuine Marxist-Leninist theory of language, that it alone is compatible with the principles of Marxism-Leninism, that it is the sole infallible instrument of Marxist-Leninist research," etc. Then the malicious fellow produced the current issue of the daily newspaper and quoted sections from an article by the same author that said, more or less: "It is obvious that Marr's theory has nothing in common with Marxism-Leninism, that it is a striking vulgarization of Marxism-Leninism, that the Marxist-Leninist conception of language must be firmly opposed to Marr's theory," etc. "What is the meaning of this?" raged the critic. "Of such a change of view within a few weeks? What a chameleon!" Confounded, the author of the quoted passages remained silent while everyone laughed merrily, until a Party activist pointed out that they should not laugh because every man had a right to change his mind and this should not in itself be considered a disgrace.

As I listened, my first impression was that the critic had been right in showing up the opportunism of the philologist and his shameful readiness to reverse his opinions with lightning speed to conform to the judgment delivered by the Greatest Philologist in the World. Only later, much later, did I realize that the embarrassed author of the pamphlet was the genuine Marxist, whereas the critic had shown himself to be completely ignorant. Because—and this is the core of the question I wish to consider—Marr's theory was truly compatible with Marxism two days before the publication of the Greatest Philologist's work, and *truly* incompatible with Marxism on the day this work appeared. Since the author of the pamphlet was an authentic Marxist he had no reason to be ashamed, but ought to have prided himself on his unshakable faithfulness to the principles of Marxism.

Principles? Perhaps this is an awkward choice of words. The point is that the term "Marxism" did not designate a doctrine with a specific content. It meant a doctrine defined purely formally, its content being in every case supplied by the decrees of the Infallible Institution which, during a certain phase, was the Greatest Philologist, the Greatest Economist, the Greatest Philosopher, and the Greatest Historian in the World.

In short, "Marxism" became a concept of institutional, rather than intellectual, content—which, by the way, happens to every doctrine connected with a church. Similarly, the word "Marxist" does not describe a man who believes in a specific world view whose content is defined. It refers to a man with a mental attitude characterized by a willingness to adopt institutionally approved opinions. From this point of view, the current content of Marxism does not matter. A man is a Marxist if he is always ready to accept as its content each recommendation of the Office. This is why, until February, 1956, the only real Marxist (which also means a revolutionary, a dialectician, a materialist) was one who agreed that there was no way to socialism except through revolutionary violence. An anti-Marxist (that is, a reformer, a metaphysician, an idealist) was anyone who thought other means could be found. As we know, after February, 1956, the reverse became true: since then the only real Marxist has been one who recognizes the possibility of a peaceful transition to socialism in certain countries. It is difficult to predict accurately who will, in regard to this problem, be a Marxist next year. But we will not be the ones to decide—the Office will settle the matter.

It is precisely for this reason, because of the institutional rather than the intellectual character of Marxism, that a true Marxist will profess beliefs he does not necessarily understand. The 1950 Marxist knew that Lysenko's theory of heredity was correct, that Hegel represented the aristocratic reaction to the French Revolution, that Dostoevski was a decadent and Babaevski a great writer, that Suvorov served the cause of progress, and also that the resonance theory in chemistry was reactionary nonsense. Every 1950 Marxist *knew* these things even if he had never heard of chromosomes, had no idea what century Hegel lived in, had never read one of Dostoevski's books or studied a high-school chemistry textbook. To a Marxist all this is absolutely unnecessary so long as the content of Marxism is determined by the Office.

In this way the concept of Marxism was defined very precisely, without any possibility of error, although the definition was purely formal; that is, it merely indicated where to look for the current content of Marxism, without actually specifying that content.

Chronologically, this appears to be the second concept of Marxism, The original one simply meant the sum total of views and theories characteristic of Karl Marx. This first, historical concept of Marxism still retains its validity and precision (in the same sense that the concepts of "Platonism," "Freudianism," and "Cartesianism" do) irrespective of whether any Marxist—meaning, in this context, a believer in Marx's views—exists in the world.

We are thus faced with a question: If the sort of Marxism in which doctrine was continuously established by the Office is now dead in the minds of most intellectuals who considered themselves Marxists, has the concept of Marxism retained any meaning at all? If so, what meaning, other than the historical one connected with the work of the man who gave his name to the doctrine? What sense is there in slogans urging the "development of Marxism," and what meaning remains in the division between Marxists and non-Marxists in science?

. . . And yet, if we wish to develop a new conceptual apparatus to analyze social stratification in types of societies unknown to Marx, we must fall back upon a certain methodological rule which he not only consistently observed but applied so forcefully and universally that it is typical of his work. According to this rule, all analyses of social life should proceed by seeking the basic divisions that separate societies into antagonistic groups. Even if it turns out that in certain societies these divisions are based on other criteria than the ones Marx formulated for the nineteenth-century bourgeois world, still the very fact of applying this extremely general rule leads the scholar to adopt Marx's characteristic methodology. From this point of view it can be said that the sociological research he is engaging in is "Marxist."

It happens, though, that the progress of knowledge requires us not only to enrich our supply of conceptual tools and methodological rules as compared with those found in Marx's works, but also to question and revise some of his concrete statements. The Office itself once proclaimed that some of Engels' assumptions about the origin of the state were false. In accordance with its usual procedures, it did not bother to justify this revision, but for the purposes of our discussion that is of secondary importance. Moreover, the Office disavowed Marx's thesis that it was impossible to build a socialist society in one isolated country. When Stalin came out with his concept of socialism in one country, Trotsky, as an orthodox and classical Marxist, rebuked him for deviating from the principles of Marxism and was, in turn, called an anti-Marxist by Stalin. Refraining for the moment from judging who was right in this dispute and whose view was verified by historical developments, we can nevertheless clearly see the scholastic sterility of a dispute conducted this way. If we say, as Stalin did, that the international situation has changed since Marx's time and that Marx himself recommended that the future of socialism be weighed in terms of the current structure of class power on an international scale, we are taking recourse to a way of thinking employed by Marx but so generalized and so common to all those who want to analyze reality rationally that it is not specifically symptomatic of "Marxist" thinking.

From the point of view of institutional Marxism, the matter is clear: In 1945 the only Marxist evaluation of Hegel was that he was a German chauvinist, an apologist for war, an enemy of the Slavic peoples, and a precursor of fascism; in 1954 Hegel had become an eminent dialectician, an idealist who played an important role in shaping Marx's philosophy. From the standpoint of an intellectual conception of Marxism, the problem looks somewhat different. There does not exist, and never will, one "truly Marxist" interpretation of Stoic philosophy, or a particular interpretation of Mickiewicz's poetry that would be "the only one compatible with Marxism." One can speak of interpreting Stoic philosophy with the help of general Marxist rules of historical methodology, but the same method may yield widely differing results. For the hope that the methodology of the social sciences may come to resemble a logarithmic table or a computer that will always enable us to proceed from a given set of facts to the same unequivocal answers is a chimera. Moreover, it is far from certain that the most rigorous application of this methodology would necessarily lead to conclusions in agreement with some particular remarks of Friedrich Engels about Stoicism—nor can it exhaust the possibilities of scientific study of the subject.

That is why disputes in which scholars try to snatch from each other the exclusive privilege of using "genuine Marxism" and to monopolize the honorable title of "consistent Marxist" are sterile verbalism. One can argue whether a given theory fulfills more or less well the requirements of scientific thinking, which include the essential rules of the method worked out by Marx. These rules, however, must be of a very general nature, and they do not contain any specific instructions on how to evaluate one or another historical phenomenon. Moreover, they always allow for many possible interpretations: the rule of historical materialism itself does not determine the type, intensity, or degree of uniformity of the influence exerted by the sum total of material conditions of life on the social thinking of people in all the epochs of history. And, a *forteriori*, historical materialism does not determine whether, for example, Pascal's philosophy is to be taken as an expression of the decadent tendencies of declining feudalism, or a representation of bourgeois thought, or something else again. In sociological investigations, and even more so in philosophical ones, there is hardly a single perfectly unambiguous term. Vacillations in meaning are inherited by even the most fundamental theses of a doctrine; none can be regarded as precise. If terms such as "matter," "social consciousness," "cognition," "superstructure," "causal determination," "relations of production," and so on are not clear, it follows that no methodological rules and no assertions of the theory in which they are involved have a precisely defined meaning.

Therefore, what we call Marxism, as understood in its intellectual function and as a method of thinking, can vary greatly in content within the limits of a very general framework. We know that it would be difficult to develop a Marxist angelology, and that we certainly could not present Bossuet's philosophy of history as Marxist. To know this, however, is not very useful, since our primary purpose in using the word "Marxist" is not to distinguish scientific thinking from the notorious irrationalism of theologians. The fact is that within the boundaries of science, where various styles of thinking and various types of methodology can very well coexist and compete, the borderline between Marxism and non-Marxism is extremely fluid.

In the history of world views one can scarcely imagine a total disappearance of doctrinal variety and a rigid monopoly by one system. That is why terms derived from the names of those who introduced into philosophy original and revealing perspectives or formulated widely accepted points of view will surely survive. "Marxism" in this sense does not denote a doctrine that must be accepted or rejected as a whole. It does not mean a universal system, but a vital philosophical inspiration affecting our whole outlook on the world, a constant stimulus to the social intelligence and social memory of mankind. It owes its permanent validity to the new and invaluable points of view it opened before our eyes, enabling us to look at human affairs through the prism of universal history; to see, on the one hand, how man in society is formed by the struggle against nature and, on the other hand, the simultaneous process by which man's work humanizes nature; to consider thinking as a product of practical activity; to unmask myths of consciousness as resulting from ever recurring alienations in social existence and to trace them back to their real sources. These perspectives enable us, furthermore, to analyze social life in its incessant conflicts and struggles which, through countless multitudes of individual goals and desires, individual suffering and disappointments, individual defeats and victories, together compose a picture of uniform evolution that—we have every right to believe—signifies, on the grand scale of history, not retrogression but progress.

* * *

Ludwig Wittgenstein (1889-1951), originally a pupil of Bertrand Russell, is one of the greatest thinkers of the twentieth century. All his books are profoundly concerned with language. He was a logician and a naturalist. The following are Dr. Samuel Anderson's comments on:

A NOTE ON LUDWIG WITTGENSTEIN'S INDUCTIVE METHOD

Wittgenstein's later works—as opposed to the *Tractatus*, which earned him his credentials in philosophical circles,—might be characterized as anecdotal linguistic theory. No longer willing to accept the formalisms of predirected calculus as valid interpretations of natural language and natural thought, he attempted to find internal criteria within the norms of hypothetical language paradigms that, he hoped, would illustrate the ways in which natural thought processes were revealed in symbols. A favorite Wittgenstein paradigm is a set of sentences, taken from an unspecified tongue of some hypothetical "tribe" (although examples are invariably rendered in German or English) to illustrate how far one might or might not go to infer linguistic confirmation of logistic principles.

In a well-known example he proposes that statement of, and therefore judgments of, competence in tribal warfare, are based on physical characteristics—e.g. visibly bulging muscles, or, perhaps, are based on the outcome of a series of performance tests: lifting weights, army swinging and skipping. Yet the statements of competence are, in fact, different propositions: "He can throw a spear" "he is fit to fight the enemy"? Wittgenstein proposes that there may be no corresponding sentences in the language for the actual performances on the tests, rather, the performances are rendered simply in "test or spear-throwing" etc. If this is the case, he argues that "skipping" "arm-swinging" and the like are English words that have no equivalents in the tribal language. To determine translatability of a word, in fact, requires knowing "the role this word plays in the whole life of the tribe". Not only statements, but questions, greetings, gestures—even facial expressions and tone of voice, must be examined to determine the translatability of human judgments. And all these things must be taken into account to represent even supposedly universal behavior such as the expression of emotions. Returning to judgments of competence, Wittgenstein suggests that our warring tribe may appear to employ the same fact to determine both a sentence of the form: "he has done so and so" and one of the corresponding form "He can do so and so." But since some performances—"more arduous ones"—imply competence for less demanding ones of the same type, Wittgenstein argues that it is a matter of circumstance whether competence is simply inferred from identical past performances or not, and the whole question has no clearly defined meaning in this case. He puts forth a further consideration of probabilistic judgments of competence, proposing that a favorite tribal pastime is betting on the outcome of athletic competitions. Even if no sentences exist in the language giving reasons for choosing to bet rather on one competitor than another, Wittgenstein argues that one can infer *causes* if one observes more betting or higher betting on athletes known to have trained well.

Yet there are many subtle behavioral cues for degrees of certainty that can be examined, apart from formal language and, if found these will demonstrate the giving of reasons. A member of the tribe might point to the size of a wrestler's biceps and then shrug, or give any of an unclearly defined set of indicators as evidence of his degree of belief in the wrestler's prowess. But although they are unclearly defined, such indicators are validly translatable into English sentences of the form: "I believe so and so *can* beat so and so in wrestling".

THE CONTEMPORARY SCENE: THE NATURALISTS

The Contemporary Scene: The Naturalists

One of the busiest areas in which contemporary linguists are working is in the study of animal languages. One of the earliest to work in this field was R. Garner (1848-1920). His theory of primate speech, and an account of his somewhat naive experiments with monkeys, follow.

THE SIMIAN TONGUE.

In coming before the world with a new theory, I am aware that it may have to undergo many repairs, and be modified by many new ideas. On entering the world of science, it begins its "struggle for life," and under the law of "the survival of the fittest" its fate must be decided. I am aware that it is heresy to doubt the dogmas of science as well as of some religious sects; but sustained by proofs too strong to be ignored, I am willing to incur the ridicule of the wise and the sneer of bigots, and assert that "articulate speech" prevails among the lower primates, and that their speech contains the rudiments from which the tongues of mankind could easily develop; and to me it seems quite possible to find proofs to show that such is the origin of human speech.

I have long believed that each sound uttered by an animal had a meaning which any other animal of the same kind would interpret at once. Animals soon learn to interpret certain words of man and to obey them, but never try to repeat them. When they reply to man, it is always in their own peculiar speech. I have often watched the conduct of a dog as he would speak, until I could interpret a meaning to his combined act and speech. I observed the same thing in other species with the same results; and it occurred to me that if I could correctly imitate these sounds I might learn to interpret them more fully and prove to myself whether it was really a uniform speech or not.

Some seven years ago, in the Cincinnati Zoological Garden, I was deeply impressed by the conduct of a number of monkeys caged with a savage rib-nosed mandril, which they seemed to fear very much. The cage was divided by a wall through which was a small doorway leading from the inner to an outer compartment, in which was a tall upright, supporting a platform at its top. Every movement of this mandril seemed to be closely watched by the monkeys that could see him, and instantly reported to those in the other compartment. The conduct of these monkeys so confirmed my belief and inspired me with new hopes and new zeal that I believed "the key to the secret chamber" was within my grasp. I regarded the task of learning the monkey tongue as very much the same as learning that of a strange race of mankind; more difficult in the degree of its inferiority, but less in volume. Year by year, as new ideas were revealed to me, new barriers arose, and I began to realise how great a task was mine. One difficulty was to *utter* the sounds I heard; another was to recall them; and yet another was to translate them. Impelled by an eternal hope, and not discouraged by poor success, I continued my studies as best I could, in the gardens of New York, Philadelphia, Cincinnati, and Chicago, and with such specimens as I could find with the travelling menagerie museum, or hand organ, or aboard some ship, or kept as a pet in some family. They have all aided in teaching me the little I know of their native tongues. But at last came a revelation! A new idea dawned upon me; and after wrestling half a night with it I felt assured of ultimate success. I went to Washington, and called upon Dr. Frank Baker, Director of the Zoological Garden and proposed the novel experiment of acting as interpreter between, two monkeys. Of course he laughed, but not in derision or in doubt, for scientific men are always credulous and believe all they are told. I then explained to him how it was possible, and he quite agreed with me. We set the time and prepared for the work. The plan was quite simple. We separated two monkeys which had been caged together, and placed them in separate rooms. I then arranged a phonograph near the cage of the female, and caused her to utter a few sounds, which were recorded on the cylinder. The machine was then placed near the cage containing the male, and the record repeated to him and his conduct closely studied. The surprise and perplexity of the male were evident.

He traced the sounds to the horn from which they came, and failing to find his mate he thrust his hand and arm into the horn quite up to his shoulder, withdrew it, and peeped into the horn again and again. He would then retreat and again cautiously approach the horn, which he examined with evident interest. The expressions of his face were indeed a study. Having satisfied myself that he recognised the sounds as those of his mate, I next proceeded to record some of his efforts, but my success was not fully up to my hopes. Yet I had secured from him enough to win the attention of his mate, and elicit from her some signs of recognition. And thus, for the first time in the history of philology, the simian tongue was reduced to record. My belief was now confirmed, and the faith of others strengthened. I noted some of the defects in my experiment, and provided against them for the future. Some weeks later, in the Chicago Zoological Garden, I made some splendid phonographic records; and thence I went to the Cincinnati Garden, where I secured, among others, a fine, distinct record of the two chimpanzees, all of which I brought home with me for study. I placed them on the machine and repeated them over and over, until I became quite familiar with the sounds and improved myself very much in my efforts to utter them. . . .

Having described to some friends who were with me the word I would use, I stood for a while with my side turned to the cage containing a capuchin monkey (*cebus capucinus*). I uttered the word or sound which I had translated "milk." My first effort caught his ear and caused him to turn and look at me. On repeating it some three or four times he answered me very distinctly with the same word I had used, and then turned to a small pan kept in the cage for him to drink from. I repeated the word again, and he placed the pan near the front of the cage and came quite up to the bars and uttered the word. I had not shown him any milk or anything of the kind. But the man in charge then brought me some milk, which I gave to him, and he drank it with great zest; then looked at me, held up the pan, and repeated the sound some three or four times. I gave him more milk, and thus continued till I was quite sure he used the same sound each time he wanted milk.

I next described to the friends who were with me a word which was very hard to render well, but I translated it "to eat." I now held a banana in front of the cage and he at once gave the word I had described. Repeated tests showed to me that he used the same word for apple, carrot, bread, and banana, hence I concluded that it meant "food," or "hunger," as also "to eat." After this I began on a word which I had interpreted "pain," or "sick," and with such result as made me feel quite sure I was not far from right. My next word was "weather," or "storm," and while the idea may seem far-fetched, I felt fairly well sustained by my tests. For many other words I had a vague idea of a meaning, and still believe that I can verify them in the end. These are only a few of many trials I have made to solve the problem of the simian tongue, and while I have only gone a step, as it were, I believe that I have found a clue to the great secret of speech, and pointed out the way which leads to its solution.

I went next to the Cincinnati Garden. When the visitors had left the monkey-house I approached the cage of a capuchin monkey, and found him crouched in the rear of his cage. I spoke to him in his own tongue, using the word which I had called "milk." He rose, answered me with the same word, and came at once to the front of the cage. He looked at me as if in doubt, and I repeated the word; he did the same, and turned at once to a small pan in the cage, which he picked up and placed near the door at the side, and returned to me and uttered the word again. I asked the keeper for milk, which he did not have, however, but brought me some water. The efforts of my little simian friend to secure the glass were very earnest, and the pleasing manner and tone assured me of his extreme thirst. I allowed him to dip his hand into the glass and he would suck his fingers and reach again. I kept the glass from reach of his hand, and he would repeat the sound and beg for more. I was thus convinced that the word I had translated "milk" must also mean "water," and from this and other tests, I at last determined that it meant also "drink" and probably "thirst." . . .

To imitate the word which I interpret "food," fix the mouth as if to whistle: draw the tongue far back into the mouth, and try to utter the word "who" by blowing. The pitch of sound is a trifle higher than the cooing of a pigeon, and not wholly unlike it. The phonics appear to me to be "wh-u-w," with the consonant elements so faint as to be almost imaginary. In music the tone is F sharp, and this seems to be the vocal pitch of the entire species, though they have a wide range of voice. The sound which I have translated "drink" or "thirst" is nearly uttered by relaxing and parting the lips, and placing the tongue as it is found in ending the German word "ich," and in this position try to utter "ch-e-u-w," making the "ch" like "k," blending the "e" and "u" like "slurred" notes in music, and suppressing the "w" as in the first case. The consonant elements can barely be detected, and the tone is about an octave higher than the word used for "food." Another sound I suspected was a "menace" or "cry of alarm," but I was unable to utter it, except with the phonograph; but during February I had access to a fine specimen of the capuchin, in Charleston, S.C. On my first visit to him I found him very gentle, and we at once became good friends. He ate from my hands and seemed to regard me very kindly. The next day, while feeding him, I uttered the peculiar sound of "alarm," whereupon he sprang at once to a perch in the top of his cage, and as I continued the sound he seemed almost frantic with fright. I could not tempt him by any means to come down. I then retired some twenty feet from the cage, and his master (of whom he is very fond) induced him to come down from the perch, and while he was fondling him I gave the alarm from where I stood. He jumped again to his perch and nothing would induce him to leave it while I remained in sight. The next day, on my approach, he fled to his perch and I could not induce him on any terms to return. It is now some time since I began my visits, and I have never, since his first fright, induced him to accept anything from me, and only with great patience can I get him to leave his perch at all, although I have not repeated this peculiar sound since my third visit, nor can I again elicit a reply from him when I say his word for "food" or "drink."

This sound may be fairly imitated by placing the back of the hand very gently to the mouth, and kissing it, drawing in the air, and producing a shrill, whistling sound, prolonged and slightly circumflexed.

Its pitch is the highest F sharp on the piano. It is not whistled, however, by a monkey, but is made with the vocal organs. While this is the highest vocal pitch of a capuchin, there are other sounds much more difficult to imitate or describe. It must be remembered that an attempt to *spell* a sound which is almost an absolute vowel, can at best convey only a very imperfect idea of the true sounds or the manner of uttering them.

I have access also to another specimen of the same variety, with which I am experimenting, but I have never tried the "alarm" on him as I do not wish to lose his friendship. He uses all the words I know in his language, and speaks them well.

My work has been confined chiefly to the capuchin monkey, because he seems to have one of the best defined languages of any of his genus, besides being less vicious and more willing to treat one civilly. So far as I have seen, the capuchin is the Caucasian of the monkey race. The chimpanzee has a strong but monotonous voice, confined to a small range of sounds, but affords a fine study while in the act of talking. I have not gone far enough with him as yet to give much detail of his language. There are only three in America now, and they talk but little and are hard to record. I have recorded but one sound made by a sooty monkey; three by a mandril; five by the white-face sapajou; and a few of less value. But from the best proof I have found I have arrived, as I believe, at some strange facts, which I shall here state.

1. The simian tongue has about eight or nine sounds, which may be changed by modulation into three or four times that number.

2. They seem to be halfway between a whistle and a pure vocal sound, and have a range of four octaves, and so far as I have tried they all chord with F sharp on a piano.

3. The sound used most is very much like "u"-"oo," in "shoot."

The next one something like "e" in "be." So far I find no a, i, or o.

4. Faint traces of consonant sounds can be found in words of low pitch, but they are few and quite feeble; but I have had cause to believe that they develop in a small degree by a change of environment.

5. The present state of their speech has been reached by development from a lower form.

6. Each race or kind has its own peculiar tongue, slightly shaded into dialects, and the radical or cardinal sounds do not have the same meanings in all tongues.

7. The words are monosyllabic, ambiguous and collective, having no negative terms except resentment.

8. The phonic character of their speech is very much the same as that of children in their early efforts to talk, except as regards the pitch.

9. Their language seems to obey the same laws of change and growth as human speech.

10. When caged together one monkey will learn to understand the language of another kind, but does not try to speak it. His replies are in his own vernacular.

11. They use their lips in talking in very much the same way that men do; but seldom speak when alone or when not necessary.

12. I think their speech, compared to their physical, mental, and social state, is in about the same relative condition as that of man by the same standard.

13. The more fixed and pronounced the social and gregarious instincts are in any species, the higher the type of its speech.

14. Simians reason from cause to effect, and their reasoning differs from that of man *in degree, but not in kind*.

To reason, they *must think*, and if it be true that *man cannot think without words*, it must be true of monkeys: hence, they must formulate those thoughts into words, and words are the natural exponents of thoughts.

15. Words are the audible, and signs the visible, expression of thought, and any voluntary sound made by the vocal organs with a constant meaning is a word.

* * *

As a result of my experience with monkeys, I shall here sum up the chief points in which their speech is found to coincide with that of man, and note those features which distinctly characterize the sounds as a form of speech.

The sounds which monkeys make are voluntary, deliberate, and articulate. They are always addressed to some certain individual with the evident purpose of having them understood. The monkey indicates by his own acts and the manner of delivery that he is conscious of the meaning which he desires to convey through the medium of the sounds. They wait for and expect an answer, and if they do not receive one they frequently repeat the sounds. They usually look at the person addressed, and do not utter these sounds when alone or as a mere pastime, but only at such times as some one is present to hear them, either some person or another monkey. They understand the sounds made by other monkeys of their own kind, and usually respond to them with a like sound. They understand these sounds when imitated by a human being, by a whistle, a phonograph, or other mechanical devices, and this indicates that they are guided by the sounds alone, and not by any signs, gestures, or psychic influence. The same sound is interpreted to mean the same thing and obeyed in the same manner by different monkeys of the same species. Different sounds are accompanied by different gestures, and produce different results under the same conditions. They make their sounds with the vocal organs and modulate them with the teeth, tongue, and lips, in the same manner that man controls his vocal sounds. The fundamental sounds appear to be pure vowels, but faint traces of consonants are found in many words, especially those of low pitch, and since I have been able to develop certain consonant sounds from a vowel basis, the conclusion forces itself upon me that the consonant elements of human speech are developed from a vowel basis. This opinion is further confirmed by the fact that the sounds produced by the types of the animal kingdom lower than the monkey appear to be more like the sounds of pipe instruments, and as we rise in the scale the vocal organs appear to become somewhat more complex and capable of varying their sounds so as to give the effect of consonants, which very much extends the vocal scope. The present state of the speech of monkeys appears to have been reached by development from a lower form. Each race or kind of monkey has its own peculiar tongue, slightly shaded into dialects, and the radical sounds do not appear to have the same meaning in different tongues. The phonetic character of their speech is equally as high as that of children in a like state of mental development, and seems to obey the same laws of phonetic growth, change, and decay as human speech. It appears to me that their speech is capable of communicating the ideas that they are capable of conceiving, and measured by their mental, moral, and social status, is as well developed as the speech of man measured by the same unit. Strange monkeys of the same species seem to understand each other at sight, whereas two monkeys of different species do not understand each other until they have been together for some time. Each one learns to understand the speech of the other, but as a rule he does not try to speak it. When he deigns an answer it is usually in his own tongue. The more fixed and pronounced the social and gregarious instincts are in any species, the higher the type of its speech. They often utter certain sounds under certain conditions in a whisper, which indicates that they are conscious of the effect which will result from the use of speech. Monkeys reason from cause to effect, communicate to others the conclusion deduced therefrom, and act in accordance therewith. If their sounds convey a fixed idea on a given subject from one mind to another, what more does human speech accomplish? If one sound communicates that idea clearly, what more could volumes do? If their sounds discharge all the functions of speech, in what respect are they not speech?

It is as reasonable to attribute meaning to their sounds as to attribute motives to their actions, and the fact that they ascribe a meaning to the sounds of human speech would show that they are aware that ideas can be conveyed by sounds. If they can interpret certain sounds of human speech, they can ascribe a meaning to their own. They think, and speech is but the natural exponent of thought; it is the audible expression of thought as signs are the visible expression of the same—born of the same cause, acts to the same end, and discharges the same functions in the economy of life. To reason is to think methodically; and if it be true that man cannot think without words, the same must be true of monkeys. I do not mean, however, to claim that such is a fact with regard to man thinking; but if such can be shown to be a fact, it will decide the question as to the invention of human speech, as it was necessary for man to think in order to invent, and by the rule he could not think a word which did not exist, and therefore could not have invented it.

Robert M. Yerkes (1876-1956), who worked at Yale, is chiefly famous for his classic monograph *The Great Apes*. The following is, however, taken from his *Almost Human* (1925).

ANTHROPOID SPEECH AND ITS SIGNIFICANCE

There is no lack of communication in the Abreu primate colony. On their part, owner and keepers talk much to, and little with, the monkeys and apes; and the animals in their various ways transfer their states of mind to one another. Time would enable the patient, trained, and skilled observer to discover the essentials of primate language at Quinta Palatino. But neither Madam Abreu nor the writer has well begun the task, much less completed it; therefore, this chapter is to be based upon the work of several observers. It is rather a summary of what is now known on the subject than a transcript from Cuban experience.

Vocalization, speech, language are terms whose meaning we should agree upon at the outset. All of the primates have a rather elaborate vocal mechanism with which they can produce varied sounds. In the apes the vocal organs are similar to the human, and they are capable of producing sounds varying widely in pitch, quality, and volume. The gorilla is notorious for the volume of its voice, the gibbon and chimpanzee for the carrying and penetrating character of some of their vocalizations.

Vocal sounds, however, are not necessarily speech. They may

be simple and monotonous cries significant of emotional crises. Only when they constitute definite and somewhat complex systems of special sounds having ideational or emotional value, do we ordinarily call them speech. To speak, then, is to vocalize with intent to express meanings, feelings, or both. Vocalization is inclusive of speech. It ranges from simple chirps or clicks to the indefinitely extensible imitative chatter of the parrot and human conversation. Although most animals have voices which are used more or less frequently and effectively in emotional expression, few speak in the sense which we have given the term.

Language, in turn, is inclusive of speech, for there are indeed many kinds, some of which do not require vocalization. Any system of symbols used to express ideas or feelings may serve as a language. Familiar examples are the finger and hand positions and movements formerly used extensively by deaf-mutes; pictographs used by various primitive peoples; hieroglyphics, and the various systems of writing which make use of modern alphabets. The signs, then, may be attitudes or movements of the person who is trying to express himself or they may be environmental objects or agencies. Ingenious children commonly invent languages for their own amusement and use. In so doing they may employ gestures, written signs, objects natural or artificial, mechanically produced signs, or their own vocalizations.

Man evidently has a special gift for the invention and development of language as a means of communication. His mental growth and his material and social progress are conditioned to a marked degree by this almost unique gift. No other living animal approaches him in this respect, but it would be rash indeed to assert that no creature other than man has developed a language. Ants, in some ways the most highly developed among animals, certainly have a system of sensory signs, probably in the main odors and contacts, which serves them much as sights and sounds serve us in establishing social contacts and in communicating significant information. Although there is no indication that they talk, there is very convincing evidence that they are able to communicate. The study of ant language is peculiarly alluring, and, in view of the interest which it has commanded, it seems strange that we do not know more about it.

But this is not a general discussion of animal communication.

The question which we set out to answer is: Does any primate, other than man, talk? It would be difficult to find a primate which does not use its voice to obvious advantage in making itself understood. We must therefore inquire how much it expresses and whether or not ideas as well as feelings are definitely indicated by sounds. To consider other than casually the vocalization or the speech of monkeys would take us far afield. Instead we shall concentrate on what has been learned about the vocal expressions of anthropoid apes and their significance.

Garner, a widely known student of primate speech who devoted the better part of his life to noting, recording, analyzing, and imitating the vocalizations of monkeys and apes, offers in his books much excellent evidence of the existence of vocal language or speech in the monkeys as well as in the great apes. For several types he describes sounds which seem to stand as words. In a given individual or species they may number from ten to a score. So definite are these vocalizations and their meaning that Garner was able to communicate with the animals. Hence, he contends that monkeys and apes speak, and states that their vocal language differs from ours in complexity and degree of development but not in its purpose or use.

As Garner was not adequately trained for his difficult research and failed to command the scientific resources of his time, his results have not been accepted generally by scientific authorities. It is nevertheless true that many of his observations have been substantially verified, while some have been proved incorrect. Probably his enthusiasm led him to exaggerate the degree of intelligence, and the power of vocal communication, of his subjects. But the writer humbly confesses that the more he learns about the great apes and the lesser primates by direct observation as contrasted with reading, the more facts and valuable suggestions he discovers in Garner's writings.

For several years, in their native habitat and also in France, Dr. Louis Boutan studied the intellectual and affective behavior of gibbons, and also their vocal expressions. Unlike Garner, he comes to the conclusion that the speech of animals is quite different from our own, and instead of being a true language is, as he terms it, a pseudo-language.

In man there is a primary language of emotions which during infancy and early childhood serves to express the feelings. This infancy and early childhood serves to express the feelings. This early rudimentary language is directed by sense impressions, images, and affective experiences. In several important respects it is like the speech of monkeys and apes. Later the child learns to express vocally ideas as well as feelings, and gradually there develops ability to communicate with one's fellows over a wide range of experience. Such is true speech in man. In pseudo-language, as Boutan thinks of it, the sounds or other indicative signs are spontaneous and innate or instinctive. By contrast, the sounds or signs which constitute the elements of a true language—such, for example, as human speech—are acquired or learned. This is possible because of the social tradition which carries from generation to generation certain conventional sounds or other signs to which definite meaning is ascribed.

Boutan, then, would say that human speech is acquired by the individual through imitation and tuition. Of course he would also admit that the individual has the power of inventing new forms of language. Whether or not he is right in his conviction that man alone possesses a true as compared with an instinctive vocal language, it remains for further research to decide. The writer suspects that the distinction is by no means so simple and clear-cut as Boutan makes out, and that both inheritance and individual acquisition contribute to languages, whatever their medium and their degree of development.

The gibbon, according to Boutan, has the best singing voice of any anthropoid ape. Its calls are sometimes agreeable, but they are often too shrill and penetrating for comfort. For the individual which he most carefully studied, four groups of sounds are described. The first are those which seem to express a state of satisfaction or well-being; the second similarly express a state of discomfort or fear; the third group seems to be intermediate in value between the first and second, and the fourth indicates states of excitement. In each of these four categories there appear several sounds which one might naturally think of as words.

Although Boutan's gibbon, in the course of his investigation, adapted very satisfactorily to conditions of life in captivity and acquired many new and useful habits, no new sounds or words were learned. Such ability to express herself vocally as she had, seems to have been instinctive. Naturally enough—indeed, inevitably—he concludes that there is a world of difference between gibbon speech and human speech.

As there is no other record of investigation to which we may appeal for further light on the speech of the gibbon, we must believe, provisionally at any rate, that it expresses feelings vocally, but not ideas, and lacks ability to learn to talk.

Although the orang-utan has a good enough voice, it is known as a silent creature whose common vocalizations are whines, screams, and groans of complaint, fear, anger, or satisfaction. No such satisfactory study of the vocal expressions of the orang-utan, as has been made by Boutan with the gibbon, is known to the writer. Consequently nothing further can be said.

Perhaps because it is more given to sociability than the other apes, and certainly also because of its delightful disposition, the vocal expressions of the chimpanzee have commanded the attention of scientists. It always seems as though this creature had something to say, and every now and then he makes one feel that he actually is saying it.

First, in order of time, Garner records of the chimpanzee that its speech consists of not more than twenty-five or thirty words, many of which seem to be "vague or ambiguous." Yet in summing up the results of his study he remarks:

> In conclusion I again assert that the sounds uttered by these apes have the characteristics of human speech. The speaker is conscious of the meaning of the sound used. The pitch and volume of the voice are regulated to suit the condition under which it is used. The ape knows the value of sound as a medium of conveying thought. These and many other facts show that their sounds are truly speech.

Not one of these statements can be accepted by the psychologist without further evidence. They may be correct, but the chances are that further research will indicate their inadequacy.

The chimpanzee shows a rudimentary gesture language. "No" is expressed by a movement of the head, as in us; similarly, definite positions and movements of the arm and hand indicate affirmation.

The vocal expressions of two young chimpanzees have been carefully observed by Mrs. William S. Learned and faithfully transcribed. Her results show a total of thirty-two sounds made by one or other of the animals, which she lists as words or elements of speech. These vocalizations she found were associated mostly with situations which have to do with food or drink and with other animals or persons. As a rule the sounds seem to be part of an emotional expression, and from Mrs. Learned's descriptions it would seem that there may be as many significant "words" as there are varieties of emotion. Whether or not a chimpanzee "word" ever stands for a definite idea, Mrs. Learned does not inform us. Her descriptions of the vocal expressions of these little creatures are particularly important and interesting because she has skilfully combined verbal picture of the situation with musical description of the vocalization. Panzee, the little female subject, is characterized as a sweet singer because of the quality and use of her voice. Chim, the little male, although also an expert vocalist, expressed himself less pleasingly.

There is no obvious reason why the chimpanzee and the other great apes should not talk, but it seems to be the consensus of opinion among expert observers, as well as those who know the animals only casually, that they do not do so. As the writer has studied the ideational behavior of these animals, he has persistently wondered why they have not developed speech and whether they may not be taught to talk. It would seem that one of the best ways to test their ability would be the attempt to teach them to speak, for if they cannot learn to express themselves by a system of vocables they probably have no true spoken language. One might very well anticipate success in such an experiment, for it is perfectly obvious that the animals learn to understand much that is said to them and have a handy vocal mechanism. Many years ago George J. Romanes, a distinguished English naturalist, wrote thus of a chimpanzee in the London Zoological Gardens:

> This ape has learned from her keeper the meaning of so many words and phrases, that in this respect she resembles a child shortly before it begins to talk. Moreover, it is not only particular words and particular phrases which she has thus learned to understand; but

> she also understands, to a large extent, the combination of these words and phrases in sentences, so that the keeper is able to explain to the animal what it is he requests her to do.

Convinced of the existence of chimpanzee ideas and suspecting that they might under favorable conditions gain expression through language, I recently tried to teach the two young chimpanzees, Chim and Panzee, to utter words. Several methods were used to induce them to respond in this way, but none succeeded. My purpose was to give the animals incentive for imitating sounds which I was certain they could reproduce. I did not actually put them through the process of making the sound, as for example, by holding the lips, tongue, or nose in proper position. Instead, I depended entirely on the imitative tendency, hoping that they might get the idea that by making a certain sound they would win a desired reward. Although the experiments, in different forms, were carried on for several months, they merely fatigued the animals, and a stage was finally reached when it was difficult to command attention. Although I admit surprise in this outcome of my effort at training the animals to speak, I am not yet convinced of their inability. This is partly because of the measure of success achieved by other investigators, but even more because of my suspicion that my methods were in various ways unsatisfactory.

Garner writes that he taught a little chimpanzee, whom he called Moses, to utter a few words. He selected the following: "mama"; the French word *feu*, fire; the German word *wie*, how; and the native Nkami word *nkgwe*, mother. He writes:

> Every day I took him on my lap and tried to induce him to say one or more of these words. For a long time he made no effort to learn them; but after some weeks of persistent labor and a bribe of corned beef, he began to see dimly what I wanted him to do. . . . In his attempt to say "mama" he worked his lips without making any sound, although he really tried to do so. . . . With *feu* he succeeded fairly well, except that the consonant element, as he uttered it, resembled "v" more than "f."

> . . . In his efforts to pronounce *wie* he always gave the vowel element like German "u" with the umlaut, but the "w" element was more like the English than the German sound of that letter.
>
> Taking into consideration the fact that he was only a little more than a year old, and was in training less than three months, his progress was all that could have been desired, and vastly more than had been hoped for.

My animals were older than Garner's Moses, but I have no reason to suppose that they were less intelligent or less capable of learning words. Perhaps it is merely a matter of long continuance of training, patience, persistence, and determination on the part of the teacher.

My humiliation is still further accentuated by the success of Dr. William H. Furness in teaching a young orang-utan to say two or three words. I cannot do justice to his interesting description except by quoting:

> In the case of the orang-utan it took at least six months of daily training to teach her to say "Papa." This word was selected not only because it is a very primitive sound, but also because it combined two elements of vocalization to which orang-utans and chimpanzees are, as I have said, unaccustomed, namely: the use of lips and an expired vowel sound. The training consisted of a repetition of the sounds for minutes at a time, while the ape's lips were brought together and opened in imitation of the movements of my lips. I also went through these same manoeuvers facing a mirror with her face close to mine that she might see what her lips were to do as well as feel the movement of them. At the end of about six months, one day of her own accord, out of lesson time, she said, "Papa," quite distinctly and repeated it on command. Of course, I praised her and petted her enthusiastically; she never forgot it after that and finally recognized it as my name. When asked, "Where is Papa?" she would at once point to me or pat me on the shoulder. One warm summer's day I carried

her in my arms into a swimming pool; she was alarmed at first but when the water came up to her legs she was panic-stricken; she clung with her arms about my neck, kissed me again and again and kept saying, "Papa! Papa! Papa!" Of course, I went no further after that pathetic appeal.

The next word I attempted to teach her to say was "cup." (Let me say that by this time she understood almost everything that it was necessary for me to say such as "Open your mouth," "Stick out your tongue," "Do this," etc., and she was perfectly gentle and occasionally seemed quite interested.) The first move in teaching her to say "cup" was to push her tongue back in her throat as if she were to make the sound "ka." This was done by means of a bone spatula with which I pressed lightly on the center of her tongue. When I saw that she had taken a full breath I placed my finger over her nose to make her try to breathe through her mouth. The spatula was then quickly withdrawn and inevitably she made the sound "ka." All the while facing her I held my mouth open with my tongue in the same position as hers so that her observation, curiosity, and powers of imitation might aid her, and I said *ka* with her emphatically as I released her tongue. After several lessons of, perhaps, fifteen minutes of this sort of training each day she would draw back her tongue to the position even before the spatula had touched it, but she would not say *ka* unless I placed my finger over her nose. The next advance was that she herself placed my finger over her nose and then said *ka* without any use of the spatula; then she found that in default of my finger her own would answer the purpose and I could get her to make this sound any time I asked her to. It was comparatively very easy from this to teach her to say "kap" by means of closing her lips with my fingers the instant she said *ka*. At the same time I showed her the cup that she drank out of and I repeated the word several times as I touched it to her lips. After a few lessons when I showed her the cup and asked "What is

> this?" she would say cup very plainly. Once when ill at night she leaned out of her hammock and said "cup, cup, cup," which I naturally understood to mean that she was thirsty and which proved to be the case. I think this showed fairly conclusively that there was a glimmering idea of the connection of the word with the object and with her desire.

Despite his notable success in training the orang-utan and his observation that both chimpanzees and orang-utans may be able to understand much that is said to them, Dr. Furness says that "if these animals have a language it is restricted to a very few sounds of a general emotional significance. Articulate speech they have none and communication with one another is accomplished by vocal sounds to no greater extent than it is by dogs, with a growl, a whine, or a bark."

There are many interesting and valuable descriptions of the emotional vocalizations of the great apes, but the essentials of what is known about their speech are indicated by the observations which have been described. It remains merely to formulate our tentative conclusion about the subject and to answer the question: Do the apes speak?

Everything seems to indicate that their vocalizations do not constitute true language, in the sense in which Boutan uses the term. Apparently the sounds are primarily innate emotional expressions. This is surprising in view of the evidence that they have ideas, and may on occasion act with insight. We may not safely assume that they have nothing but feelings to express, or even that their word-like sounds always lack ideational meaning. Perhaps the chief reason for the ape's failure to develop speech is the absence of a tendency to imitate sounds. Seeing strongly stimulates to imitation; but hearing seems to have no such effect. I am inclined to conclude from the various evidences that the great apes have plenty to talk about, but no gift for the use of sounds to represent individual, as contrasted with racial, feelings or ideas. Perhaps they can be taught to use their fingers, somewhat as does the deaf and dumb person, and thus helped to acquire a simple, nonvocal, "sign language."

R. Allen Gardner and Beatrice T. Gardner are, respectively, professor of psychology and research associate and lecturer in psychology at the University of Nevada, Reno. What follows is condensed from a paper published in 1969.

TEACHING SIGN LANGUAGE TO A CHIMPANZEE[13]

The extent to which another species might be able to use human language is a classical problem in comparative psychology. One approach to this problem is to consider the nature of language, the processes of learning, the neural mechanisms of learning and of language, and the genetic basis of these mechanisms, and then, while recognizing certain gaps in what is known about these factors, to attempt to arrive at an answer by dint of careful scholarship. An alternative approach is to try to teach a form of human language to an animal. We chose the latter alternative and, in June 1966, began training an infant female chimpanzee, named Washoe, to use the gestural language of the deaf. Within the first 22 months of training it became evident that we had been correct in at least one major aspect of method, the use of a gestural language. Additional aspects of method have evolved in the course of the project. These and some implications of our early results can now be described in a way that may be useful in other studies of communicative behavior. Accordingly, in this article we discuss the considerations which led us to use the chimpanzee as a subject and American Sign Language (the language used by the deaf in North America) as a medium of communication; describe the general methods of training as they were initially conceived and as they developed in the course of the project; and summarize those results that could be reported with some degree of confidence by the end of the first phase of the project. . . .

A serious disadvantage is that human speech sounds are unsuitable as a medium of communication for the chimpanzee. The vocal apparatus of the chimpanzee is very different from that of man. More important, the vocal behavior of the chimpanzee is very different from that of man. Chimpanzees do make many different sounds, but generally vocalization occurs in situations of high excitement and tends to be specific to the exciting situations. Undisturbed, chimpanzees are usually silent. Thus, it is unlikely that a chimpanzee could be trained to make refined use of its vocalizations. . . .

Use of the hands, however, is a prominent feature of chimpanzee behavior; manipulatory mechanical problems are their forte. More to the point, even caged, laboratory chimpanzees develop begging and similar gestures spontaneously, while individuals that have had extensive contact with human beings have displayed an even wider variety of communicative gestures. In our choice of sign language we were influenced more by the behavioral evidence that this medium of communication was appropriate to the species than by anatomical evidence of structural similarity between the hands of chimpanzees and of men. . . .

We chose a language based on gestures because we reasoned that gestures for the chimpanzee should be analogous to bar-pressing for rats, key-pecking for pigeons, and babbling for humans.

American Sign Language. Two systems of manual communication are used by the deaf. One system is the manual alphabet, or finger spelling, in which configurations of the hand correspond to letters of the alphabet. In this system the words of a spoken language, such as English, can be spelled out manually. The other system, sign language, consists of a set of manual configurations and gestures that correspond to particular words or concepts. Unlike finger spelling, which is the direct encoding of a spoken language, sign languages have their own rules of usage. Word-for-sign translation between a spoken language and a sign language yields results that are similar to those of word-for-word translation between two spoken languages: the translation is often passable, though awkward, but it can also be ambiguous or quite nonsensical. Also, there are national and regional variations in sign languages that are comparable to those of spoken languages.

We chose for this project the American Sign Language (ASL), which, with certain regional variations, is used by the deaf in North America. . . . The ASL can be compared to pictograph writing in which some symbols are quite arbitrary and some are quite representational or iconic, but all are arbitrary to some degree. For example, in ASL the sign for "always" is made by holding the hand in a fist, index finger extended (the pointing hand), while rotating the arm at the elbow. This is clearly an arbitrary representation of the concept "always." The sign for "flower," however, is highly iconic; it is made by holding the fingers of one hand extended, all five fingertips touching (the tapered hand), and touching the fingertips first to one nostril then to the other, as if sniffing a flower. While this is an iconic sign for "flower," it is only one of a number of conventions by which the concept "flower" could be iconically represented; it is thus arbitrary to some degree. Undoubtedly, many of the signs of ASL that seem quite arbitrary today once had an iconic origin that was lost through years of stylized usage. Thus, the signs of ASL are neither uniformly arbitrary nor uniformly iconic; rather the degree of abstraction varies from sign to sign over a wide range. This would seem to be a useful property of ASL for our research.

The literate deaf typically use a combination of ASL and finger spelling; for purposes of this project we have avoided the use of finger spelling as much as possible. A great range of expression is possible within the limits of ASL. We soon found that a good way to practice signing among ourselves was to render familiar songs and poetry into signs; as far as we can judge, there is no message that cannot be rendered faithfully (apart from the usual problems of translation from one language to another). Technical terms and proper names are a problem when first introduced, but within any community of signers it is easy to agree on a convention for any commonly used term. For example, among ourselves we do not finger-spell the words *psychologist* and *psychology*, but render them as "think doctor" and "think science." Or, among users of ASL, "California" can be finger-spelled but is commonly rendered as "golden playland." (Incidentally, the sign for "gold" is made by plucking at the earlobe with thumb and forefinger, indicating an earring—another example of an iconic sign that is at the same time arbitrary and stylized.)

The fact that ASL is in current use by human beings is an additional advantage. The early linguistic environment of the deaf children of deaf parents is in some respects similar to the linguistic environment that we could provide for an experimental subject. This should permit some comparative evaluation of Washoe's eventual level of competence. For example, in discussing Washoe's early performance with deaf parents we have been told that many of her variants of standard signs are similar to the baby-talk variants commonly observed when human children sign.

Washoe. Having decided on a species and a medium of communication, our next concern was to obtain an experimental subject. It is altogether possible that there is some critical early age for the acquisition of this type of behavior. On the other hand, newborn chimpanzees tend to be quite helpless and vegetative. They are also considerably less hardy than older infants. Nevertheless, we reasoned that the dangers of starting too late were much greater than the dangers of starting too early, and we sought the youngest infant we could get. Newborn laboratory chimpanzees are very scarce, and we found that the youngest laboratory infant we could get would be about 2 years old at the time we planned to start the project. It seemed preferable to obtain a wild-caught infant. Wild-caught infants are usually at least 8 to 10 months old before they are available for research. This is because infants rarely reach the United States before they are 5 months old, and to this age must be added 1 or 2 months before final purchase and 2 or 3 months for quarantine and other medical services.

We named our chimpanzee Washoe for Washoe County, the home of the University of Nevada. Her exact age will never be known, but from her weight and dentition we estimated her age to be between 8 and 14 months at the end of June 1966, when she first arrived at our laboratory. . . .

Laboratory conditions. At the outset we were quite sure that Washoe could learn to make various signs in order to obtain food, drink, and other things. For the project to be a success, we felt that something more must be developed. We wanted Washoe not only to ask for objects but to answer questions about them and also to ask us questions. We wanted to develop behavior that could be described as conversation. With this in mind, we attempted to provide Washoe with an environment that might be conducive to this sort of behavior. Confinement was to be minimal, about the same as that of human infants. Her human companions were to be friends and playmates as well as providers and protectors, and they were to introduce a great many games and activities that would be likely to result in maximum interaction with Washoe.

In practice, such an environment is readily achieved with a chimpanzee; bonds of warm affection have always been established between Washoe and her several human companions. We have enjoyed the interaction almost as much as Washoe has, within the limits of human endurance. A number of human companions have been enlisted to participate in the project and relieve each other at intervals, so that at least one person would be with Washoe during all her waking hours. At first we feared that such frequent changes would be disturbing, but Washoe seemed to adapt very well to this procedure. Apparently it is possible to provide an infant chimpanzee with affection on a shift basis.

All of Washoe's human companions have been required to master ASL and to use it extensively in her presence, in association with interesting activities and events and also in a general way, as one chatters at a human infant in the course of the day. The ASL has been used almost exclusively, although occasional finger spelling has been permitted. From time to time, of course, there are lapses into spoken English, as when medical personnel must examine Washoe. At one time, we considered an alternative procedure in which we would sign and speak English to Washoe simultaneously, thus giving her an additional source of informative cues. We rejected this procedure, reasoning that, if she should come to understand speech sooner or more easily than ASL, then she might not pay sufficient attention to our gestures. Another alternative, that of speaking English among ourselves and signing to Washoe, was also rejected. We reasoned that this would make it seem that big chimps talk and only little chimps sign, which might give signing an undesirable social status.

The environment we are describing is not a silent one. The

human beings can vocalize in many ways, laughing and making sounds of pleasure and displeasure. Whistles and drums are sounded in a variety of imitation games, and hands are clapped for attention. The rule is that all meaningful sounds, whether vocalized or not, must be sounds that a chimpanzee can imitate.

Training methods

Imitation. The imitativeness of apes is proverbial, and rightly so. Those who have worked closely with chimpanzees have frequently remarked on their readiness to engage in visually guided imitation. Consider the following typical comment of Yerkes: "Chim and Panzee would imitate many of my acts, but never have I heard them imitate a sound and rarely make a sound peculiarly their own in response to mine. As previously stated, their imitative tendency is as remarkable for its specialization and limitations as for its strength. It seems to be controlled chiefly by visual stimuli. Things which are seen tend to be imitated or reproduced. What is heard is not reproduced. Obviously an animal which lacks the tendency to reinstate auditory stimuli—in other words to imitate sounds—cannot reasonably be expected to talk. The human infant exhibits this tendency to a remarkable degree. So also does the parrot. If the imitative tendency of the parrot could be coupled with the quality of intelligence of the chimpanzee, the latter undoubtedly could speak."

. . . As a method of prompting, we have been able to use imitation extensively to increase the frequency and refine the form of signs. Washoe sometimes fails to use a new sign in an appropriate situation, or uses another, incorrect sign. At such times we can make the correct sign to Washoe, repeating the performance until she makes the sign herself. (With more stable signs, more indirect forms of prompting can be used—for example, pointing at, or touching, Washoe's hand or a part of her body that should be involved in the sign; making the sign for "sign," which is equivalent to saying "Speak up"; or asking a question in signs, such as "What do you want?" or "What is it?") Again, with new signs, and often with old signs as well, Washoe can lapse into what we refer to as poor "diction." Of course, a great deal of slurring and a wide range of variants are permitted in ASL as in any spoken language. In any event, Washoe's diction has frequently been improved by the simple device of repeating, in exaggeratedly correct form, the sign she has just made, until she repeats it herself in more correct form. On the whole, she has responded quite well to prompting, but there are strict limits to its use with a wild animal—one that is probably quite spoiled, besides. Pressed too hard, Washoe can become completely diverted from her original object; she may ask for something entirely different, run away, go into a tantrum, or even bite her tutor.

Chimpanzees also imitate, after some delay, and this delayed imitation can be quite elaborate. The following is a typical example of Washoe's delayed imitation. From the beginning of the project she was bathed regularly and according to a standard routine. Also, from her 2nd month with us, she always had dolls to play with. One day, during the 10th month of the project, she bathed one of her dolls in the way we usually bathed her. She filled her little bathtub with water, dunked the doll in the tub, then took it out and dried it with a towel. She has repeated the entire performance, or parts of it, many times since, sometimes also soaping the doll.

This is a type of imitation that may be very important in the acquisition of language by human children, and many of our procedures with Washoe were devised to capitalize on it. Routine activities—feeding, dressing, bathing, and so on—have been highly ritualized, with appropriate signs figuring prominently in the rituals. Many games have been invented which can be accompanied by appropriate signs. Objects and activities have been named as often as possible, especially when Washoe seemed to be paying particular attention to them. New objects and new examples of familiar objects, including pictures, have been continually brought to her attention, together with the appropriate signs. She likes to ride in automobiles, and a ride in an automobile, including the preparations for a ride, provides a wealth of sights that can be accompanied by signs. A good destination for a ride is a home or the university nursery school, both well stocked with props for language lessons.

Some of Washoe's signs seem to have been originally acquired by delayed imitation. A good example is the sign for "toothbrush." A part of the daily routine has been to brush her teeth after every meal. When this routine was first introduced Washoe generally resisted it. She gradually came to submit with less and less fuss, and after many months she would even help or sometimes brush her teeth herself. Usually, having finished her meal, Washoe would try to leave her highchair; we would restrain her, signing "First, toothbrushing, then you can go." One day, in the 10th month of the project, Washoe was visiting the Gardner home and found her way into the bathroom. She climbed up on the counter, looked at our mug full of toothbrushes, and signed "toothbrush." At the time, we believed that Washoe understood this sign but we had not seen her use it. She had no reason to ask for the toothbrushes, because they were well within her reach, and it is most unlikely that she was asking to have her teeth brushed. This was our first observation, and one of the clearest examples, of behavior in which Washoe seemed to name an object or an event for no obvious motive other than communication.

Following this observation, the toothbrushing routine at mealtime was altered. First, imitative prompting was introduced. Then as the sign became more reliable, her rinsing-mug and toothbrush were displayed prominently until she made the sign. By the 14th month she was making the "toothbrush" sign at the end of meals with little or no prompting; in fact she has called for her toothbrush in a peremptory fashion when its appearance at the end of a meal was delayed. The "toothbrush" sign is not merely a response cued by the end of a meal; Washoe retained her ability to name toothbrushes when they were shown to her at other times.

The sign for "flower" may also have been acquired by delayed imitation. From her first summer with us, Washoe showed a great interest in flowers, and we took advantage of this by providing many flowers and pictures of flowers accompanied by the appropriate sign. Then one day in the 15th month she made the sign, spontaneously, while she and a companion were walking toward a flower garden. As in the case of "toothbrush," we believed that she understood the sign at this time, but we had made no attempt

TABLE 1. Signs used reliably by chimpanzee Washoe within 22 months of the beginning of training. The signs are listed in the order of their original appearance in her repertoire.

Signs	*Description*	*Context*
Come-gimme	Beckoning motion, with wrist or knuckles as pivot.	Sign made to persons or animals, also for objects out of reach. Often combined: "come tickle," "gimme sweet," etc.
More	Fingertips are brought together, usually overhead. (Correct ASL form: tips of the tapered hand touch repeatedly.)	When asking for continuation or repetition of activities such as swinging or tickling, for second helpings of food, etc. Also used to ask for repetition of some performance, such as a somersault.
Up	Arm extends upward, and index finger may also point up.	Wants a lift to reach objects such as grapes on vine, or leaves; or wants to be placed on someone's shoulders; or wants to leave potty-chair.
Sweet	Index or index and second fingers touch tip of wagging tongue. (Correct ASL form: index and second fingers extended side by side.)	For dessert; used spontaneously at end of meal. Also, when asking for candy.
Open	Flat hands are placed side by side, palms down, then drawn apart while rotated to palms up.	At door of house, room, car, refrigerator, or cupboard; on containers such as jars; and on faucets.
Tickle	The index finger of one hand is drawn across the back of the other hand. (Related to ASL "touch.")	For tickling or for chasing games.
Go	Opposite of "come-gimme."	While walking hand-in-hand or riding on someone's shoulders. Washoe usually indicates the direction desired.

Out	Curved hand grasps tapered hand; then tapered hand is withdrawn upward.	When passing through doorways; until recently, used for both "in" and "out." Also, when asking to be taken outdoors.
Hurry	Open hand is shaken at the wrist. (Correct ASL form: index and second fingers extended side by side.)	Often follows signs such as "come-gimme," "out," "open," and "go," particularly if there is a delay before Washoe is obeyed. Also, used while watching her meal being prepared.
Hear-listen	Index finger touches ear.	For loud or strange sounds: bells, car horns, sonic booms, etc. Also, for asking someone to hold a watch to her ear.
Toothbrush	Index finger is used as brush, to rub front teeth.	When Washoe has finished her meal, or at other times when shown a toothbrush.
Drink	Thumb is extended from fisted hand and touches mouth.	For water, formula, soda pop, etc. For soda pop, often combined with "sweet."
Hurt	Extended index fingers are jabbed toward each other. Can be used to indicate location of pain.	To indicate cuts and bruises on herself or on others. Can be elicited by red stains on a person's skin or by tears in clothing.
Sorry	Fisted hand clasps and unclasps at shoulder. (Correct ASL form: fisted hand is rubbed over heart with circular motion.)	After biting someone, or when someone has been hurt in another way (not necessarily by Washoe). When told to apologize for mischief.
Funny	Tip of index finger presses nose, and Washoe snorts. (Correct ASL form: index and second fingers used; no snort.)	When soliciting interaction play, and during games. Occasionally, when being pursued after mischief.

Please	Open hand is drawn across chest. (Correct ASL form: fingertips used, and circular motion.)	When asking for objects and activities. Frequently combined: "Please go," "Out, please," "Please drink."
Food-eat	Several fingers of one hand are placed in mouth. (Correct ASL form: fingertips of tapered hand touch mouth repeatedly.)	During meals and preparation of meals.
Flower	Tip of index finger touches one or both nostrils. (Correct ASL form: tips of tapered hand touch first one nostril, then the other.)	For flowers.
Cover-blanket	Draws one hand toward self over the back of the other.	At bedtime or naptime, and, on cold days, when Washoe wants to be taken out.
Dog	Repeated slapping on thigh.	For dogs and for barking.
You	Index finger points at a person's chest.	Indicates successive turns in games. Also used in response to questions such as "Who tickle?" "Who brush?"
Napkin-bib	Fingertips wipe the mouth region.	For bib, for washcloth, and for Kleenex.
In	Opposite of "out."	Wants to go indoors, or wants someone to join her indoors.
Brush	The fisted hand rubs the back of the open hand several times. (Adapted from ASL "polish.")	For hairbrush, and when asking for brushing.
Hat	Palm pats top of head.	For hats and caps.
I-me	Index finger points at, or touches, chest.	Indicates Washoe's turn, when she and a companion share food, drink, etc. Also used in phrases such as "I drink," and in reply to questions such as "Who tickle?" (Washoe: "you"); "Who I tickle?" (Washoe: "Me.")

Shoes	The fisted hands are held side by side and strike down on shoes or floor. (Correct ASL form: the sides of the fisted hands strike against each other.)	For shoes and boots.
Smell	Palm is held before nose and moved slightly upward several times.	For scented objects: tobacco, perfume, sage, etc.
Pants	Palms of the flat hands are drawn up against the body toward waist.	For diapers, rubber pants, trousers.
Clothes	Fingertips brush down the chest.	For Washoe's jacket, nightgown, and shirts; also for our clothing.
Cat	Thumb and index finger grasp cheek hair near side of mouth and are drawn outward (representing cat's whiskers).	For cats.
Key	Palm of one hand is repeatedly touched with the index finger of the other. (Correct ASL form: crooked index finger is rotated against palm.)	Used for keys and locks and to ask us to unlock a door.
Baby	One forearm is placed in the crook of the other, as if cradling a baby.	For dolls, including animal dolls such as a toy horse and duck.
Clean	The open palm of one hand is passed over the open palm of the other.	Used when Washoe is washing, or being washed, or when a companion is washing hands or some other object. Also used for "soap."

to elicit it from her except by making it ourselves in appropriate situations. Again, after the first observation, we proceeded to elicit this sign as often as possible by a variety of methods, most frequently by showing her a flower and giving it to her if she made the sign for it. Eventually the sign became very reliable and could be elicited by a variety of flowers and pictures of flowers. . . .

Almost from the first she had a begging gesture—an extension of her open hand, palm up, toward one of us. She made this gesture in situations in which she wanted aid and in situations in which we were holding some object that she wanted. The ASL signs for "give me" and "come" are very similar to this, except that they involve a prominent beckoning movement. Gradually Washoe came to incorporate a beckoning wrist movement into her use of this sign. In Table 1 we refer to this sign as "come-gimme." As Washoe has come to use it, the sign is not simply a modification of the original begging gesture. For example, very commonly she reaches forward with one hand (palm up) while she gestures with the other hand (palm down) held near her head. (The result resembles a classic fencing posture.)

Another sign of this type is the sign for "hurry," which, so far, Washoe has always made by shaking her open hand vigorously at the wrist. This first appeared as an impatient flourish following some request that she had made in signs; for example, after making the "open" sign before a door. The correct ASL for "hurry" is very close, and we began to use it often, ourselves, in appropriate contexts. We believe that Washoe has come to use this sign in a meaningful way, because she has frequently used it when she, herself, is in a hurry—for example, when rushing to her nursery chair. . . .

The sign for "open" had a similar history. When Washoe wanted to get through a door, she tended to hold up both hands and pound on the door with her palms or her knuckles. This is the beginning position for the "open" sign (see Table 1). By waiting for her to place her hands on the door and then lift them, and also by imitative prompting, we were able to shape a good approximation of the "open" sign, and would reward this by opening the door. Originally she was trained to make this sign for three particular doors that she used every day. Washoe transferred this sign to all doors; then to containers such as the refrigerator, cupboards, drawers, briefcases, boxes, and jars; and eventually—an invention of Washoe's—she used it to ask us to turn on water faucets.

In the case of "more" and "open" we followed the conventional laboratory procedure of waiting for Washoe to make some response that could be shaped into the sign we wished her to acquire. We soon found that this was not necessary; Washoe could acquire signs that were first elicited by our holding her hands, forming them into the desired configuration, and then putting them through the desired movement. Since this procedure of guidance is usually much more practical than waiting for a spontaneous approximation to occur at a favorable moment, we have used it much more frequently.

Combinations. During the phase of the project covered by this article we made no deliberate attempts to elicit combinations or phrases, although we may have responded more readily to strings of two or more signs than to single signs. As far as we can judge, Washoe's early use of signs in strings was spontaneous. Almost as soon as she had eight or ten signs in her repertoire, she began to use them two and three at a time. As her repertoire increased, her tendency to produce strings of two or more signs also increased, to the point where this has become a common mode of signing for her. We, of course, usually signed to her in combinations, but if Washoe's use of combinations has been imitative, then it must be a generalized sort of imitation, since she has invented a number of combinations, such as "gimme tickle" (before we had ever asked her to tickle us), and "open food drink" (for the refrigerator—we have always called it the "cold box").

Four signs—"please," "come-gimme," "hurry," and "more" —used with one or more other signs, account for the largest share of Washoe's early combinations. In general, these four signs have functioned as emphasizers, as in "please open hurry" and "gimme drink please."

Until recently, five additional signs—"go," "out," "in," "open," and "hear-listen"—accounted for most of the remaining combinations. Typical examples of combinations using these four are, "go in" or "go out" (when at some distance from a door), "go sweet" (for being carried to a raspberry bush), "open flower" (to be let through the gate to a flower garden), "open key" (for a locked door), "listen eat" (at the sound of an alarm clock signaling mealtime), and "listen dog" (at the sound of barking by an unseen dog). All but the first and last of these six examples were inventions of Washoe's. Combinations of this type tend to amplify the meaning of the single signs used. Sometimes, however, the function of these five signs has been about the same as that of the emphasizers, as in "open out" (when standing in front of a door).

Toward the end of the period covered in this article we were able to introduce the pronouns "I-me" and "you," so that combinations that resemble short sentences have begun to appear.

Concluding Observations

From time to time we have been asked questions such as, "Do you think that Washoe has language?" or "At what point will you be able to say that Washoe has language?" We find it very difficult to respond to these questions because they are altogether foreign to the spirit of our research. They imply a distinction between one class of communicative behavior that can be called language and another class that cannot. This in turn implies a well-established theory that could provide the distinction. If our objectives had required such a theory, we would certainly not have been able to begin this project as early as we did.

In the first phase of the project we were able to verify the hypothesis that sign language is an appropriate medium of two-way communication for the chimpanzee. Washoe's intellectual immaturity, the continuing acceleration of her progress, the fact that her signs do not remain specific to their original referents but are transferred spontaneously to new referents, and the emergence of rudimentary combinations all suggest that significantly more can be accomplished by Washoe during the subsequent phases of this project. As we proceed, the problems of these subsequent phases will be chiefly concerned with the technical business of measurement. We are now developing a procedure for testing Washoe's ability to name objects. In this procedure, an object or a picture of an object is placed in a box with a window. An observer, who does not know what is in the box, asks Washoe what she sees through the window. At present, this method is limited to items that fit in the box; a more ingenious method will have to be devised for other items. In particular, the ability to combine and recombine signs must be tested. Here, a great deal depends upon reaching a stage at which Washoe produces an extended series of signs in answer to questions. Our hope is that Washoe can be brought to the point where she describes events and situations to an observer who has no other source of information.

At an earlier time we would have been more cautious about suggesting that a chimpanzee might be able to produce extended utterances to communicate information. We believe now that it is the writers—who would predict just what it is that no chimpanzee will ever do—who must proceed with caution. Washoe's accomplishments will probably be exceeded by another chimpanzee, because it is unlikely that the conditions of training have been optimal in this first attempt. Theories of language that depend upon the identification of aspects of language that are exclusively human must remain tentative until a considerably larger body of intensive research with other species becomes available. . . .

Leaving the apes for the moment, we find John Lilly concentrating on dolphins. The following notes are from a transcript of a talk given at Big Sur, California.

ON DOLPHINS

The brain of the dolphin is first-class. It has everything that the human brain has, plus more cerebral cortex. The shark has a body weighing forty tons and a tiny brain; the whale has just brain enough for survival; why has the dolphin so much brain? It is not there just for us to admire. It has forty percent more than we have, though the brain-body ratio is roughly the same as ours. Dolphins can reply to questions of all kinds, including questions about life-situations. They have three voices, independently controlled, and can detect and use patterns ten times per second faster than we can. Everything the dolphin perceives it perceives acoustically: its sight is minimal. It uses its sonar against sharks. Dolphins perceive by echoes, and their nostrils transmit sound which is reflected off their internal organs. Dolphins breathe air, but deliberately, as we walk: the first thing a mother dolphin teaches her child is to breathe, and no dolphin can breathe automatically, so if it is anesthetized it dies, unless artificial respiration is continually given.

The dolphin has an X-ray acoustic medium by which it can "see" lungs, heart; but it can "see" humans only when they are submerged. It is possible that the stories of dolphins rescuing drowning men are true, for they can "see" when a human body is in distress.

All communication is limited by the language one knows, so the dolphin can only communicate acoustically. A dolphin's hearing goes up from 1000 cycles per second to 170 kilocycles. When communicating with human beings, they abandon the upper cycles and come down to our band. They communicate ten times faster than we do, using their larynx to whistle. They also have a clicking system.

Peter Marler, of Rockefeller University, has raised general theoretical questions about animal language, querying whether general linguistic theory, heretofore conceived only in connection with human language, may have significant implications for animal communication.

* * *

BIRDSONG AND SPEECH DEVELOPMENT: COULD THERE BE PARALLELS?[14]

Ever since Aesop animals have served as a kind of mirror for man, although the reflections are usually viewed with some sense of condescension on our part. It is obvious to anyone who thinks even half seriously about the matter that man and the animals are fundamentally different, or so we are told. Yet it may be that the chances of solving some of the questions that plague us about human behavior would be increased if we remind ourselves that man still has much in common with his animal ancestry. Some of our confusion about the position to take vis-a-vis our animal ancestors surely stems from uncertainty concerning the appropriate questions to ask about the causes of our own behavior. If we can only achieve a more thorough understanding of the rules that govern the behavior of animals, we may then be in a better position to develop more revealing hypotheses about ourselves.

Human Relevance of Animal Studies

Curiously, many people are still unconvinced of the relevance of animal studies to man, at least with regard to psychology. At the level of cellular biology and physiology, even that of the nervous system, we all accept the many parallels between animals and man, and much of the science of medicine is based on the assumption that studies on rats, dogs, and monkeys have a bearing on human medicine. But the same notion seems much harder to accept at the psychological level. We are tempted to think that the extent to which our behavior is shaped by cultural influences in general—and by language in particular—removes us so far from the condition in other organisms that any parallels are remote and essentially irrelevant to the understanding of the behavior of anyone more mature than a babe in arms. My own view is that animal studies are as relevant in the psychological realm as in physiology in understanding the human condition. If this is not yet obvious to most people, I believe it is because our understanding of animals is still so incomplete.

In past years my colleagues and I have spent a good deal of time studying the behavior of birds. The results have no direct human import, but I would like to present some of them within the framework of a comparison with our own language, to try to show that there are parallels worthy of note. Specifically, I want to suggest that the processes by which sounds develop in animals have several properties that are echoed in children.

If one were looking for parallels with the process of human vocal learning, the most obvious place to look would be in our closest surviving relatives, the apes and monkeys. Surprisingly, no one has yet discovered a non-human primate with any facility for vocal imitation. It is true that several apes have been taught a few words of human speech. In a famous experiment conducted in the thirties two young psychologists took a baby chimpanzee into their home and raised it as a child. One of their primary aims was to teach this young female chimpanzee, Vicki, to utter some words of human speech.

After considerable labor they were successful (Kellogg 1968). However, if you study the methods that were necessary to achieve these few words—"mama," "papa," and "cup"—it becomes clear that this was accomplished not by imitation in the usual sense but by gradual shaping of the separate movements of lips and jaw that produce the words. The labor and concentration involved, both for experimenter and subject, are on a quite different scale from the effortless mimicry of the human infant. Thus Vicki's vocal accomplishments are interesting, but they do not throw any light on the processes involved in speech development.

In searching for parallels, it is necessary to go beyond other primates and, with the possible exception of dolphins, even beyond other mammals, to the birds, to find any facility for vocal imitation at all. Parrots and mynah birds are commonly kept in homes because their ability to mimic sounds amuses their owners. Several investigators have been convinced that study of speech learning in mynah birds might illuminate our understanding of human speech development. Some of the results are interesting, but I am convinced that the inferences to be drawn from trying to teach birds human sounds are limited. Would it not be more illuminating to find a species in which learning plays a key role in the normal vocal development and analyze the processes involved there, and then attempt a comparison with ourselves? That at any rate is what we have tried to do with several species of wild birds, and the results do indeed suggest parallels with human vocal development.

In both our own species and in certain birds, learning of young from adult plays a major role in the development of natural patterns of vocalizations. In both cases dialects arise as a consequence of that learning. There is in both a certain critical period of life during which the ability for vocal learning is at its maximum. We can see in both child and bird predispositions emerging during this critical period which have the effect of guiding the learning in certain directions. Hearing plays a special role in both cases, not only to allow the young organism to hear sounds of adults of its species, but also in allowing it to hear its own voice, as a vital factor in normal development. There are early stages of vocal development, the so-called babbling of infants and what we call subsong in birds, which have a number of properties in common that are probably not coincidental. The process of vocal imitation may prove to be essentially self-reinforcing in both cases and thus basically independent of reward by the parent. And finally, there is a remarkable parallel in the tendency for one side of the brain to assume dominant control of the sound-producing equipment, the larynx in man, the syrinx in birds.

If we record and analyze the sounds that a species uses in the course of its life cycle, they can be arranged in categories according to their physical structure. From such an analysis it is possible to estimate the size of the acoustical repertoire for a species. Although our knowledge is limited, some generalizations are beginning to emerge. The largest repertoires to be found among birds and mammals are considerably greater than those of frogs and fish and invertebrate animals. As far as one can tell there is no great difference between birds and mammals in this regard. For example, an estimate of the number of basic vocalizations in the adult repertoires of animals might reveal a range of 5 to 14 sounds in birds and 5 to 17 in various monkeys and apes. Actually such comparisons provoke considerable argument, since in some species the sounds are organized in discrete, non-overlapping categories, whereas in others they grade into one another with a variety of subtle distinctions. In such cases, it is difficult to derive a meaningful estimate of repertoire size by descriptive analysis alone.

Functions of Birdsong and Calls

In birds, there is usually no difficulty in distinguishing between a variety of sounds, or calls, in which the fundamental acoustical unit is short, and the song, in which sequences of sounds are given in a more or less highly organized pattern. The song is usually the prerogative of the male. It is often the loudest sound in the repertoire. As we shall see, learning plays little part in the development of calls, but is often very important in the development of the male song.

A consideration of the situations in which birds utter sounds helps in understanding why calls and songs might differ in their development. As with other behavior, so the sounds of birds are given in more or less well-defined contexts. Some are characteristic of a particular age. Some vocalizations are heard the year around while others are restricted to birds in breeding condition. For example, adult chaffinches in non-reproductive condition use only two vocalizations at all commonly, a flight call and a social call (Marler 1956). These two calls evidently suffice for adequate organization of behavior in the winter flock. In the spring the flock breaks up, males stake out territories, each is typically joined by a female, and they raise a brood. As the level of sex hormones in the blood rises, several new vocalizations enter the repertoire, especially in the male.

Some of the new sounds that herald the coming breeding season—courtship and alarm calls, for example—occur only in a particular situation: approach of the mate or appearance of a predator, say. This is not true of the male song. Although it sometimes occurs in response to social stimulation, it more often seems to occur spontaneously.

The male song typically serves both to attract and retain a mate and to maintain the spacing of territorial males. Both functions require the male to broadcast evidence of his presence more or less continuously. By the same token, the male song serves for communication over long distances. In the breeding season of many bird species, the sound with the greatest volume and the highest frequency of utterance is the song of the male.

Reflection on the different functions served by the song and some of the calls may lead us to speculate about the rates of change that might be required in the course of evolution if the functions are to be served efficiently. For example, the alarm calls used by certain woodland birds are very similar, and this resemblance surely correlates with their frequent use in the interspecific communication of danger (Marler 1955). There is little for neighbors to gain by evolving very different alarm calls if they are endangered by the same predators. Thus in the case of alarm calls efficient functioning requires only a minimum of specific divergence in the course of evolution. Quite the reverse is true of the male song. For a male white-crowned sparrow to attract a female white-crowned sparrow and to repel other male white-crowns, it is important that there be no danger of confusion with the songs of other species. It is surely no accident that even close relatives usually have highly divergent song patterns if they are sympatric.

Given the recent multiplication of the numbers of species of song birds and the fact that many species are to be heard in any given area, the functions of song require a high rate of structural change in the course of evolution. This may be important to maintain separation not only from other species but even from separate populations of the same species. With different rates of change required for different vocalizations within the repertoire, the stage is set for some radical innovation in the mechanisms of development. If there is a dominant role for learning in the development of the male song of some birds, this may perhaps be viewed as a response to an evolutionary demand for rapid change.

The White-crowned Sparrow

The song of the male white-crowned sparrow, which we studied in California, has a distinctive and elaborate acoustical pattern that is normally learned in nature. A male raised in social isolation from five days of age, with no opportunity to hear other sparrows, develops an abnormal song. To correct the sequence of development into normal channels, it is sufficient, under the same experimental conditions, to play recorded songs to the young male—about 60 songs a day for three weeks. He will subsequently develop normal song. Field study reveals that the learning generates local dialects; groups of birds only a few miles apart have song patterns that are in certain respects distinctively and consistently different from one another (Marler and Tamura 1962).

On exploring the nature of the learning processes involved, by varying the age at which the young male is exposed to recorded song, we find that there are constraints upon the time of life at which learning will take place, and constraints on what sounds will be learned. A period from 10 to 50 days of age seems to be critical in learning a song pattern to which a male is exposed. Whether song develops normally or abnormally, additional auditory experience has no further effect (Marler 1970).

Another kind of constraint emerges if we present during this period recordings not of one sound but of two, for example his own specific song and the song of another species. Under these conditions he learns his own and rejects the other. If he is exposed only to alien song during this period, it is likewise rejected and song develops as in an isolated bird. With another kind of approach, we find that the ability of the bird to hear itself has a special role. There is normally a delay of several months between learning and singing. If we deafen a bird during this interval, he subsequently develops a highly abnormal song (Konishi 1965); he has to be able to hear himself if he is to translate what is learned into the motor pattern of song. If, on the other hand, the deafening is postponed until song development is complete, then it has little or no effect on the motor pattern. Here and elsewhere, one may already perceive some distant but intriguing parallels with human speech development.

I am also trying to make another point: if we had set out to try to teach sparrows human speech, or to teach children birdsong for that matter, the results would have been negative. This would, of course, have told us something, but something of limited value. As it is, we have made some progress in understanding how learning plays a part in vocal development in this species, and we find it makes sense in terms of the general biology of the species. This may in turn serve to remind us that human language is a biological phenomenon with an evolutionary history.

The predispositions brought to the task of vocal learning have a special interest. In the sparrows they play a prominent role in determining the course development will take. And if we think back to the environmental situation in which learning occurs, it becomes clear that such predispositions are important if the learning process is not to lead to the incorporation into the repertoire of biologically inappropriate sounds. In the habitat in which the white-crowned sparrows are common, one can stand by the nest, and as often as not the closest singing bird will be a member of another species, namely the song sparrow. A male white-crowned sparrow who had learned song sparrow song would be a social misfit. At best he might waste a great deal of time before finding a deaf female white-crowned sparrow for a mate, at worst he might have to make do with a female song sparrow and run the risk of infertile offspring. Viewed in this light, it seems natural, indeed almost inevitable, that a species would evolve constraints on the learning process. We are prone to forget that the very openness that learning brings with it can lead to biological hazards as well as advantages.

Karl von Frisch carries investigation of speech from the animal to the insect world.

THE LANGUAGE OF BEES[15]

Training experiments designed to throw light on the co-ordination of the bee's various sense organs [require] . . . for their success that the trainees should make their appearance at the place where we intend to train them. To attract them to it, a simple device can be used: a few sheets of paper liberally smeared with honey are placed on the experimental table. It may take many hours or days even before a foraging worker appears; but once her attention is aroused by the smell of honey, she will soon regale herself greedily with the rich food. From now on we have an easy task, and we may start preparing our experiment, assured that not only will our first bee return to her food a few minutes later, but that dozens, nay hundreds, of newcomers will appear at our table within a few hours. If we try to trace their origin we shall find that almost without exception they came from the same colony as the first discoverer of the feeding-place. Hence it appears that in some way or other this first-comer must not only have announced her rich find to the other bees in the hive, but must also have led some of them out to it so that they might exploit it for themselves.

What we should like to know is *how* she did it. There is one way, and one way only, of obtaining a clear idea of the course of these events: this is actually to watch the behaviour of the returning bee as well as that of her companions who respond to her. This would not be feasible in an ordinary beehive but it can be done in a specially constructed observation hive. . . . By the side of such a hive we place a little dish filled with food. As soon as a visitor alights on it we mark her with paint so as to be able to distinguish her from her companions amidst the bustle of the hive, and not lose sight of her again. In this way we shall see her coming in through the entrance hole, running up the combs, and presently stopping, to remain seated motionless for a short time, surrounded by her hive-mates. She then disgorges from her stomach all the honey she has just collected. This honey, which appears as a glistening droplet in her mouth, is immediately sucked up by two or three of her companions who face her with their tongues outstretched. These are the bees who are responsible for disposing of the honey; they walk along the combs and, according to the colony's immediate needs, either feed their hungry companions or place the honey in the storage cells—internal matters these, with which the forager bee does not waste her time. While all these activities are going on, a drama is being enacted worthy of the pen of one of those great classical poets who have sung the praises of the bee. But, alas! it had not been discovered during their life-time. The kindly reader will therefore have to content himself with the following prosaic description.

A Round Dance as Means of Communication

The foraging bee, having got rid of her load, begins to perform a kind of "round dance". On the part of the comb where she is sitting she starts whirling around in a narrow circle, constantly changing her direction, turning now right, now left, dancing clockwise and anti-clockwise in quick succession, describing between one and two circles in each direction. This dance is performed among the thickest bustle of the hive. What makes it so particularly striking and attractive is the way it infects the surrounding bees; those sitting next to the dancer start tripping after her, always trying to keep their outstretched feelers in close contact with the tip of her abdomen. They take part in each of her manoeuvrings so that the dancer herself, in her madly wheeling movements, appears to carry behind her a perpetual comet's tail of bees. In this way they keep whirling round and round, sometimes for a few seconds, sometimes for as long as half a minute, or even a full minute, before the dancer suddenly stops, breaking loose from her followers to disgorge a second or even a third droplet of honey while settling on one, or two other parts of the comb, each time concluding with a similar dance. This done, she hurries towards the entrance hole again to take off for her particular feeding-place, from where she is sure to bring back another load; the same performance being enacted at each subsequent return.

Under normal circumstances, the dance takes place in the darkness of a closed hive. Thus the dancer cannot be seen by her comrades. If they notice her behaviour and run after her every time she turns, they can only do so through their sense of feeling and smell.

What is the meaning of this round dance? One thing is obvious: it causes enormous excitement among the inmates of the hive sitting nearest to the dancers. Moreover, if we watch one of the bees in the dancer's train, we may actually see her preparing to depart, cleaning herself perfunctorily, then hurrying off in the direction of the entrance hole to leave the hive. In this case it is not long before the original discoverer of the feeding-place is joined there by the first newcomers. After returning with their loads, the new bees will dance in their turn; the greater the number of dancers, the greater will be the number of newcomers crowding around the feeding place. The relation between these two factors has now been established beyond any doubt: it is the dancing inside the hive that announces a rich find of food to the colony. But the problem that still remains unsolved is, how do the bees thus informed manage to find the *exact place* where the food is to be found?

The following explanation suggests itself: at the end of the dance, the bees informed by it might perhaps start rushing towards the entrance hole at the same time as the dancer, to fly after her on her next visit to the feeding-place. But this is definitely not the case. By keeping a close watch on the hive we may satisfy ourselves that no other bee ever keeps pace with the dancer during her hasty run over the combs towards the entrance hole; and, watching the dancer on her arrival at the feeding place, we may be equally sure that not a single bee has actually followed her in her flight. The arrival of newcomers at the feeding-place is sudden and unexpected, and quite independent of whether the honey has been replaced by a dish of pure sugar-water to avoid any attraction by scent. The method by which the position of the feeding place is communicated remained a mystery for quite a long time.

Then suddenly the mystery was solved in a very simple way in so far as targets situated near the hive were concerned. Suppose our feeding-place is situated at a distance of a little over ten yards to the south of the hive. Here, to a little dish of sugar-water, we manage to attract a group of about twelve bees which are marked immediately on their arrival. They go on collecting, and on their return to the hive they will each perform their dance on the combs. Next we place on the grass several glass dishes containing sugar-water, with a little honey added to make it easier for the bees to find them; these dishes are placed at a distance of about twenty yards, at all four points of the compass, north, south, east, and west of the hive. A few minutes after the first bees have started dancing, forager bees belonging to our colony will appear at *each* of the dishes. They do not know exactly where the dancers had been foraging; they just swarm out in all directions. There is such a crowd that at least some of them are bound to find the original feeding place almost at once, joining as newcomers those bees that had been marked before; while the rest discover the remaining dishes placed all round the hive. About the same number of bees will be found at each dish.

Hence a further question arises: how big is the area over which the search flights are extended?

In the following experiment, while retaining our first feeding-place near the hive, we place the remaining feeding-dishes further and further away. The greater the distance the longer the time it will take the newcomers to find them. However, even in our last experiment, with the little feeding-dish placed at a distance of more than half a mile away in the middle of a vast meadow, where it looked quite lost in the long grass, and where it was separated from the hive by valleys as well as by wooded hills, even there the bees arrived in the end, if only in small numbers and after four hours' delay. All the bees who settled on this dish were marked at once, and their departure from the feeding place was then reported to the people waiting at the hive by means of signals passed along a chain of relays, so that before many minutes had passed we knew that those bees had not just been chance visitors dropping in from one of the neighbouring apiaries, but had been members of our observation hive that had been summoned by their own dancers.

Suppose we remove the little sugar-water dish from our feeding table, so that our marked bees find that there is no food in the usual place? They will behave exactly as they would if their natural food, the honey flow, had dried up owing to bad weather, when their usual flowers temporarily cease to provide them with nectar. The bees will stay at home, and stop dancing. From then on the little honey dishes laid out round the hive may have to wait on the lawn for hours or even days on end before a single bee will visit them again.

This may surprise the reader who knows that those few bees marked at our feeding-place are by no means the only foragers in our colony. While they were frequenting our sugar-water dishes, hundreds if not thousands of their hive mates must have been foraging on various flowers, collecting pollen as well as honey; and they must have gone on foraging long after the flow of sugar-water at our artificial feeding place had been suspended.

Why have those other foragers on their return from the flowers not aroused their companions by dancing, and sent them off in their turn searching in all directions, so that among other things they would also find the dishes? The answer is this: those who have found a *rich* source of nectar will certainly send their companions off to seek for food; not to sugar-water dishes, however, but to exactly the same sort of flowers that they themselves have just been successfully exploiting.

New Light on the Biological Significance of Flower Scent

Flowers, not glass dishes, are the bee's natural drinking vessels. We shall come nearer to natural conditions by offering at our feeding site a little bunch of flowers, e.g. cyclamen, instead of our dish of sugar-water. To enable us to use any kind of flower we like for feeding purposes, regardless of how much nectar it happens to secrete at the time, each blossom is provided with a drop of sugar-water, replenished as soon as it is sucked up. So that the bees may go to the flowers only, and not pick up any sugar-water drops which may fall on the table, we stand the vase in a fairly large bowl of water. The marked bees, finding a rich source of food provided for them by the cyclamen, will perform their usual dances on the combs.

In another place, selected a random, we arrange on the grass a bowl of cyclamen *without* any sugar-water, by the side of a bowl of flowers of a different kind, e.g. phlox. Soon the alarm given by the dancers begins to have its effect: bees begin to appear all over the meadow, swarming about in their search for food. Having discovered our flower bowls, they make for the cyclamen, in which they bury themselves with a persistence suggesting that they are convinced that something is to be found there. But they pass by the bowl of phlox without taking the slightest interest in it.

Next, the cyclamen at our original feeding-site are replaced by phlox blossoms which in their turn have been richly doped with sugar-water. Now the same foragers, which not long ago had been busy on cyclamen, make for the phlox. On the lawn our arrangement of vases, though itself unchanged, will provide a completely new picture within a few minutes: while interest in the cyclamen begins to slacken, the newcomers start visiting phlox, and what is more, we can see them flying into the neighbour's garden as well, where they busy themselves with all the phlox plants they can find. This is a strange sight for those who know that none but a butterfly's very long tongue can penetrate the deep floral tubes of the phlox blossoms. The bee, with her short proboscis, is quite unable to reach the nectar hidden deep down in the flower and is therefore normally not seen on phlox. Obviously the foraging bees know exactly what to look for, which means that the dancers inside the hive must have told them exactly what sort of flower had offered them so rich a reward.

The experiment described here is sure to be successful; no matter whether the food is offered on cyclamen or phlox, on gentian or vetch, thistle blossom or ranunculus, beans or immortelles. If we consider the conditions prevailing in nature we soon realize how appropriate this behaviour is on the part of the bee: whenever a plant newly come into flower is discovered by the scout bees, they announce their discovery by means of a dance; their companions thus aroused are then able to go straight to the flowers whose rich nectar secretion has provoked the dancing, instead of wasting their time fruitlessly seeking among flowers which may have nothing to offer. But how is this behaviour to be explained?

It is unbelievable that the bee language should possess a separate expression for every variety of flower. Yet such is the case. Revealed to us here is a language of flowers in the true sense of the word—incredibly simple, charming, and well-designed for its purpose. While the forager-bee is sucking the sweet juice out of a flower, a trace of its scent adheres to her body. While dancing on her return she still carries this scent. Her companions who trip after her briskly examining her with their feelers—which act as their organs of smell—are able to perceive it. They commit it to memory and then go out in search of it, swarming all over the place in consequence of this latest "alarm".

We can make this relation even more evident if we replace our natural flowers by essential oils or by an artificial scent. . . .

The "Wagging Dance" Tells the Distance of the Food Supply

For many years we carried on experiments with the feeding-place set up close to the hive. Accordingly it did not strike us as peculiar that, in the tests which followed each training, newcomers swarming out from the hive arrived at the place near the hive earlier and in greater numbers than they did at places which were farther off. There came a day, however, when we moved our feeding-place to a site several hundred yards from the hive. The number of newcomers to be seen searching near the hive immediately diminished; but large numbers of them kept arriving at the distant feeding-place. For the first time we began to suspect that the dancing might reveal, among other things, the distance that the foragers had to cover.

If bees from our observation hive are trained in such a way that one group of marked insects collects food from a place near the hive, while a second group, differently marked, collects it from a more distant place, we see this astonishing scene being enacted on the combs: while all the bees belonging to the first group perform their usual round dances, those belonging to the second group perform what I have called "wagging dances" (*Schwänzeltänze*). In these dances the bee runs along a narrow semi-circle, makes a sharp turn, and then runs back in a straight line to her starting point. Next she describes another semi-circle, this time in the opposite direction, thus completing a full circle, once more returning to her starting point in a straight line. She does this for several minutes, remaining on the same spot all the time: semi-circle to the left, straight back, then semi-circle to the right, straight back, and so on indefinitely. The characteristic feature which distinguishes this "wagging dance" from the "round dance" is a very striking, rapid wagging of the bee's abdomen performed only during her straight run. This wagging dance commands just as much attention among the bees tripping behind the dancer as does the round dance.

If our feeding-place is gradually moved from a place close to the hive to one further away from it, the round dance will begin to merge into a wagging dance when a distance of between fifty and one hundred yards is reached. If, on the other hand, we start at a distant feeding-place and move it step by step towards the hive, then the wagging dance will give way to a round dance, again at approximately the same distance. The round dance and the wagging dance represent two different words of the bee language: the round dance indicates the presence of a food source fairly near the hive, and the wagging dance points to one further afield. That this meaning is understood by the inmates of the hive was proved by experiment.

We know that the bee's range of flight extends two or three miles all round the hive. Therefore the knowledge that food was to be found either "less than a hundred yards away" or "more than a hundred yards away" from the hive would not in itself be very helpful. When in a new series of experiments we began to move the feeding-place in very small steps towards the outer boundary of the bee's range of flight, we finally discovered the law ruling the performance of the wagging dance, a law that enables bees as well as men to derive from observation of the dance much more precise information than could have been anticipated. It is this:

With a distance of a hundred yards between hive and feeding-place, the dances are hastily performed, the separate turns following each other in quick succession. But as the distance of the food supply increases these turns follow each other at longer and longer intervals, making the dances appear more and more stately, the straight waggle run at the same time gradually becoming more prolonged and more vigorous. Using a stop-watch we found that the bee travels along the straight part of the waggle run between nine and ten times in a quarter of a minute if the distance between the hive and the feeding-place is a hundred metres, six times at a distance of five hundred metres, four to five times at a distance of a thousand metres, twice at five thousand, and barely more than once at a distance of ten thousand metres. The agreement between measurements taken on different days, in different years, or even with different colonies, is simply amazing. This is all the more remarkable as the bees do not carry watches. Obviously they must possess a very acute sense of time, enabling the dancer to move in the rhythm appropriate to the occasion, and her companions to comprehend and interpret her movements correctly. Can they really do all this? And how accurately do the newcomers keep to the distance indicated to them by the wagging dance? In order to discover this, several numbered bees were fed with sugar-water to which a little lavender scent had been added, at a definite distance from the hive; similarly scented bait, but no food, was placed at other, varying, distances. The foragers danced on the combs, sending their comrades to look for the source of the lavender scent. During this experiment, the feeding-place was 750 metres away from the hive; scented boards without food were placed in the same direction at regular intervals of 75, 200, 400, 700, 800, 1,000, 1,500, 2,000, and 2,500 metres. An observer sat at each of these points, noting each bee that flew there in the course of an hour and a half. The numbers of new bees arriving at the different points are registered; the curve shows the result. In another test, the feeding-place was 2,000 metres from the hive and the scented bait lay at distances of 100, 400, 800, 1,200, 1,600, 1,950, 2,050, 2,400, 3,000, 4,000, and 5,000 metres. The bees, which had been notified by the dance, followed its indication beyond all expectation, persistently searching by the hour at the correct distances.

How do they know at all how far they have flown? Let us take a look at their measuring system in windy weather. If they encounter a head wind on their flight to the feeding-place, on their return they indicate a greater distance than if there had been no wind; with a following wind, a shorter distance is indicated. If there is no wind and they have to fly up a steep hillside to reach the feeding-place, the dance is affected as though the distance were longer; if the flight is downhill, the effect on the dance is as though the distance were shorter. It seems, therefore, that their calculation of distance depends on the time required or the strength exerted.

The Wagging Dance Also Indicates the Direction of the Food Supply

It would be of little use to the bees if they knew that a limetree was in full flower a mile away from the hive if at the same time they were ignorant of its direction. In fact, the wagging dance gives them this information as well. It is contained in the direction of the "wagging" runs during the figure of the dance.

For showing the right direction, bees use two different

methods, depending on whether the dance takes place (as it usually does) inside the hive on the *vertical* comb or outside on the *horizontal* platform. Direction-finding from a horizontal surface is probably older in the history of the bee folk. It is also easier to understand, so we shall begin with it. It should be remembered that the sun is used as a compass. When the foraging bee flies from the hive to the feeding-place with the sun at an angle of 40° to the left and in front of her, she keeps this angle in her wagging dance and thus indicates the direction of the feeding-place (fig. 43). The bees who follow after the dancer notice their own position with respect to the sun while following the wagging dance; by maintaining the same position on their flight, they obtain the direction of the feeding-source. This applies only if the dancer can see the sun—or at least blue sky—for instance during a dance on the alighting board. This takes place quite frequently when some of the inmates of the hive await the homecoming foragers outside on the board during warm weather. One can also take a comb out of the hive and hold it in a horizontal position in mid-air. The dancers are not easily fooled. They point in the direction in which they have been foraging, and if we rotate the horizontal comb like a railway turntable, they allow the dance floor to turn under their feet and keep their direction like a compass needle. But if we hide the sky from their eyes, they dance at random and become completely disorientated.

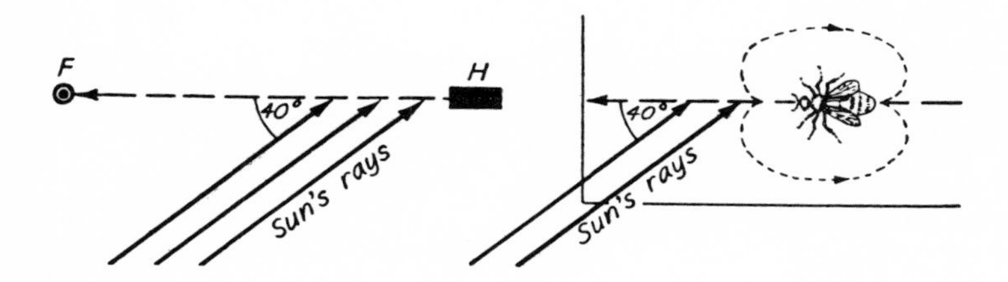

Fig. 43. Giving the sun's bearing in a wagging dance on a horizontal surface. Left: H, hive. F, feeding-place. Right: wagging dance on a horizontal surface. - - -, direction of flight to feeding-place.

Inside the hive it is dark, the sky is invisible; besides, the comb surfaces stand upright and so an indication of direction in the way we have just described is impossible. Under these circumstances the bees use the second method, a very remarkable one. Instead of using the horizontal angle with the sun, which they followed during their flight to the feeding-place, they indicate direction by means of gravity, in the following way: upward wagging runs mean that the feeding-place lies towards the sun; downward wagging runs indicate the opposite direction; upward wagging runs 60° to the left of the vertical point to a source of food 60° to the left of the direction of the sun (fig. 44) and so on. Experience gained by the newcomers in this way, in the darkness of the hive, by means of their delicate sense of feeling for gravity is transferred to a bearing on the sun once they are outside the hive.

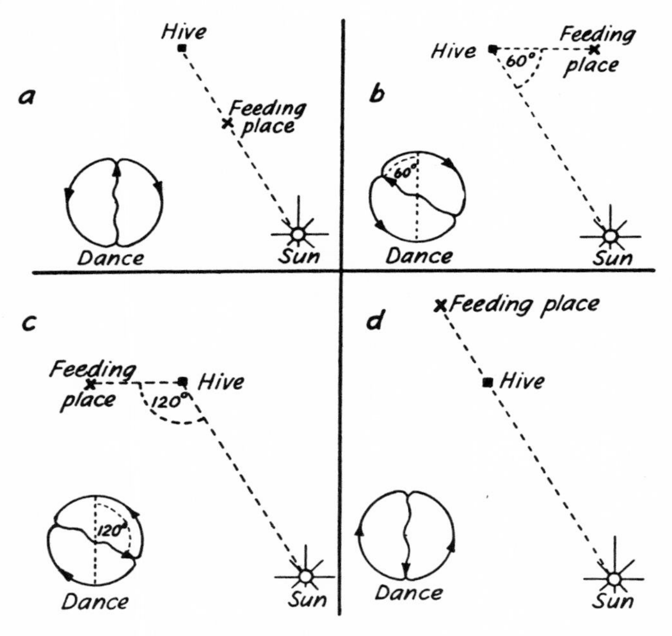

Fig. 44. Giving the sun's bearing in a dance on a vertical comb surface. The little diagrams on the left of each drawing show the dance as it appears on the vertical comb.

Just as we discovered from the "step experiment" whether the instructions about distance had been followed, so now we shall see by the "fan experiment" whether the bees really fly in the direction they have been given. Fig. 45 shows the results of such an experiment. A few numbered bees were fed on a scented foundation F, 250 yards away from the hive. Similar scented objects, this time without food, were arranged in the shape of a fan at angles of 15° from the hive and at a distance of 200 yards from it. The numbers in the diagram indicate the number of newcomers that arrived at the observation points during a test period of 1-1/2 hours. Only a few of the bees deviated from the right path.

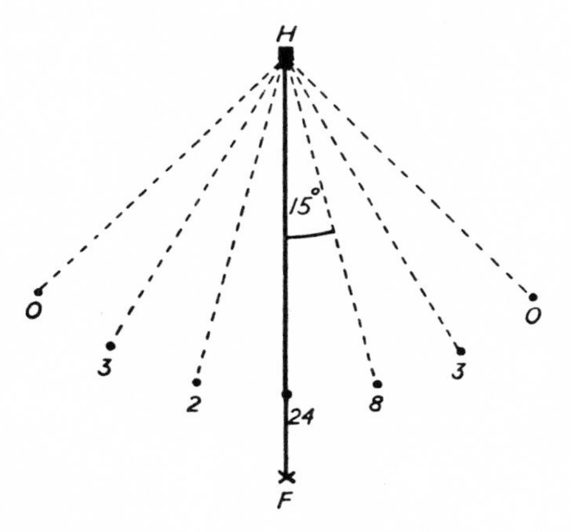

Fig. 45. The results of a "fan" experiment: H, hive. F, feeding-place. The black dots represent scented bait without *food, the numbers by each one indicate the humber of bees that arrived at each point.*

In mountainous country even flying creatures cannot always reach their objective by the most direct route. By what means will the bees show their hive-mates how to reach a source of food by an indirect route? There was plenty of opportunity to answer this question in the mountainous country near the Wolfgangsee. One day our observation hive was placed behind a ridge of rock on the Schafberg; a quickly-made feeding-place with numbered bees was set out at the foot of a cliff. . . . The sketch in fig. 46 shows a plan of the positions and distances in the area of the experiment. The foragers flew up and down along the track marked by two sides of the acute-angled triangle, but in their dances they indicated the direction neither of the take-off from the hive nor of the second part of the route to the objective—as in both cases they would have confused their fellows. The wagging run indicated the "bee-line" to the feeding-place, although actually they never flew along it. This was the only way they could guide their fellows to the right place; the latter flew in the direction shown for a limited period, since they knew from the dances what the correct *distance* should be and so they found their objective even with the detour. The behaviour of the guides was thus adjusted to the situation and was completely sensible. That they are able to fly by an indirect route and yet reconstruct the true direction without the aid of ruler, protractor, or drawing-board, is one of the most wonderful accomplishments in the life of the bee and indeed in all creation.

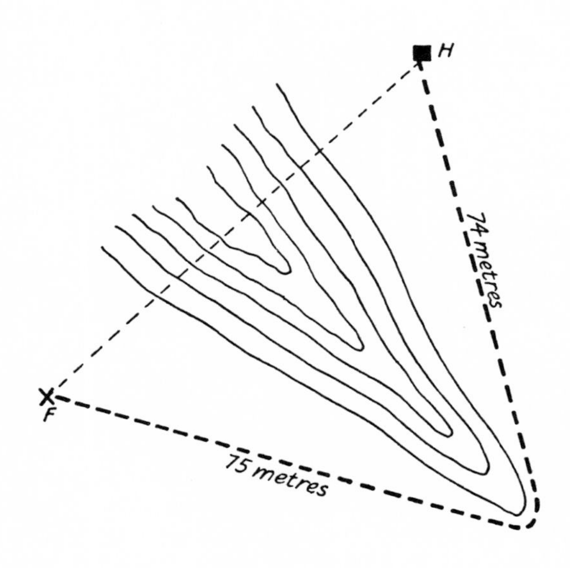

Fig. 46. Sketch of the "indirect route" experiment on the Shafberg. H, *hive.* F, *feeding-place.* - - - - - *course taken.* - - - - - *direct line to object.*

David Premack proposes that we consider the chimpanzee as a drawing board upon which we may perform selected experiments directly derivable from formal theories not only of language but also of logical inference. What follows was published in 1971.

From LANGUAGE IN CHIMPANZEE?[16]

SYMBOLIZATION: WHEN IS A PIECE OF PLASTIC A WORD?

When does a piece of plastic cease to be a piece of plastic and become a word? We might answer, When it is used as a word: that is, when it occurs along with other words of appropriate grammatical class in sentences and when it occurs as the answer or part of the answer to questions. For example, we consider a small piece of blue plastic to be the word for apple because (i) it is used when, for example, the subject requests apple and (ii) it is used by the subject to answer, "What is the name of apple?" We might add that the piece of plastic is a word when the properties ascribed to it by the subject are not those of the plastic itself, but those of the object it designates.

We can determine whether this condition obtains by using the matching-to-sample procedures again—this time to obtain independent analyses of the features of both the word and its referent. An analysis of the features of the apple was made by giving Sarah a series of trials. On each trial she was given the apple and a pair of alternatives and was required to indicate which of the alternatives she considered to be more like the apple. The alternatives were red versus green; round versus square; square with stemlike protuberance versus plain square; and plain round versus square with protuberances. The alternatives could be words or objects instancing the properties named by the words. That is, the subject could be required to decide whether the apple was more like the words "red" versus "green" or more like a red patch versus a green patch. Our use of the latter approach was dictated by Sarah's limited vocabulary.

After obtaining a features analysis of the apple, we repeated the test exactly with the word "apple" (a piece of blue plastic). The subject assigned the same properties to the plastic that she had earlier assigned to the apple. The properties she assigned to the word "apple" show that her analysis of the word was based not on the physical form of the blue piece of plastic, but on the object that the plastic represents.

Strictly speaking, we do not know the necessary and sufficient conditions for this effect, or even the specific point in training when the effect first becomes demonstrable. There are several intermediate possibilities, but consider the two major alternatives: (i) in the course of acquiring language, the organism learns how to symbolize; (ii) symbolization is an integral property of perhaps all learning and makes language possible. What form would symbolization take in lower organisms if the latter were true? A pigeon exposed to the fact that a vertical line preceded food A, and a horizontal line food B, would ascribe to the vertical line whatever features it ascribed to food A, and to the horizontal line whatever features it ascribed to food B. A nonlaboratory example may make the point still clearer. A dog noses a leash in a hallway. Is a walk into the house or out of it? into the fields or into town? with birds or without? squirrel scent or not? and so forth. When asked these questions of the walk, in one case, and of the leash, in the other, the dog's answers should be the same. We do not know if this is so, but can find out simply by adapting the procedures we used with the chimpanzee to the other species.

Assumption (ii) above seems the more reasonable, since it does not require the further assumption that it is possible to teach an organism that does not symbolize in the first place to symbolize. Of course it may be possible, but I do not see how, any more than I can see how to teach an organism that does not transfer to do so. Symbolization and transfer both lie at the heart of language learning. I suspect they have in common the fact that neither is instilled by the present training procedures, but is a capacity of the organism that is utilized by the training.

Premack's "assumption ii" (that symbolization underlies any process of learning and is therefore unlearned) resembles the position taken by Chomsky on human language, to be discussed in another section. The linguist Jakobson has remarked that it may be no accident that biology discovers, in the mechanism of the genetic code, a context-sensitive phrase structure grammar at the same time linguistics discovers that underlying each human language there **appears to exist a context-sensitive phrase structure grammar.**

The significant key that links together the new discoveries in molecular biology and the ever more precise attempts to formalise language is expressed by Jacques Monod, the Nobel Prize winner in genetics, who pays his tribute to George Boole in his *Chance and Necessity*.

From CHANCE AND NECESSITY[17]

The conclusions of a long study of this wonderfully and almost miraculously teleonomic phenomenon are summarized in Fig. 4. Here we need not discuss the right-hand part of the diagram, which represents the operation of messenger-RNA synthesis and its translation into polypeptide sequences. Let us simply observe that since the messenger has a rather brief existence (it lives for only a few minutes), its rate of synthesis determines the three proteins' rate of synthesis. Our chief interest is in the components of the regulatory system. They are:

the "regulator" gene, i
the "repressor" protein, R
the "operator" segment of the DNA, o
the DNA "promoter" segment, p
a molecule of inducer galactoside, *B*G

Its functioning is as follows:

1. The regulator gene directs the synthesis, at a constant and very slow rate, of the repressor protein.
2. The repressor specifically recognizes the operator segment to which it binds, with it forming a very stable complex (corresponding to a F of some 15 Kcal).

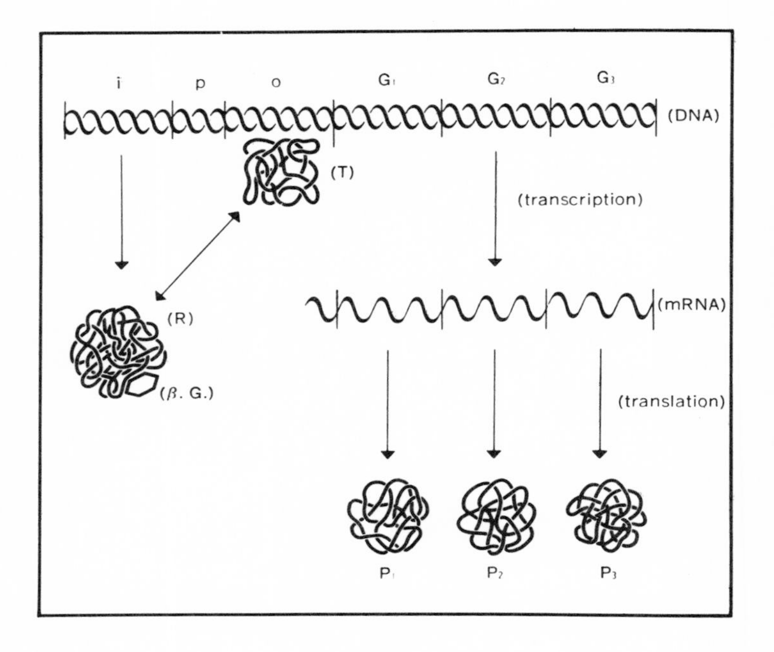

Fig. 4. Regulation of the synthesis of the enzymes in the "lactose system."
R: repressor-protein, in state of association with the galactoside inducer shown by the hexagon.
T: repressor-protein in state of association with operator segment (o) of DNA.
i: "regulator gene" governing synthesis of the repressor.
p: "promoter" segment, point of initiation for synthesis of messenger RNA (m RNA).
G_1, G_2, G_3: "structure" genes governing synthesis of the three proteins in the system, marked P_1, P_2, P_3. (See text, p. 75.)

3. In this state, synthesis of messenger (implying the intervention of the enzyme RNA polymerase) is blocked, presumably by simple steric hindrance, the beginning of this synthesis having to occur on the level of the promoter.

4. The repressor also recognizes *B*-galactosides, but binds them firmly only when in a free state: hence, in the presence of *B*-galactosides the operator-repressor complex is dissociated, this

permitting the synthesis of messenger and consequently of protein.

It is important to note that both interactions of the repressor are noncovalent and reversible, and that, in particular, the inducer is not modified through its binding to the repressor. Thus the logic of this system is simple in the extreme: the repressor inactivates transcription; it is inactivated in its turn by the inducer. From this double negation results a positive effect, an "affirmation." The logic of this negation of the negation, we may add, is not dialectical: it does not result in a new statement but in the reiteration of the original one, written within the structure of DNA in accordance with the genetic code. The logic of biological regulatory systems abides not by Hegelian laws but, like the workings of computers, by the propositional algebra of George Boole.

THE CONTEMPORARY SCENE II

The Contemporary Scene II

Victoria A. Fromkin is Professor of Linguistics and Chairman of the Department of Linguistics at the University of California, Los Angeles. She is a fellow of the Acoustical Society of America. What follows is excerpted from a recent article in *Scientific American.*

From SLIPS OF THE TONGUE

by Victoria A. Fromkin

What makes it possible for a person to produce and understand novel sentences? If we are to understand the nature of language, we must be able to explain this ability. It cannot be accounted for simply by listing all possible sentences; in principle the number of sentences is infinite. For any sentence of length n one can produce a sentence of length $n+1$. For example: "This is the house that Jack built. This is the malt that lay in the house that Jack built. It is questionable that this is the malt that lay in the house that Jack built. I know that it is questionable that this is the malt that lay in the house that Jack built."

Given the finite storage capacity of the brain, one cannot store all possible sentences of a language. We can of course store the words of a language because they are finite in number. In no language, however, are sentences formed by putting words together at random. "Built Jack that house the is this" is not an English sentence.

Furthermore, although the number of words in a language is finite, the speakers of a language have the ability to create and adopt new word , for example Brillo and Kleenex. But just as there are rules for well-formed sentences, so there are rules for well-formed words; "Glooper" could be an acceptable word for a new product, but "nga" would never be used in English even though it is a perfectly good word in the Twi language of the Ashanti in western Africa.

Knowledge of a language must therefore include rules for the formation of words and sentences. In order to account for a speaker's ability to form a potentially infinite set of sentences and for his linguistic judgments concerning the well-formedness of words and sentences, linguistic theorists posit that what is learned in language acquisition is a grammar that includes a finite set of basic elements and a finite set of rules for their combination, including a recursive element to allow the formation of sentences of unlimited length (*see illustration.*) Furthermore, there must be a hierarchy of such elements: discrete elements of sound (phonemes) combine in restricted ways to form syllables, which combine to form meaningful units (morphemes or words), which are combined to form phrases, which are combined into sentences.

All attempts to describe language and to account for our linguistic abilities assume the discreteness of each of these linguistic units. Yet the sounds we produce and the sounds we hear when we are talking are continuous signals, and examination of the physical properties of these acoustic signals does not reveal individual discrete sounds, words or phrases. It has been impossible, however, to account for our linguistic abilities without positing a grammar consisting of discrete units and rules. This has always been intuitively accepted, as is indicated by the ancient Hindu myth in which the god Indra is said to have broken speech down into its distinct elements, thereby creating language. The classical Greeks also recognized the difference between the continuous nature of speech and the discrete nature of language. The messenger of the gods, Hermes, is also the god of speech because he was always on the move. In Plato's *Cratylus* dialogue (the oldest, extant philosophical essay dealing exclusively with language) one of Hermes' namesakes, Hermogenes, asks Socrates if language can be analyzed by taking it apart. Socrates answers that doing so is the only way one can proceed.

The reality of the discrete elements of language and their rules of

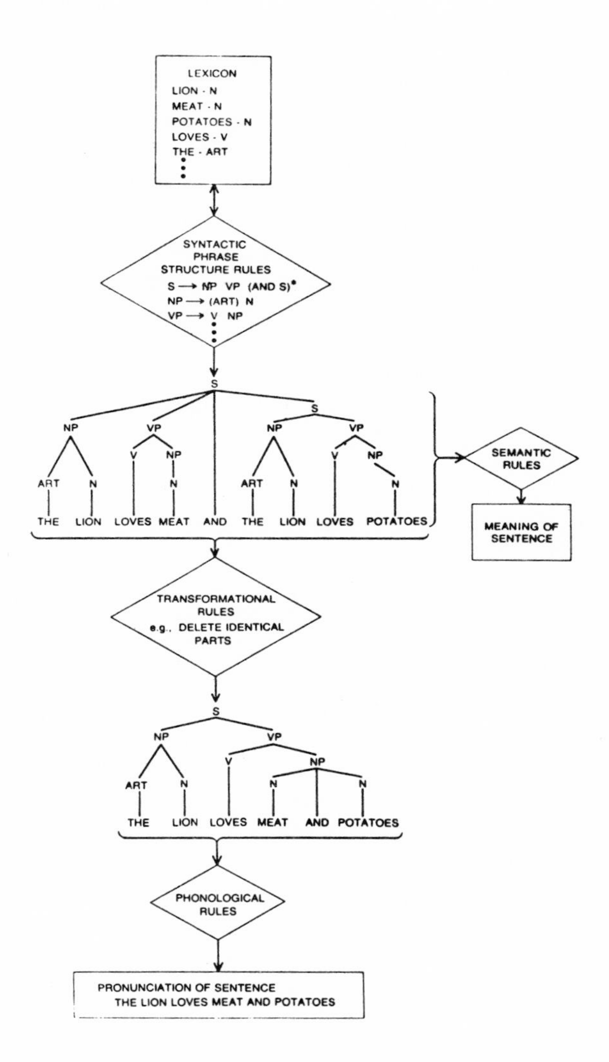

GRAMMAR OF A LANGUAGE consists of a finite set of basic elements (lexicon) and a finite set of rules for combining the basic elements such as nouns (*N*), verbs (*V*), articles (*ART*) and so forth. In order to generate a sentence (*S*), noun phrases (*NP*) and verb phrases (*VP*) are combined according to syntatic rules. The semantic rules determine whether or not the sentence generated is meaningful. Transformational rules enable a speaker to permute the sentence without altering its meaning. Phonological rules determine how the sentence is articulated. Errors at various stages can result in production of a deviant sentence, for example "The meat loves lion and potatoes" of "The lion loves peat and motatoes."

combination cannot be found by looking into the brains of speakers. It is here that systematic errors of speech can yield useful evidence.

Looked at from the viewpoint of linguistic behavior or performance, speech can be considered a communication system in which the concept to be conveyed must undergo a number of transformations. The message is generated in the brain of the speaker, encoded into the linguistic form of the language being spoken and transformed into neural signals that are sent to the muscles of the vocal tract, which transform the message into articulatory configurations. The acoustic signal must then be decoded by the listener to recover the original message. Thus the input signal that presumably starts as a string of individual discrete sounds organized into phrases and words ends up as a semicontinuous signal that the receiver must change back into the original string of discrete units. The grammar that represents our knowledge of the language allows us to encode and decode an utterance.

Difficulties are encountered in attempts to model the actual behavior of a speaker because the only phenomena in this communication system that can be examined are the semicontinuous muscular movements of the vocal tract, the dynamic articulatory configurations and the acoustic signals. As in other communication systems, however, noise in any of the stages or connecting channels involved in speech can distort the original message. Most errors of speech would seem to be the result of noise or interference at the stage of linguisitc encoding. Such errors can tell us something about a process that is not otherwise observable, and about the abstract grammar that underlies linguistic behavior.

Over the past five years I have recorded more than 6,000 spontaneous errors of speech. In order to prevent the inclusion of errors of perception each item has been attested to by at least one other person. The deviant utterances that I give as examples hereafter are taken from this corpus.

According to all linguists who have analyzed spontaneous speech errors, the errors are nonrandom and predictable. Although one cannot predict when an error will occur or what the particular error will be, one can predict the kinds of error that will occur. Such predictions are based on our knowledge of the mental grammar utilized by speakers when they produce utterances. For example, many errors involve the abstract, discrete elements of sound we call phonemes. Although we cannot find these elements either in the moving articulators or in the acoustic signal, the fact that we learn to read and write with alphabetic symbols shows that they exist. In addition, if these discrete units were not real units used in speaking, we could not explain speech errors in which such segments must be involved. Substitution of one segment for another occurs: a later phoneme may be anticipated ("taddle tennis" instead of "paddle tennis"); a phoneme may persevere ("I can't cook worth a cam" instead of "I can't cook worth a damn"), or two segments may be transposed ("Yew Nork" instead of "New York"). Such segmental errors can involve vowels as well as consonants ("budbegs" instead of "bedbugs"). Moreover, two consonants that form a cluster can be either split or moved as a unit ("tendahl" instead of "Stendahl" and "foon speeding" instead of "spoon feeding"). Such errors demonstrate that even though we do not produce discrete elements of sound at the stage of muscular movement in speech, discrete segments do exist at some earlier stage.

It is not the phonetic properties of sounds alone that determine the more abstract representation of phonemes. Sounds such as those represented by the "ch" in "church" and the "j" and "dge" in "judge" are clusters of two consonants on the phonetic level. This is shown by the fact that in the regular tempo of conversation the following two sentences will be pronounced identically by most people: " 'Why choose,' she said" and " 'White shoes,' she said." Yet linguists have posited that in words such as "choose," "church," "chain" and "judge" these phonetic clusters are single phonemes. The fact that the "ch" and "j" sounds in such words are never split in speech errors, although other consonant clusters such as "sp" and "gl" are, bears out this analysis. When these sounds are involved in speech errors, they always move as a single unit, as in "chee cane" instead of "key chain" and "sack's jute" instead of "Jack's suit." In cases where they represent two discrete phonemes, however, they can be independently disordered as in "Put the white boos in the shocks" for "Put the white shoes in the box." Speech errors therefore support the abstract analysis of linguists.

Segmental errors are constrained by rules of grammar that dictate the allowable sequence of sounds. Although "slips of the tongue" can be incorrectly uttered as "stips of the lung," it cannot be uttered as "tlip of the sung" because the sound "tl" is not allowed as the beginning of an English word. It is not the inability to say "tl" that inhibits such errors; we can say it easily enough. Rather it is a grammatical constraint in the English language. It is in this sense that speech errors are predictable and nonrandom.

Phonemic segments have been classified into intersecting sets dependent on shared properties. Thus the sounds that are produced by a closure of the lips, such as /p/, /b/ and /m/ (the diagonals are used to distinguish the sounds from the alphabetic letters), are classified as labials. The sounds produced by raising the tip of the tongue to the top of the teeth, such as /t/, /d/ and /n/, are alveolars. The sounds produced by raising the back of the tongue to the soft palate, such as /k/, /g/ and the /ng/ in "sing," are velvars.

Such classes have been used to describe the sounds of all languages, but they had no basis in linguistic theory until recently. Roman Jakobson suggested a set of universal features that could be used to describe the sound system of all languages. These features, somewhat revised, were then incorporated into the theory of generative phonology by Morris Halle, who developed them further in collaboration with Noam Chomsky. It was shown that if segments are not viewed as being composites of features in the grammar of a language, certain regularities would be obscured, and the grammar written by the linguist would fail to correctly model a speaker's linguistic knowledge.

There has been some debate in linguistic circles over whether or not these universal features have any psychological reality. Some argue that they merely provide an elegant description of the sound system and do not exist as elements in the mental grammar of speakers. Just as speech errors show that discrete segments are real units, so also do they attest to the reality of phonetic features. Among the features posited in the universal set are the binary-valued features: voiced/voiceless and nasal/oral. Sounds produced with vocal-cord vibrations are voiced; sounds produced with an open glottis are voiceless. Nasal sounds are produced by lowering the soft palate to allow some air to escape through the nose while making a sound; oral sounds are produced by raising the soft palate to block off the nasal passage. In speech errors a single feature can be disordered while all other features remain as intended; for example, "clear blue sky" was transposed to "glear plue sky." There was a voicing switch: the voiceless velvar /k/ became a voiced /g/ and the voiced labial /b/ became a voiceless /p/.

Unless the individual features have an independent existence in the mental grammar such errors cannot be accounted for. Prior to or simultaneous with the stage in the production process when neural signals are sent to the appropriate muscles, the specifications for voicing or not voicing must have been disordered. Similar transpositions can occur with nasal/oral features.

Speech errors involve more than sound units. In all languages different meanings are expressed by different strings of phonemes. That is, knowing a language enables one to associate certain sounds with certain meanings. One learns the vocabulary of the meaningful units of a language by learning not only the sounds but also what the sounds mean. Since the words of a language can consist of more than one meaningful element, words themselves cannot be the most elemental units of meaning. "Tolerant," "sane," "active" and "direct" are all English words; so are "intolerant," "insane," "inactive" and "indirect." The latter set includes the meanings of the former plus the meaningful unit "in-," which in these instances means "not."

In learning a language we learn these basic meaningful elements called morphemes and how to combine them into words. Speech errors show that there can be a breakdown in the application of the rules of word formation. The result is an uttered word that is possible but nonexistent. For example, "groupment" was said instead of "grouping," "intervenient" for "intervening," "motionly" for "motionless," "ambigual" for "ambiguous" and "bloodent" for "bloody." It is clear from such examples that rules for word formation must exist; otherwise there is no way to explain the deviant word forms. Obviously we do not have such words stored in our mental dictionary. Speech errors suggest that we learn morphemes as separate items and the rules for their combination. This ability enables us to create new words.

Many morphemes have alternative pronunciations depending on their context. The indefinite-article morpheme in English is either "a" or "an" depending on the initial sound of the word that follows: a coat, a man, an orange coat, an old man. This rule of language depends on the morpheme and not on the sound. We do make the "a" sound before a vowel ("America is") and the "an" sound before a consonant ("Roman court"). But errors such as "an istem" for "a system" or "a burly bird" for "an early bird" show that when segmental disordering occurs that changes a noun beginning with a consonsant to a noun beginning with a vowel, or vice versa, the indefinite article is also changed so that it conforms to the grammatical rule. The rule also operates when entire words are disordered, as when "an example of courage" was produced as "a courage of example."

This operation is accomplished automatically, and such errors tell us something about the ordering of events in the brain. The disordering of the words or the phonemic segments must occur before the indefinite article is specified, or alternatively the rule that determines the indefinite article must reapply or feed back after the disordering has occurred. Furthermore, the monitoring function of the grammatical rule must specify the sounds of the indefinite article prior to the stage where neural signals are sent to the vocal muscles, since the rule does not change a structure such as "Rosa is" to "Rosan is." The existence of similar rules, called morphophonemic rules, and the ordering of their application are shown over and over again in speech errors.

The errors I have cited show that when we speak, words are structured into larger syntactic phrases that are stored in a kind of buffer memory before segments or features or words are disordered. This storage must occur prior to the articulatory stage. We do not select one word from our mental dictionary and say it, then select another word and say it. We organize an entire phrase and in many cases an entire sentence. This process can be demonstrated by the examination of errors in disordered phrases and sentences: "Nerve of a vergeous breakdown" instead of "Verge of a nervous breakdown"; "Seymour sliced the knife with a salami" instead of "Seymour sliced the salami with a knife"; "He threw the window through the clock" instead of "He threw the clock through the window"; "I broke the whistle on my crotch" instead of "I broke the crystal on my watch."

If these phrases had not been formed in some buffer storage, the transpositions could not have occurred. Furthermore, the intonation contour (stressed syllables and variations in pitch) of the utterance often remains the same as it is in the intended phrase even when the words are disordered. In the intended utterance

"Seymour sliced the salami with a knife" the highest pitch would be on "knife." In the disordered sentence the highest pitch occurred on the second syllable of "salami." The pitch rise is determined by the grammatical structure of the utterance. It must be constructed prior to articulation and is dependent on the syntactic structure rather than on the individual words. Thus syntactic structures also are shown to be units in linguistic behavior.

When words are exchanged, they are usually exchanged with words of the same grammatical category; nouns are exchanged with nouns, adjectives with adjectives and so on. This phenomenon shows that words are represented in memory along with their grammatical characteristics. Indeed, when different grammatical classes are involved in a speech error, there is often a restructuring of the words to correct what otherwise would be syntactically incorrect. "I think it is reasonable to measure with care" was not transformed into "I think it is care to measure with reasonable" but rather into "I think it is careful to measure with reason." Such corrections reveal that there is constant monitoring at different stages of the speech-production chain. Although some errors emerged, a compounding of errors does not usually occur. In speech errors we never find a total disruption of the permissible syntactic structure, such as "Breakdown nervous a of verge."

Speech errors can involve entire words. A common type of error is a blend of two words: "shrig soufflé" for "shrimp and egg soufflé," "prodeption of speech" for "production and perception of speech." A more interesting blend, called a portmanteau word by Lewis Carroll, combines two words with similar meanings into one: "instantaneous" and "momentary" into "momentaneous," "splinters" and "blisters" into "splisters," "shifting" and "switching" into "swifting" and "edited" and "annotated" into "editated." This type of error reveals that the idea of the message is generated independently of the particular words selected from the mental dictionary to represent these concepts. A speaker seems to match the semantic features of words with the semantic notion to be conveyed. When there are alternatives, synonyms or near-synonyms, the speaker may be unsure of what word will best express his thoughts and in the moment of indecision may select two words and blend them.

The involuntary substitution of one word for the intended word shows that the meaning of a word is not an indissoluble whole. The semantic representation of a word is a composite of hierarchically ordered semantic features. In word selection one finds that the substituted and the original word often fall into the same semantic class: "blond eyes" for "blond hair," "bridge of the neck" for "bridge of the nose," "When my tongues bled" for "When my gums bled," "my boss's husband" for "my boss's wife" and "There's a small Chinese—I mean Japanese—restaurant."

Some errors show that antonyms are substituted: "like" for "hate," "big" for "small," "open" for "shut" and "hot" for "cold." Whatever the psychological causes of such slips, they show the ways we represent language in our stored mental grammar. The person who substituted "dachshund" for "Volkswagen" apparently selected a word with the semantic features "small, German." In the selection he underspecified the features to be matched.

There are many other varieties of speech error. All of them must be accounted for in a model of speech production. By positing the same units and rules required in a linguistic grammar, many of the errors can be categorized and explained. Speech therefore does provide a window into the cerebral life. By carefully studying speech errors we can get a view of the discrete elements of language and can see the grammatical rules at work. We also can look into the mental dictionary and get some notion of the complexity of the specifications of words and how the dictionary is organized. Throughout history men have speculated, theorized and conjectured about the nature of human language. Speech errors provide good data for testing some of these theories.

The following is reprinted from Peter Farb's *Word Play,* Alfred A. Knopf, 1973.

BABY TALK

Parents usually do not realize that they unconsciously speak differently to children, even those 6 or 7 years old, than they do to adults.

They exaggerate changes in pitch and sometimes they speak almost in singsong; they utter their words more slowly; they use simple sentence structures. And the sounds of their speech are much more precise, as seen, for example, in the pronunciation of *butter.* Most English-speaking adults talking to other adults pronounce it almost as if it were spelled *budder,* but in speaking to a child they usually use the strong *t* sound of *table.*

Such careful attention to speech when talking to children is, however, different from the baby-talk words like *choo-choo* and *itsy-bitsy.* Baby talk, rather than representing a "natural" vocabulary that a child instinctively uses, actually is taught to children by adults—who, after a few years, then force the children to stop using it.

Baby talk is simply a variation of the adult language, invented by adults for the sole purpose of talking to very young children. Once baby talk becomes part of the language system of speech communities, it persists for long periods. Some Latin baby-talk words are still being used in Romance languages after 2000 years, like today's Spanish *papa,* "food," which derives from the Latin word *pappa.*

Baby-talk vocabulary has been compared in six quite different languages from around the world: two major European languages (English and Spanish), two major languages of Asia with strong literary traditions (Arabic and Marathi), one language of a small nonliterate community in Siberia (Gilyak), and one language of a small non-literate community in North America (Comanche). The actual baby-talk words in the six languages were, of course, different; nevertheless, the vocabularies revealed surprising similarities in linguistic characteristics.

All the languages simplified clusters of consonants (as English speakers do when they substitute *tummy* for *stomach);* they replaced *r* with some other consonant (such as *wabbit* for *rabbit);* they reduplicated syllables *(choo-choo, wee-wee);* and most of the languages dropped unstressed syllables (as when *goodbye* becomes *bye).* The six languages altered words to form diminutives (such as the English *y* in *doggy, horsey,* and *dolly)* and substituted words to eliminate pronouns *(Daddy wants* instead of *I want).*

We might expect that people from six widespread cultures would want to talk about different things with their children—but the items in the baby-talk vocabularies were very much the same. Almost all the words referred to bodily functions, good or bad behavior, sensations like hot and cold, names of common animals, and kinship terms for close relatives.

Since children are not born to speak baby talk, what could possibly be the explanation for its prevalence around the world? Most adults in the six cultures claimed that baby talk made it easier for children to learn to speak. It is indeed true that in most cases baby-talk words have simpler consonant arrangements and fewer vowels than adult language.

On the other hand, some baby-talk systems, such as that of Arabic, employ difficult sounds which children do not ordinarily master until they have considerable experience in speaking the adult language. And is it really easier for an English-speaking child to say *itsy-bitsy* than *tiny?*

Despite such exceptions, folk wisdom about baby talk apparently is correct; it does give children practice in speaking. Baby talk presents the child with a stock of simple utterances, and reduplication increases practice in their use. These utterances can gradually be discarded when adult words begin to be used, by which time they have served their purpose.

Reduplication does, however, persist into adult speech, to a much greater extent in some languages than in English, which has comparatively few examples like *helter-skelter, fiddle-faddle, hocus-pocus, mish-mash, and teeny-weeny.* Other languages sometimes make reduplication serve functional uses, as when Indonesians say *igi-igi-igi-igi* to emphasize the idea of "multitudes," and when the Ewe of Africa form the reduplicated *gadagadagada* to express intensity, in this case the heat of a fire.

Chinese in particular has found uses for reduplication with various parts of speech. A reduplicated noun adds the meaning "every," as when *tian,* "day," becomes *tian-tian,* "every day." Reduplication applied to verbs adds a transitory meaning to the action: *zou* means "to walk," but *zouzou* signifies "to take a walk." Adjectives are converted to adverbs by reduplication plus the addition of the suffix *de*—as when *kuai,* "quick," becomes *kuaikuaide,* "quickly."

The most common sounds in baby talk—the consonants made with the lips, such as *p, b,* and *m*—are the first ones the child can make, probably because the lips are used early for nursing. The next three consonants a child learns are formed with the teeth and gums—*t, d,* and *n*—and they are almost as important in the early stages of speech as the first three.

So it is not surprising that the earliest words infants speak are those like *papa, dada, baba, mama,* and *nana.* At first children simply utter these sounds without reference to any particular people—and so most parents are incorrect when they believe the sounds refer to a recognition of father, brother, mother, and nursemaid.

Child-development specialists occasionally argue over whether or not adults should speak baby talk to their children. Some believe that it retards the child in developing normal language; others feel that baby talk affords good practice in producing sounds. Apparently, speaking baby talk does no harm, and it may even be a valuable aid in the early stages of acquiring a language. On the other hand, if a child continues to speak it beyond the first several years of life, it may retard his speech at a babyish level.

Children normally begin to speak as early as 18 months, occasionally as late as 28 months; in the exceptional case of Albert Einstein, the onset of speech did not occur until he was nearly 3 years old. Certainly all mothers have not mutually agreed that it is time to teach infants to talk when they are approximately 2 years old.

But the effort to learn what triggers a child's speech is somewhat like a problem presented to engineering students. They are shown the outside of a black box, with input wires leading to it and other wires leading out that produce an electrical result. The students must then try to infer the internal wiring of the box solely on the basis of the input-output relationships.

The child's mind presents a similar sort of problem. It is a black box (or "language-acquisition device," as it has been called) that cannot be looked into in the living child. The linguist knows only that the language-acquisition device receives input in the form of relatively few utterances, which emerge as utterances in accordance with the grammar of the child's native tongue.

Furthermore, the mysterious device in the child's mind works wherever he happens to spend the first several years of life, with the result that the language he learns is that of his native community.

Noam Chomsky has given fresh insights to psychologists and linguists who are attempting to discover how the language-acquisition device works. In an earlier period of psycholinguistic research, many psychologists were influenced by behaviorists such as B. F. Skinner and Ivan P. Pavlov.

The behaviorists visualize the child's mind at birth as a blank state which lacks any inborn capacity to acquire language. The fact that the child does eventually speak is attributed solely to training, in much the same way that an animal can be conditioned to learn by offering it rewards and other reinforcements. The behaviorists think in terms of the child as building up his language piece by piece in accordance with the orders given by the adult generation, which rewards him when he speaks correctly and ridicules him when he speaks incorrectly. This view looks upon learning language as little different from learning correct table manners.

Chomsky instead regards language as a creative instrument that is the birthright of all healthy human children, who acquire it as a by-product of growing up, simply by exposure to it. They are born with a blueprint for language which they use to analyze the utterances heard in their speech community and then to produce their own sentences. To Chomsky, the influence of training is minimal—a view which is the direct opposite of behaviorist theories that a child learns the grammar of his language as a result of social pressures, conditioning, or simply the trial-and-error imitation of adults.

Chomsky feels that his theory can account for a basic and mystifying fact about language acquisition. The child hears a relative small number of utterances, most of which are grammatically incorrect or misunderstood—yet, on the basis of this scanty and flawed information, in his pre-school years and with no special instruction, he discovers for himself the complex grammatical rules of his speech community. This fact can be explained only by assuming that the child is born with competence in the structure of language, in the same way that a child is genetically endowed at birth with numerous other abilities that make him human.

The situation is somewhat like learning to walk. The child possesses at birth the blueprint for the muscular coordination that he will develop later in order to walk. No one tells him how to lift his legs, bend his ankles or knees, or place his feet on the ground. He does not consciously arrive at the skill of balancing himself on his legs, any more than a 3-year-old consciously figures out the rules for grammatical transformations. The child walks and the child talks—and in neither case does he know exactly how he did it.

A simple example of the way in which a child can be seen putting together the rules for his language's grammar is the English word *hisself*, an "erroneous" form of *himself* which most children use until about the age of 4, despite attempts by parents to correct them. So persistent is this "error" that it has been known since the time of Chaucer and survives in several dialects of English. What is the explanation for its persistence? And why is it constructed by children who usually have never heard it before.

The answer is that *hisself* strictly follows the rules of English grammar that the child is acquiring. *Hisself* is a reflexive pronoun like *myself, yourself*, and *herself*—each of which is formed by combining the possessive pronoun *my, your*, or *her* with *self*. The masculine possessive in this set is *his* and therefore, when combined with *self*, should rightly produce the reflexive *hisself*.

But English is inconsistent in this instance, as all languages are in one instance or another, and the preferred form is *himself*. So children, by insisting upon *hisself* until the age when they acquire knowledge about the irregularities of English, show that they have internalized a basic rule of their grammar and follow it for a long time, despite adult attempts to correct them.

Strong evidence supports Chomsky's view. Only human children learn to speak, thus indicating that some sort of blueprint for language must be transmitted from generation to generation in our species. And human children everywhere develop a language without instruction, unless they are isolated as "wolf children" during the critical acquisition years or unless they suffer from extreme mental deficiency.

Bright children and stupid children, trained children and untrained children, all learn approximately the same linguistic system. Some street urchins do not have parents to instruct them, but they learn to speak nevertheless—and, as can be seen in international cities like Tangiers and Singapore, the homeless child may speak several languages fluently. All children show equal aptitude for language in their early years.

At the same time that the child is acquiring grammatical rules, he is also learning rules for the correct use of his language in the various speech situations of his community. By the age of 2 or so, children already use speech to get what they want, to talk about things they know will interest the listener, and to influence the social behavior of others. They know some of the occasions on which it is proper to shout or to whisper; they know that it is permissible to say *gimme* to certain people but that they should use *please* in other speech situations; they have some idea of differences in age and rank of listeners and the kinds of speech appropriate with a child or an adult, with a stranger or a neighbor.

Only a little later children begin to play word games and to make up nonsense rhymes—clear evidence that they have already internalized the rules and can exploit the alternative possibilities of their language. Although most children acquire their grammar at a steady rate, largely insulated from major influences in the social environment, learning the appropriate use of language depends upon the speech community in which the child grows up and the social group to which he belongs.

Princeton linguist William Moulton has declared that linguistics is "the most scientific of the humanities and the most humanistic of the sciences." Thirty U.S. universities currently offer Ph.D.'s in linguistics, and linguistic scholars today may include psychology, biology, mathematics, electrical engineering and analytic philosophy in their disciplines.

While everyone in the linguistic field accepts naturalism, contemporary linguists can be divided into naive naturalists who disregard theory, neo-rationalists who hark back to the eighteenth century, and those who seek their theory only in the doctrine of empiricism.

The founder of the neo-rationalist school is Noam Chomsky, and his most sensitive critic is Charles Hockett.

Noam Chomsky, of the Massachusetts Institute of Technology, has developed what he calls the theory of generative grammar, for which he has proposed mathematical demonstrations to prove that this theory is powerful enough to constitute an explicit formal basis for all of linguistic theory.

The following account of the differences between Noam Chomsky and Charles Hockett is from Ved Mehta's book *John is Easy to Please*.

From JOHN IS EASY TO PLEASE[18]

Linguists are stirring up quite a lot of intellectual dust just now with a theory of language known as transformational, or generative, grammar, which was first enunciated, in 1957, by Noam Chomsky, the leader of the linguistic vanguard, and which was recently denounced by Charles F. Hockett, a stalwart of the linguistic rearguard, as "a theory spawned by a generation of vipers." The two factions are polarized not only by rhetorical excess—Chomsky is a master of polemics in his own right—but also by actual issues, which are constantly being debated in the literature on the subject. Although Chomsky's two most influential books are "Syntactic Structures," which his disciples call the Old Testament, and "Aspects of the Theory of Syntax," which they call the New Testament, the clearest statement of the theory for someone unschooled in the technical jargon of transformational grammar is to be found in "Language and Mind," an expanded version of three lectures that Chomsky, a professor of linguistics at the Massachusetts Institute of Technology, gave in 1967 at the University of California at Berkeley. In the book, Chomsky took specific examples of grammatical rules relating to English phonology and syntax, and tried to demonstrate that their application was subject to certain universal conditions. These conditions, he argued, were the principles of "universal grammar" and provided "a highly restrictive schema to which any human language must conform." He wrote, "The study of universal grammar, so understood, is a study of the nature of human intellectual capacities. It tries to formulate the necessary and sufficient conditions that a system must meet to qualify as a potential human language, conditions that are not accidentally true to the existing human languages, but that are rather rooted in the human 'language capacity,' and thus constitute the innate organization that determines what counts as linguistic experience and what knowledge of language arises on the basis of this experience." He claimed that the human mind was equipped at birth with a mental representation of the universal grammar, and that this grammar, by means of formal operations he called "transformations," enabled a speaker of any language to generate an indefinite series of sentences. Indeed, he argued, the human mind was uniquely equipped to learn "natural" languages, and a child would fail to learn, as a first language, either the language of another planet or an artificial language that did not meet the universal conditions. Unlike earlier students of language, who had been content merely to describe usage, Chomsky hoped to discover and catalogue the conditions that he believed underlay not just usage but the acquisition of language. Venturing into philosophy, he revived the classic rationalist notion—first stated by Descartes in the seventeenth century—that certain ideas were implanted in the mind as innate equipment. In fact, for the purposes of his argument, he adopted the Cartesian distinction between mind, the essence of which was understanding and will, and body, the essence of which was extension and motion, and contended that the central problem on which Cartesianism foundered (If mind and body were separate substances, how did they interact in man?) could be solved through the study of language, for the creative use of language, the ability to produce and understand sentences, was what most obviously distinguished man from animal. . . .

After spending some time with Chomsky's works on linguistics, I discover that he has all the ingenuity of a Daedalus, so I take a big ball of thread with me when I go to meet him for the second time. I step through the door of his office and boldly ask him to explain transformational grammar.

"The traditional multi-volume grammars that you find on the shelves of libraries present and classify precisely the examples that appear in them, and nothing else," he says. "But we transformationalists try to answer the mysterious and, I think, rather profound question: What qualities of intelligence does a human being possess that make it possible for him to use language creatively, to generate from the limited set of examples that he hears an infinite set of sentences? But perhaps the clearest way to explain the theory of transformational grammar is to show how transformations operate in sentences. Sentences consist of phrases of various types—noun phrases, verb phrases, adverbial phrases, and so on. O.K.? For purposes of analysis, every sentence can be enclosed within brackets, and its parts enclosed within smaller brackets and marked, and the parts of the parts enclosed within still smaller brackets and marked, and so on. O.K.? You end up with a sentence that's properly bracketed, or parenthesized, in the technical sense that every left parenthesis is associated with a right parenthesis and the entire structure is exhausted at every stage of the analysis. Take the sentence 'John kept the car that was in the garage.' " From my reading, I recognize the sentence as a variation of one of Chomsky's stock examples, "John kept the car in the garage." "It consists of the noun phrase—in this case, really a noun—'John'; the verb 'kept'; and the noun phrase 'the car that was in the garage.' O.K.? The noun phrase 'the car that was in the garage' consists, in turn, of the noun 'car' and the sentence 'that was in the garage'; the shorter sentence 'that was in the garage' consists, in turn, of other phrases; and so on. O.K.? The whole sentence can be bracketed and labelled with abbreviations —sentence, noun phrase, noun, verb phrase, verb, article, and so on."

He diagrams the sentence on a sheet of paper:

[*S* [*N* John]*N* [*VP* [*V* kept]*V* [*NP* [*NP* [*Art* the]*Art* [*N* car]*N*]*NP*

[*S* [*NP* [*N* that]*N*]*NP* [*VP* [*V* was]*V* [*PP* [*P* in]*P* [*NP* [*Art* the]*Art*

[*N* garage]*N*]*NP*]*PP*]*VP*]*S*]*NP*]*VP*]*S*

"Now, the fundamental idea of transformational grammar is that the bracketed and labelled representation of a sentence is its surface structure, and associated with each sentence is a long sequence of more and more abstract representations of the sentence—we transformationalists call them phrase markers—of which surface structure is only the first," he continues. "For example, underlying the surface structure of 'John kept the car that was in the garage,' which might be represented by the phrase marker P_1, there would be, embedded and unspoken, a somewhat more abstract phrase marker, P_1, which would be converted into P_1 by what we call a transformation, transformation being our term for the operation by which less abstract phrase markers are generated from more abstract ones. And underlying P_2 would be a still more abstract phrase marker, P_3, which would be converted into P_2 by another transformation, and so on, back farther and farther, until you reach the almost abstract phrase marker of all, which we call the deep structure of the sentence. Whereas the surface structure in general is not closely related to the meaning of the sentence, the deep structure appears to be closely related to meaning. O.K.? . . ."

I try to draw him away from examples by asking him how he regards the workings of these rules and conditions. "Surely they are not conscious?" I say.

"In the normal use of the language, we unconsciously and instantaneously make use of abstract representations," he says.

"If these rules and conditions are in fact unconscious, then why think of them in formal terms as structures—as mental representations?" I ask.

"Let me answer your question in this way," he says. "Take two examples somewhat more complex than the sentences we've been talking about: 'John is eager to please' and 'John is easy to please.' O.K.?" I immediately recognize these sentences as the most famous examples of Chomsky's school. "We could assign to these two sentences their respective surface structures—a noun, 'John,' followed by a verb, 'is,' followed by a certain kind of adjective phrase, 'eager to please' in one case, 'easy to please' in the other. But the surface structures don't tell the whole story. If we say 'John is eager to please,' 'John' is the subject of 'please'—John is doing the pleasing. We attribute to John the property of being eager to do something. Now, if we say 'John is easy to please,' 'John' is the direct object of 'please.' We mean that pleasing John is easy and we attribute to the proposition 'please John' the property of being easy. O.K.? Although the two sentences differ considerably in the grammatical relation between their parts—in what is predicated of what—these differences are not represented in their surface structures. In the case of 'John is eager to please,' the surface structure and the deep structure are really identical—that 'John' is the subject of 'please' is already explicit in the surface structure. But in the case of 'John is easy to please' the surface structure, 'John is easy to please,' is quite different from the deep structure, 'To please John is easy' or 'For us to please John is easy,' and it requires a long sequence of operations to transform this deep structure into its surface structure. I won't try to explain all these transformations now, because they're a little too complicated. But in the deep structure of 'John is easy to please' the verb-object relation between 'to please' and 'John' is explicit, whereas in the surface structure the relation is not explicit at all. It is possible, however, to conceive of a surface structure for this particular meaning—the meaning 'To please John is easy'—in which the verb-object relation between 'John' and 'to please' would be explicit. This would be true for the surface structure 'To please John is easy.' To transform the deep structure 'To please John is easy' into the surface structure 'To please John is easy' involves only the simplest of operations."

"But in another language—say, in French or Latin—wouldn't the difference between what is predicated of what in 'John is eager to please' and in 'John is easy to please' be expressed by the case of the noun, or by the addition of a preposition?" I ask. "If so, then what you speak of as the contrast between the deep structures and the identity of the surface structures of these two sentences might be relevant only to English."

"Yes," he says. "In French or Latin, the surface structures of the two sentences would certainly not be identical, but the two surface structures would still show greater similarity to each other than the two deep structures would. O.K.? In French or Latin, these sentences would retain in their surface structures things like cases, which are a sort of residual deep structure. But in English they don't, so you get an amusing and striking example of sentences whose surface structures are identical but whose deep structures are radically different."

"But does the contrast between 'John is eager to please' and

'John is easy to please' actually matter to someone using English?" I ask.

"The real contrast between the two sentences shows up in the way in which we perform certain syntactic operations on them, like the operation of nominalization," he says. "If we have the sentence 'John is weak,' we can perform the operation of nominalization and produce the noun phrase 'John's weakness.' If we have 'John is eager to please,' by the same operation we can produce the noun phrase 'John's eagerness to please.' But if we perform the same operation on 'John is easy to please,' we produce 'John's easiness to please.' This is not a properly formed noun phrase. You can say 'John's eagerness to please surprised me,' but you can't say 'John's easiness to please surprised me.' If somebody said it, you would know what he meant, but you would also know that he didn't know how to speak English properly. Thus, the contrast between 'John is eager to please' and 'John is easy to please' appears as a difference in grammaticality when we perform the operation of nominalization. This simple example illustrates the fact that when we perform certain operations, we perform them not on actual sentences but on mental representations, on the sequences of abstract structures that underlie sentences. For what we transformationalists are saying is that grammar is really in the mind—that it is a fixed, finite set of internalized rules and conditions which associates the surface structures of sentences with particular sounds and particular meanings and makes it possible for the speaker of a language to generate an infinite number of sentences."

I ask him what he thinks the relationship between sound and meaning is.

"It has to do with the phonological, syntactic, and semantic components of grammar that form the framework of our theory. Transformationalists are divided over the precise boundaries of these components, but my view is that the phonological component assigns, among other things, an intonational structure—a stress and pitch contour—to each surface structure. For example, the phrase 'lighthouse keeper,' meaning the keeper of a lighthouse, would be bracketed one way—"

A diagram:

[[[light] [house]] [keeper]]
NP N A A N N N N N NP

"—and the phrase 'light housekeeper,' meaning a housekeeper who isn't a heavy person, would be bracketed in a different way."

Another diagram:

[[light] [[house] [keeper]]]
NP A A N N N N N N NP

"In the first instance 'lighthouse' is a lexical unit, in the second instance 'housekeeper' is a lexical unit, and when we hear these two phrases, which have different stress and pitch contours, we mentally reconstruct their surface structures. In fact, we rely upon an abstract representation to interpret even the simplest words we hear. Take the words 'explain' and 'explanation.' It's obvious that they are almost identical, so there has to be a single underlying representation for them."

I observe which phonemes occur before 'a-t'—'p,' 'b,' 't,' and so on. I observe that 'eh' never occurs before '-at'; there is no such word as 'ehat.' So I call phonemes that can precede the sound 'at' without altering it consonants. I proceed in this manner with different segments of your utterances, and I observe that certain sequences of phonemes occur in a regular way. 'Khat,' which has three phonemes, occurs in a lot of places and in similar ways. I conclude that 'khat' is a morpheme, the minimal meaning-bearing unit. I follow the same procedure with morphemes that I followed with phonemes, and I observe that 'slept' and 'sleep' are two variants of a single morpheme, because one, 'slep,' occurs only before 't,' and the other, 'sleep,' occurs only in isolation. I therefore set up an abstract morpheme of which 'slept' and 'sleep' are two manifestations. I go on to develop categories of morphemes, such as nouns and verbs. Then I look at certain possible sequences of these categories—such as article-noun, 'the cat,' and article-adjective-noun, 'the sleeping cat'—and I keep going until I arrive at the notion of a sentence. The record of all the segments and all the categories, all the data that I have collected —that record is my grammar."

The greatest exponent of structural linguistics in the United States was Leonard Bloomfield, who lived from 1887 to 1949. He studied Algonquian, Malayo-Polynesian, and Indo-European languages, especially Germanic phonology and morphology, but he is best remembered for his book "Language," an attempt to synthesize the science of linguistics. In an obituary for Bloomfield, the Yale linguist Bernard Bloch wrote:

> In his long campaign to make a science of linguistics, the chief enemy that Bloomfield met was that habit of thought which is called mentalism: the habit of appealing to mind and will as ready-made explanations of all possible problems. Most men regard this habit as obvious common sense; but in Bloomfield's view, as in that of other scientists, it is mere superstition, unfruitful at best and deadly when carried over into scientific research. In the opposite approach—known as positivism, determinism, or mechanism—Bloomfield saw the main hope of the world; for he was convinced that only the knowledge gained by a strictly objective study of human behavior, including language, would one day make it possible for men to live at peace with each other.

The most prominent of Bloomfield's living disciples is Charles Hockett, who with the publication of "The State of the Art," in 1968, established himself as Chomsky's most vocal critic as well. Hockett teaches at Cornell, and I meet him by arrangement at his house in Ithaca. It is a large, prefabricated, Techbuilt structure, with a lot of glass. . . .

I ask him if he thinks that Chomsky and his school have made any contribution at all to linguistics.

He is again slow to answer, but finally says, "Given the avidity with which some of the younger transformationalists are applying themselves, one has to concede that their approach is revealing some interesting things about English syntax. The notion of working by ordered rules from underlying forms to spoken forms is very nice indeed, but the transformationalists confuse the machinery of analysis with the object being analyzed. They claim that these underlying forms exist independently of their investigations. That's tripe. They are only convenient tools. To take a simple case, in English the plural of 'boy' is made with a 'z' sound and the plural of 'cat' is made with an 's' sound. You can invent an underlying form to include 'z' and 's,' and make rules that will tell you when the plural of a noun should be pronounced with a 'z' and when with an 's'—and, for that matter, when with an 'e-s.' But you must always keep in mind that although 'z' and 's' are intrinsic to the language, the hunk of stuff—the underlying form—is something that you have brought in for your own convenience. . . ."

I ask him why it is, in his opinion, that transformational grammar has received so much attention.

He reflects for some time, and just as I am beginning to think that he has forgotten the question, he says, "Since the Second World War, Western society has tended to make science a scapegoat for the threat of nuclear destruction. It has tended to confuse genuine science with mere technology and to blame our lack of control of technology upon the methods of science. Chomsky epitomizes this trend. To prove his theory of language, he postulates certain entities that cannot be confirmed by the empirical method. . . ."

I ask him if he has any other objections to Chomsky's theory.

Again he puffs at his pipe for a time before answering. "In a field like linguistics, which is not very well developed, it's easy to win kudos by rejecting simple old explanations and coming up with abstruse new theories," he says, at last. "This makes you look brave, because you are attacking something supposedly very difficult."

"Do you really think this is what Chomsky is doing?" I ask.

"Not consciously," he says. "But a good scientist shouldn't be blind to evidence that might contradict his theory. . . ."

I ask him where he would place himself in the linguistic tradition.

He refills his pipe and lights it. "Of course, I'm a structural linguist and I'm a physicalist," he says. "My position is that the behavior of an organism is tied up with its physical structure. We human beings all share certain anatomical features, we all eat, we all breathe, we are all subject to certain natural laws. Because we are all human, all our languages are bound to be somewhat alike. But transformationalists forget that linguistic universals can be only guesses. As you know from reading 'The State of the Art,' my basic philosophical objection to Chomsky's theory has to do with the mathematical concept of well-defined and ill-defined systems. The point here is that the issues that linguists are tinkering with go beyond linguistics into the field of anthropology, biology, physics, and philosophy. In human experience, there are two kinds of systems—well-defined and ill-defined. For well-defined systems we can formulate rules that, if they are applied correctly, will accurately predict results, but for ill-defined systems we cannot do this. The hunk of stuff we call numerals, for instance, is a well-defined system. We have an unlimited series of signs in written notation, and this guarantees that no matter how large a numeral we write, we can always write a larger one. Numbers —the collection of things out there—on the other hand, are an ill-defined system. We represent them by numerals, but numbers exist independently of our representations of them; a hundred stars would still be a hundred stars even if we had no numerals to represent that number of stars with. I think that in the present state of our knowledge all physical phenomena fall into the category of ill-defined systems. If one assumes that one well-defined system can be derived only from another well-defined system, then one must conclude that well-defined systems, like ill-defined systems, have always existed. In other words, one must assume that at creation, instead of mind and matter, there was an ill-defined system, the physical universe, and a well-defined system, the logical universe. But I myself don't think that well-defined systems have been here since the creation. I think that they are the product of human beings, who themselves are ill-defined systems. Human language is a well-defined system if it was created by man. It is an ill-defined system if it was created at the same time as man, as part of his evolutionary heritage. What we scholars have learned about language in the course of a hundred and fifty years of backbreaking work persuades me that language is an ill-defined system, and that it is part of the total physical human experience that has made it possible for man to invent well-defined systems in the first place. Implicit in everything Chomsky does, however, is the assumption that language is a well-defined system, and that our heads are simply so many black boxes with inputs and outputs. In short, either you believe that human life is the product of two different systems or you believe in the purely Platonic, idealistic position that only well-defined systems really exist and all ill-defined systems are shadows—illusions of the well-defined system."

Footnotes

1. (*Current Trends in Linguistics*, edited by Thomas A. Seboek, vol. V, p. 495. The Hague: Mouton, 1969.)
2. (J. F. Staat, "Sanskrit Philosophy of Language," in *Current Trends in Linguistics*, vol. V, p. 500. The Hague: Mouton, 1969.)
3. Trans. by Madeleine Biardeau, (Paris, 1964)
4. *Cratylus* from The Dialogues of Plato, B. Jowett. Macmillan. 1894.
5. From *The Complete Works of Aristotle*.
6. John I:1-14 (King James translation, Authorized Version)
7. Pp. 89-93; 134-139.
8. De Bonald, *Legislation Primitive* (Paris, 1803), part 1, p. 54.
9. De Bonald, *Grammaire Generale* (Paris, 1799), part 2, p. 117.
10. Jean-Jacques Rousseau, *The Origin of Language* (Frederick Ungar Publishing Co., N.Y., 1966.)
11. Johann Gottfried Herder, *Essay on the Origin of Language*. (Frederick Ungar Publishing Co., N.Y., 1966.)
12. George Boole, *Studies in Logic and Probability* (Open Court Publishing Company, Chicago, 1952).
13. R. Allen Gardner and Beatrice Gardner, *Science*, Vol. 165, pp. 684-687.
14. Peter Marler, *American Scientist*, Nov.-Dec., 1970, Vol. 58, no. 6, pp. 669-672.
15. Karl von Frisch, *The Dancing Bees*, (Harcourt Brace, and World, N.Y., 1955).
16. David Premack, *Language in Chimpanzees,* "Science," Vol. 172, May, 1971.
17. Jacques Monod, *Chance and Necessity* (Knopf., N.Y., 1971.)
18. Farrar, Straus & Giroux, 1971.

Bibliography

Baader, F. *Writings & Fragments on Esthetics*, London, 1789
Ballet, N. *Die Innerliche Sprache*, Berlin, 1890
Barthes, R. *Le Degré zéro l'écriture*, Paris 1953
Bastian, H. *Brain as an Organ of the Mind*, N.Y. 1883
Beamzee, N. *Grammaire Générale*, Paris 1809
Benveniste, E. *Problèmes de Linguistique*, Paris 1966
Bloomfield, L. *Language*, N.Y. 1933
Boehme, J. *Six Theosophic Points*, London 1920
Boethius, *On Aristotle's Commentaries*, Basle, 1750
Boole, G. *An Investigation of the Laws of Thought*, London, 1854
Brazier, *Revue philosophique*, Oct. 1892
Brossees, C. *Traité de la formation mécanique des langues*, Paris, 1765
Campanella, T. *Grammatica Speculativa*, Florence, 1951
Cassirer, E. *The Philosophy of the Enlightenment*, Boston, 1955
Condillac, E. *Varia Linguistica*, Paris, 1822
Croce, B. *Estetica come Scienza dell Espressione e Linguistica*, Turin, 1903
Cusa, N. *De Docta Ignorantia*, Hamburg, 1927
Dante. *De Vulgari Eloquio*, N.Y. 1953
Darmesteter, A. *La Vie des mots*, Paris, 1887
Diderot, D. *Lettre sur les sourds et les muets*, Paris, 1751
Egger, E. *La Parole intérieure*, Paris, 1904
Foucault, M. *Les Mots et les choses*, Paris 1966
Fritsch, K. *The Language of Bees*, Ithaca, 1971
Jespersen, O. *The Philosophy of Grammar*, London, 1935
Jones, C. *Medieval Literature in Translation*, N.Y., 1950
Kant, I. *Critique of Pure Reason*, London 1848
Labedz, L. *Reply to Stalin on Linguistics*, N.Y., 1962
Leibniz, G. *Origini dell'Alfabeta*, Milan, 1908
Lindoworski, P. *Manual of Experimental Psychology*, N.Y. 1939
Martinet, A. *Eléments de linguistique*, Paris, 1967
Meillet & Cohen, *Les langues du monde*, Paris, 1952
Michaelis, C. *Dissertation sur l'influence réciproque des langues*, Paris, 1759
Panini, A. *The Astavhiyi: in English by Srisa Chandra Vasu*, 1891
Paulhan, F. *La Double fonction du langage*, Paris, 1912
Plato, *Cratylus*, Cambridge, Mass., 1962
Renan, E. *Origines du Langage*, Paris, 1886
Rousseau, C. *Essai sur l'origine des langages*, Paris, 1912
Saussure, F. *Cours de linguistique générale*, Geneva, 1957
Stalin, J. *Concerning Marxism*, Moscow, 1953
Vico, G. *Scienza Nuova*, Bari, 1911